THOMAS CAMPBELL:
MAN OF THE BOOK

THOMAS CAMPBELL:

MAN OF THE BOOK

BY

LESTER G. McALLISTER

WIPF & STOCK · Eugene, Oregon

Wipf and Stock Publishers
199 W 8th Ave, Suite 3
Eugene, OR 97401

Thomas Campbell
Man of The Book
By McAllister, Lester G.
Publication date 12/1/2012
Previously published by The Bethany Press, 1954

Thomas Campbell

This portrait, now in possession of the Seventh Street Christian
Church, Richmond, Virginia, was painted about 1834 by
John Blennerhassett Martin

This study of an eighteenth- and nineteenth-century minister, educator, and reformer is dedicated in love and affection:

TO CLARA EDNA AND LESTER G. MCALLISTER, SR., MY PARENTS
TO THE MEMORY OF JOHNNIE AARON BROWN, MY GRANDMOTHER

who first introduced me to the church universal

ACKNOWLEDGMENTS

There is a surprising amount of information available about Thomas Campbell. Unfortunately it is widely scattered and the writer's principal task has been to assemble this diverse material, to sift through it, and to organize it into coherent form. This could not have been achieved without the kind help of Mr. Stillson Judah, librarian of Pacific School of Religion, who assisted primarily with background books and Mr. Claude Spencer, Curator of the Disciples of Christ Historical Society, Nashville, Tennessee, whose help in making available the *Millennial Harbinger* and other primary sources is especially appreciated. For many helpful criticisms and suggestions the writer is deeply grateful to Dr. Ralph Hyslop, Dr. Wayne Rood, and other members of the faculty of the Pacific School of Religion and to Mr. Daniel Sexton of the University of California, Berkeley.

Appreciation is due the following publishers who have authorized quoted material: Oxford University Press, New York; The Bethany Press, St. Louis, Missouri; The Standard Publishing Company, Cincinnati, Ohio; and Yale University Press, New Haven. The Seventh Street Christian Church, Richmond, Virginia, very graciously consented to the use of the Thomas Campbell portrait.

CONTENTS

FOREWORD 11
I. YEARS IN IRELAND AND SCOTLAND 21
   Birth and Ancestry 21
   University and Seminary 24
   Marriage and Ministry 30
   Influences at Rich Hill 44
   Removal to America 56
II. EXPERIENCES ON THE FRONTIER 60
   The American Frontier 1790-1807 60
   Arrival and Settlement in Pennsylvania 67
   Trouble in the Chartiers Presbytery 72
   Appeal to the Associate Synod 84
   Withdrawal from Presbytery and Synod 91
   Formation of the Christian Association 95
   The Family Arrives in America 101
III. THE DECLARATION AND ADDRESS 105
   Background and Description 105
   The Declaration 107
   The Address 110
   Philosophical Background 125
   Importance of the Declaration and Address . . . 132
   The Appendix and Postscript 133
IV. THE MOVEMENT IS LAUNCHED 138
   Effect of the Declaration and Address 138
   Approach to the Synod of Pittsburgh 140
   Alexander Emerges as a Strong Leader 144
   The Association Becomes a Church 148
   Adoption of Immersion 152
   Matters of Faith and Worship 161
   Next Steps 167

Contents

V. ALEXANDER GAINS AN ABLE ASSISTANT 172
    Migrations of 1813-1819 172
    Thomas Campbell Returns "Home" 183
    Activity on the Western Reserve 197
    Editor *Pro-tem* 205
    Separation from the Baptists 209
    Sydney Rigdon and Mormonism 214

VI. VENERABLE FATHER CAMPBELL 216
    Efforts on Behalf of the Disciples 216
    Discussion with Stone on the Atonement 221
    Last Active Decade: 1833-1843 225
    Retirement and Reflection 246
    Views on Slavery 252
    "Faithful Unto Death" 256

VII. THE SUMMING UP 262

NOTES 279
BIBLIOGRAPHY 287
INDEX 291

FOREWORD

The story of Thomas Campbell's life is a human rather than a spectacular one and in its various phases reflects the shifting religious and social ideas of the ninety-one years in which he lived. A Scotch-Irish Seceder Presbyterian minister who came to the United States from northern Ireland in the early part of the nineteenth century, he became part of a religious movement on the Western frontier which at the time of his death numbered many thousands of members. He was a man of humble spirit driven by deep convictions to give himself devotedly to the advocacy of the primacy of the Scriptures for the guidance of Christians. He was a man who lived long and experienced much but remained always true to what he believed to be right.

Historians, when they have mentioned him at all, have spoken of him along with Barton W. Stone and Walter Scott as one of the founders of the movement known today as "Disciples of Christ," and as the father of Alexander Campbell. But Thomas Campbell was more than that. He was a transitional figure, forming a link between the religious traditionalism of the Old World and the spirit and zeal of the New—a man who, like so many in America at that time, lived the first half of his life in Ireland and the last half on the American frontier.

Migrating to the frontier of western Pennsylvania on his arrival in America, Campbell became increasingly aware of the sectarian spirit brought from Europe by the settlers and, at the same time, was sensitive to the infinite opportunities for Christian union which a new and free country offered. His dominant hope was that every Christian could be made to see the necessity of following the guidance of the Scriptures, especially the New Testament, so that the way could be opened for a union of all Christians. Thomas Campbell's contemporaries saw in him the graciousness and kindliness of a Christian gentleman and almost without exception praised him for his courtesy and gentleness. Charles Louis Loos, who was professor in the early days of Bethany College and who knew him personally, recorded a typical impression of refinement of manners and deep, unaffected piety. Loos was quick to suggest, however, that for all his courtesy and gentleness of disposition Campbell was unyielding on important matters of conscience, especially when the word of God was at stake.[1]

That Thomas Campbell was one of the pioneers of Disciples of Christ is beyond question, but he was so overshadowed by his dynamic son that it is difficult to unravel his life facts and properly to evaluate his influence. The son, Alexander Campbell, took over the leadership of the uniquely American religious movement that emerged on the frontier of western Pennsylvania and gave it his own interpretation, but it must not be forgotten that he built on ideas and foundations laid by the father, and their execution was under way even before Alexander left Scotland for America. It may be said then that the father created the movement and that the son gave it life, that Alexander was the popularizer and Thomas the creative genius behind the movement. In most writings by or about Disciples of Christ, the father all but disappears historically after the publication of his *Declaration and Address* in 1809. But it must not be forgotten that for over forty-five years after that date he remained a wise counselor and guide for his son and his influence as such should not be overlooked.

Seldom in history has it been possible for a father and son to work so cooperatively and so fully to complement each other in personality and intellect. Because he was more aggressive than his father, Alexander has virtually usurped from Thomas the place which he earned. Yet no attempt can be made to understand the more famous son without some understanding of the contribution made by the father. This, of course, presents the first and most difficult problem to the one who seeks to evaluate the contribution of Thomas Campbell. It is the persistent problem of anyone who tries to study the secondary figure in history. The man's life and work were important, but the man himself is always seen in the background of another man's life.

In the life of Thomas Campbell the foreground character is his son, Alexander, and always in Alexander's life one finds the figure of the father in the background. The problem is to try to make Thomas Campbell come alive, to have him take on a character and personality of his own.

The fact that there is so little direct or compiled information on the father poses the second major problem in studying the life and work of Thomas Campbell. The story of his life must first be written before it can be evaluated and the sources which exist are few and inadequate. For most of the facts on his life one is dependent on Robert Richardson's detailed, two-volume, *Memoirs of Alexander Campbell*. Richardson was a lifetime friend of the Campbells, both father and son, and his life spanned most of the first fifty years of the movement of Disciples of Christ; he was thus in a position to know intimately the history of this period. It must be remembered, however, that Richardson was primarily concerned with recording the life story of Alexander and only incidentally reveals information and facts concerning the elder Campbell. Richardson is most helpful in studying Thomas Campbell's years in Ireland and Scotland and must be read carefully to glean to the fullest the later infrequent references to him. However, even Richardson is subject to error and must be corrected by knowledge received from other sources.

Alexander Campbell in the last years of his life was urged to write a biography of his father, but was either too busy or too tired to do a proper work. His *Memoirs of Elder Thomas Campbell* (Cincinnati: Bosworth, Chase and Hall, 1871) is at best the reflections of an old man about an old man. He put into this volume various papers of his father, a few of his letters, his obituary notices, and added to these one or two sketches written by members of the family. Alexander was seventy-three years old at the time and was recalling the life and experiences of a man who had died just seven years previously. In the Preface to this volume Alexander said:

> This memoir has been long called for. My apology is and has been, the multiplicity and the variety of public calls upon my time at home and abroad . . . I have long been waiting for a more convenient season, but it still seemed to be in the future . . . But, under all the circumstances that surrounded me, and all the duties incumbent upon me, I have done the best I could.[2]

Even though it falls short of being a well-written biography, this work is an invaluable source for the early writings and papers of Thomas Campbell and gives dates and events not mentioned anywhere else. As one reads Richardson, it is obvious that he had access to the material found in Alexander's book. Alexander Campbell's book and the two volumes of Richardson are the chief sources for the happenings and events of Thomas Campbell's life. The pages of the *Christian Baptist* for 1823-1830 and of the *Millennial Harbinger* from 1830 until Thomas Campbell's death in 1854 give valuable firsthand knowledge of the views and beliefs of the elder Campbell.

One additional source must be mentioned. William Herbert Hanna, doing research in the history of Disciples of Christ, brought to light the minutes of the Chartiers Presbytery and the Associate Synod of North America, which contain the record of Thomas' trial and the appeal to the synod during the years 1808 and 1809. The results of his study were published nineteen years ago under the title, *Thomas Campbell, Seceder and Christian Union Advocate* (Cincinnati: The Standard Publishing Company, 1935). Although this proves excellent source material for the years in which the trial and the appeal to the synod occurred, it is in no sense a definitive biography, for almost no attention is paid to the formative years of his life; his early years in Ireland, the Scottish backgrounds, or to his contribution after 1809.

As has been already pointed out, the materials on Thomas Campbell are scattered throughout the literature of Disciples of Christ. The method of procedure for this biography has been to read every book or document written by or containing a reference to Thomas Campbell, to collect every known fact, and to seek the essence of that which represents the truth about Thomas Campbell. On the pages which follow the results of that search have been organized logically, and almost always chronologically, to present them as far as possible in an objective manner; allowing events and, wherever possible, Campbell's own words to speak for themselves. Only in the final chapter is an attempt made to evaluate Thomas Campbell in terms of his contribution and influence. This would seem to be the best way to arrive at a satisfactory and definitive biographical study of the life of Thomas Campbell.

It is helpful to see the life of the elder Campbell as it is related to the religious movement known as Disciples of Christ. When he died in 1854, the movement was becoming increasingly important on the Western frontier and its subsequent growth has consistently followed the westward flow of American history. Statistics are interesting but unreliable. Estimates abound, but accurate accounts simply do not exist. Robert Richardson wrote in 1844, when Thomas Campbell's active days were past, that "the whole number of communicants in the United States, so far as has been ascertained, is believed to fall but little short of 200,000."[3]

The influence of the American frontier on the thinking of Thomas Campbell and his concept of the Christian life will be considered in its proper place. It is sufficient to note for the present that two basic ideas were in the minds of the men whose work led to the beginnings of the movement. The first was that the church ought to be without sectarian divisions. The second was that the church was divided because "human opinions" had been added to the practice of the early church as it was revealed in the New Testament. The tragedy of the last one hundred years of history of Disciples of Christ, and of the life of Thomas Campbell, has been that the emphasis has been placed on the second of these two propositions. By emphasizing a literal interpretation of the New Testament, division rather than union has resulted. These two ideas, the reunion of all Christians and the restoration of the essentials of primitive Christianity, have roots that run centuries back into Christian history. The genius of the movement which emerged in western Pennsylvania in the first decade of the nineteenth century, based on Thomas Campbell's principles, is that it conceived of the restoration of simple New Testament Christianity not only as a Christian duty, but also as a means to the promotion of Christian union. When Campbell adopted the familiar formula of restoring the authority of the New Testament church, he combined with it the almost forgotten ideal of Christian union. When later his son, Alexander, and others interpreted and amplified this combination they produced a strikingly different result.

In the beginning there was no thought of the organization of a new sect or religious party. Such an idea was repugnant to the mind of Thomas Campbell and he was drawn only reluctantly to such a conclusion. The *Declaration and Address* was careful to state that the Christian Association was not to be considered a church. With the acceptance, however, of the ideas of simple New Testament Christianity and Christian union, there arose, first an "association" of like-minded believers of many parties; then, a "movement" within existing churches; and finally, as a last alternative, a separate religious body, which through the years has continued to struggle to bring about Christian union on the authority and teaching of the New Testament. The difficulty has always been the lack of a uniform interpretation of the teaching contained in the Scriptures. Disciples of Christ, however, have remained decidedly anticreedal, and have taught that creeds are divisive and that they should be abolished, yet have frequently made ordinances tests of fellowship. Disciples of Christ have urged a return to the simple practices of the New Testament in such matters as baptism and communion, have believed that the ordinances do not have efficacy in and of themselves, and have rejected the conception that they are carriers of divine grace or that, without them, salvation cannot be obtained.

Those interested in Disciples of Christ today need to understand more fully both the greatness of Thomas Campbell's insight and the incipient tragedy in his life. The entire story of the elder Campbell as an advocate of a scriptural basis for the Christian experience as it reflects itself in the family, the church, and the state, needs to be presented. It is the purpose of this biographical study to reveal Campbell's character and personality in its truest nature. The following pages seek to develop his life story, as far as it can be reconstructed from the materials available, from the early years in Ireland and Scotland, through his experiences on the frontier, to the writing of the *Declaration and Address*, with particular attention to the years after 1809 to his death in 1854.

This is a particularly appropriate time for an examination of the life and contribution of Thomas Campbell to the history of Disciples of Christ. In the first place, January 4, 1954, marked the one hundredth anniversary of the death of Campbell and the intervening century gives the student of the man and his work an advantage of perspective which preceding scholars were not in a position to have. Secondly, within five years the

Disciples of Christ will observe the one hundred and fiftieth anniversary of the publication of Thomas Campbell's major literary contribution, the *Declaration and Address,* one of the most important documents in the history of Disciples of Christ. More important, however, than the coincidence of these dates is the fact that, although detailed studies have been made of most of the early leaders of Disciples of Christ, Thomas Campbell has been all but ignored. This is undoubtedly due to the fact that the movement has emphasized the leadership of Walter Scott and Alexander Campbell which has tended to focus attention on them and to obscure the influence of such leaders as Barton W. Stone and Thomas Campbell. Whatever the case, it seems to this writer that the lack of a definitive study of Thomas Campbell has left the history of our brotherhood as incomplete as a portrait in which the background has been left unpainted. It is hoped that this study of Thomas Campbell may help to paint in some of the missing colors.

Each chapter which follows is but a "spelling out" of the one driving and compelling force of Thomas Campbell's life: the appeal to the Scriptures for everything in the Christian experience. Viewed in this light it is seen that no other appellation reveals more clearly his true nature than that of Thomas Campbell: Man of the Book. Such a study of an eighteenth- and nineteenth-century minister, educator, and reformer may be of assistance to those in the twentieth century who would strive for a united church. Thomas Campbell in his day sought an answer to the problem of Christian union on a voluntary rather than a compulsory basis and found it, he was convinced, in a pattern clearly discernible in the New Testament. We today must restudy these past efforts, carefully evaluating their successes and failures, if we would build solidly the ecumenical church.

LESTER G. MCALLISTER

BETHANY COLLEGE
BETHANY, WEST VIRGINIA

THOMAS CAMPBELL:
MAN OF THE BOOK

CHAPTER ONE

YEARS IN IRELAND AND SCOTLAND

Birth and Ancestry

THOMAS CAMPBELL'S father, Archibald, had served as a soldier in the British army and had fought with General James Wolfe in 1759 on the Plains of Abraham in the struggle for Quebec. There was, in fact, a tradition in the Campbell family that General Wolfe died in his arms during the battle, but this has never been verified. Five generations of Archibald's immediate family have been traced in Ireland.[1] The Campbells had migrated from the west of Scotland in the late seventeenth or early eighteenth centuries, probably as a part of the project of the British to colonize crown lands in the northern part of Ireland. Their Scottish background had been an illustrious one and their ancestors had belonged to the Clan Campbell, which the Duke of Argyle headed.

Upon his return from war (presumably the engagement at Quebec) Archibald Campbell married and established a home near Newry, County Down. He had been reared a Roman Catholic but at the time of his marriage he became a member of the Church of England, worshiping God, as he said: "according to the act of Parliament." He was a strict Anglican until his death at eighty-eight and is thought to have been somewhat eccentric, but genial and warm in his feelings. We know nothing of Thomas Campbell's mother.

Thomas, the first child of Archibald and his wife, was born on February 1, 1763, and was probably named for his grandfather. In all there were eight children, four boys and four girls. The four boys, Thomas, James, Archibald, and Enos, reached maturity but the four daughters, who were born into the family and all named Mary, died in infancy. All of the sons were sent to a military regimental school not far from their home and there received an excellent English classical education, consisting of studies in English grammar and reading, Latin and Greek, writing and arithmetic. When still quite young, the boys started teaching school in the country near the village of Sheepbridge, about two miles from Newry. Thomas was the first, and was followed in his profession by his younger brothers, James and Archibald. James apparently led an unsettled life and was thought to have gone to Canada, although there is no further record of him so far as is known. Archibald and Enos afterward opened an academy in the town of Newry and taught successfully for many years. Of all Archibald Campbell's sons, Thomas is said to have been closest to him, and Richardson suggests that the quiet and studious Thomas had considerable influence over his father. Even Thomas at times, however, felt the effects of the elder Campbell's easily aroused temper.

Thomas was a thoughtful young man and early in life turned to a study of the Scriptures. He was of a deeply religious nature, but failing to find the Church of England congenial to his temperament, soon sought fellowship with a group of Seceder Presbyterians. The church of the Seceder Presbyterians had been created by those who refused to give up the right to select their own ministers when, after 1712, the Church of Scotland sought to limit selection. Young Campbell found their type of religious life and order preferable to the cold formality of the Church of England, attended all their meetings, and finally put himself under their religious guidance. For several years he sought that evidence of an "effectual calling" which was considered necessary to conversion by the Seceders and made earnest and diligent use of prayer, seeking assurance of forgiveness and acceptance. It is recorded that walking in the fields one day, alone and meditating,

> ... he felt a divine peace suddenly diffuse itself throughout his soul. ... His doubts, anxieties and fears were at once dissipated. ... From this moment he recognized himself as consecrated to God, and thought only how he might best appropriate his time and his abilities to his service.[2]

With this conversion there came the feeling he had been called to be a minister and he immediately determined to devote his life to the preaching of the gospel in the Seceder branch of the Presbyterian church. Thomas' brothers, Archibald and Enos, also became members of the Secession church and Archibald served as ruling elder of the congregation at Newry for many years.

Out of respect Thomas talked with his father about his desire to become a minister. Although there is no record of this conversation, it is known that the father did not favor the proposal, for he had not looked with pleasure on Thomas' change of church. Either the father agreed to think it over or there was a mutual understanding that the matter would be dropped, for we find Thomas leaving shortly to teach school in the province of Connaught. Connaught was a poverty-stricken section of Ireland, and it was partly to satisfy his longing to serve humanity that Campbell chose to go there. He soon established an English academy which attracted a large number of pupils, but had not been there long when, for a reason which is not known, he was suddenly summoned by his father to return, and as soon as he could make the necessary arrangements, he went back home.

A good school was then obtained for him at Sheepbridge through the influence of a fellow Seceder, a John Kinley, who lived in the village. Apparently a man of prominence and means, Kinley was so impressed with Thomas' innate ability and promise that he offered to finance his education if Thomas would carry out his original intention of entering the ministry. Reluctantly the father gave his consent and it was agreed that Thomas might enter university at the next session with Mr. Kinley providing the means. Accordingly, at the appropriate time, Thomas Campbell packed his meagre possessions and took the boat for Scotland, probably from Belfast, entering the University of Glasgow in 1783 shortly after his twentieth birthday.[3]

University and Seminary

When Thomas Campbell entered the University of Glasgow, it was over three hundred and thirty years old. It had been founded in the middle of the fifteenth century by the medieval church on authority of Pope Nicholas V. Through the years its fortunes had fluctuated but during the eighteenth century it had become a very famous center of learning.

The governing body at that time included a chancellor, elected for life; a principal, also elected for life; and a rector with his council of four deputies, elected triennially by the students voting in "nations" according to their birthplace. Other officers of the university were the scribe or registrar; the bursarius or treasurer; the promoter, corresponding to the modern admissions office; and the bedellus, who combined the offices of sergeant-at-arms and janitor. In the beginning there were only four faculties or colleges: Arts, Theology, Canon Law, and Medicine; and each was organized separately. All the teachers in these colleges were required by oath to maintain peace and harmony among the various faculties. At first all the officers of the university had lived together in one building; but through the centuries many buildings and faculty members had been added. Shortly before Thomas Campbell entered the university a vigorous building program had been instituted and some members of the faculty complained that the noise was disturbing to their classes. The eighteenth century has been called the "golden age" of Scottish thought. Campbell's years at the university were at the height of a brilliant intellectual awakening. George Stewart in his survey of Scottish education says:

... the eighteenth century was in many ways the most brilliant in the intellectual history of Scotland. A galaxy of distinguished names adorned it, and almost every branch of human interest and mental achievement—science, art, literature, medicine and theology, can claim an equal share in its triumphs.[4]

Scotland was now reaping the rich harvest of past struggles for intellectual and religious freedom. It was a remarkable period in literature, in philosophy, in commerce, in economic and social science, as well as in the development of the church. There was indeed great progress in almost every department of human activity. This was due partly to the better understanding existing between Scotland and England, to commercial expansion, to the growing sympathy between the Highlands and the Lowlands; but largely it was the result of increased educational interest.

Scotland was small but, out of all proportion to its size, greatly influenced the intellectual world of the eighteenth century. Skepticism and rationalism were rampant in England and on the continent but Scotland stood as a stronghold of the faith. The teachers of the University of Glasgow were more or less successful in relating the principles of inductive reasoning and the Christian faith, while other teachers and universities were sacrificing either one or the other.

It was during the student days of Thomas Campbell at the University of Glasgow that scientific study came into its own. It became extremely popular, and even the common man found opportunity for such study. During this period such organizations for the promotion of scientific study as the British Scientific Society, the Royal Society of London, and the French Academy were established. The conclusions of these societies were brought before the public in books, journals, and encyclopedias, and the belief became widespread that science was going to conquer all truth, reveal all the secrets of the universe, and provide the answers to all human questions.

Thomas Campbell attended the University of Glasgow from 1783 to 1786 and was but one of the many Thomas Campbells who, from time to time, signed the registration roll. He was probably enrolled in the regular course in the faculty of Arts. The University of Glasgow at this time was in the forefront of those institutions teaching the new science and as Bacon and Newton were studied more and more, Aristotle was studied less. A laboratory, astronomical observatory, and a natural history museum were added to the university and the new school for the scientific study of medicine was a going concern in Thomas Campbell's time. Several of the university's outstanding professors either taught or influenced Campbell.

One of these was Thomas Reid, whose first book of importance, *An Inquiry Into the Human Mind, on the Principles of Common Sense,* was published in Edinburgh in 1764. This book resulted from a study of Hume, and led to Reid's system being called a "philosophy of common sense." He was professor of moral philosophy at the University of Glasgow from 1764 until his death in 1796, lecturing on theology, ethics, political science, and rhetoric. Reid may have retired a year or so before Campbell went there as a student but in any event the influence of Reid on the university would have been strong during Thomas' student days. Starting with the empiricism of Locke and the rationalistic philosophy of Hume, Reid contended that the eye of the mind conveys irresistible and necessary convictions, which we both feel and judge to be true, and his emphasis on the power of spiritual perception gave rise to the intuitionalism by which his philosophy was described. He maintained that spiritual insight revealed as self-evident: 1) the real existence of the external world; 2) the necessary causal connection of natural events; 3) the moral character of actions; and 4) the existence of the soul. These were the principles of common sense, the innate powers of the human understanding. This "common sense" philosophy was a conservative reaction against the skepticism of Hume, and Reid's school was about the only current British philosophy which gave hearty support to orthodox Christian faith. Reid's philosophy undoubtedly had a profound influence on the later development of Thomas Campbell's deepest convictions.

The highly respected John Young, professor of Greek at the university from 1774-1820 was also one of Thomas Campbell's teachers and years later Campbell would occasionally quote Young.[5] Young was spoken of at the time as "the profound grammarian and master of elocution" and apparently gave lectures in science as well as Greek, adopting ingenious methods of instruction. In order to encourage his students in the study of geology, Professor Young one day announced he would be prepared to classify any interesting specimens of stones or minerals which the students might bring to class. Several students dutifully bought specimens for examination, but one student cunningly painted a brick to deceive the professor. When Young came to deal with the specimens, he classified them as follows: "This, gentlemen, is a specimen of gold-bearing quartz. Here we have a very satisfactory sample of porphyry . . . And here," taking up the brick, "we have a specimen of what

... fools come to my class." Young was very influential and at his death the following epitaph was prepared for his memorial in Glasgow Cathedral:

With the profoundest subtility he explored and with the happiest talent laid open to the minds of his students the whole structure of language, and restored the majesty of ancient learning.... He was a man fitted by genius and education for almost every liberal study, a curious observer of nature, a poet of respectable power, an eloquent speaker, an ingenious writer, and a philosopher of profound sagacity.[6]

Another of the great Glasgow teachers of the eighteenth century who taught Thomas Campbell was George Jardine, professor of logic and *belles-lettres*. Jardine was assistant and successor to Professor James Clow during the years 1775-1787. Thomas Campbell, the poet, who finished his course at Glasgow in 1796, spoke of Jardine as the "amiable . . . the benign . . . the philosophic Jardine." Jardine believed students should know Latin and used the writings of Quintilian as a textbook in rhetoric. It was said that his favorite textbook was the *Novum Organum* of Bacon.

Jardine was a great educationalist and introduced many improvements in university teaching. He had great faith in oral examination and held that written essays plus such an examination were more useful to the student than hearing lectures. Carrying his theory into practice Jardine required papers to be written weekly for homework, to be gone over later by him and returned to the student with comments and criticisms added. There were also oral examinations. It was said of him that he had "plain downright common sense, and his great aim and object was to make his pupils think for themselves on a variety of subjects." Both he and Young were the most successful teachers in awakening the mind of young Thomas Campbell.

Aside from his study under such teachers as these Campbell attended the lectures in the medical school which had been established shortly before he entered the university. It was then regarded as proper for ministers to have enough knowledge of medicine to enable them to render any necessary attention to their poorer parishioners. It is recorded that Campbell attended classes and lectures with punctuality and gave strict attention to study.

It should be pointed out that the university, though emphasizing the scientific method, strongly repudiated the natural theology which attempted to make science the basis of religion. The professors took care to insist that science only gave a method and that the world must continue to look to revealed religion for spiritual motivation.

About 1786 Thomas Campbell completed his literary course with honors and the next year entered the theological school maintained by the Anti-Burgher branch of the Seceder church. The Anti-Burghers differed with the Seceders over the question as to whether the burgesses of the Scottish cities could properly swear to support the established church. Young Campbell took the Anti-Burgher position. The Reverend Archibald Bruce was at this time the professor of the Anti-Burgher seminary and the school was located at Whitburn, a village midway between Edinburgh and Glasgow. Bruce was then the minister of the Anti-Burgher Seceder congregation in Whitburn and the school was located there because it was the custom to transfer the school to the place where the professor, appointed by the synod, happened to live. Bruce was highly qualified and was popular with the students. Appointed to office in September, 1786, he held the post for twenty years, writing and publishing many studies on worship and doctrine.

The usual class during this period consisted of from twenty to thirty students and to gain admission to "Divinity Hall," as the theological school was called, it was necessary to be examined on proficiency in Latin and Greek by the presbytery within whose bounds the student lived. The student was likewise examined also on the various branches of philosophy he had studied at the university and on his personal religious beliefs.

The course of study, leading to licensing and ultimately to ordination, consisted of attendance at five annual sessions of eight weeks each. Some exceptions were made for missionaries and, if the synod needed preachers badly enough, a shorter course could be arranged. The week's activity, with occasional variation, required one meeting a day at twelve o'clock. On Monday, a general lecture was given by the professor. On Tuesday, there were sermons by the students and on Wednesday, a lecture in Latin on systematic theology, for which the *Markii Medulla* (a treatise on systematic theology by Mark of Leyden, seventeenth-century Dutch Covenanter professor) was used as a textbook. On Thursday, there was an examination on the theology taught the previous day, and on Friday, more sermons by the students. On Saturday, there was a lecture on the Confession of Faith, with conferences on some practical subject suggested by the professor. In addition to all this, the students organized debates in which theological questions were discussed.

Completing this five-year course in 1791, Thomas Campbell returned to his home presbytery and there submitted to the usual examination and trials for license. After this he became a probationer which meant that he was to preach the gospel under the supervision of the synod to such churches as did not have a regular or located minister.

Marriage and Ministry

After entering the theological school at Whitburn, Thomas Campbell actually alternated between school in

Scotland and teaching in northern Ireland. It is recorded that he attended five annual sessions of the school from 1787 to 1791. Inasmuch as the school was in session for only eight weeks each year he must have spent the long period between sessions in Ireland. An incident arising out of one of the long periods in Ireland is indicative of a characteristic which was to become more pronounced in Campbell in later years and should be included here. While home on vacation from Whitburn, Thomas had been permitted to lead the family devotions. His father was afflicted with rheumatism in his knees at the time, and the son failed to remember the fact. He lost himself in prayer so long that it turned his father's devotion into anger. When at long last Thomas said the "Amen" and everyone rose to his feet, he was no doubt surprised to feel his father's cane on his back. The caning seemingly did not produce the desired results, for Thomas Campbell was always longwinded.

On what occasion Thomas first met his future wife is not known. Her name was Jane Corneigle. She lived not far from the village of Ballymena, near the shores of beautiful Loch Neagh in County Antrim. It was probably while teaching school at Ballymena, during one of his vacations from theological school, that Thomas Campbell first met this descendant of a French Huguenot family who was to become his wife and beloved companion through the years.

The Huguenots had fled from France on the revocation of the Edict of Nantes by Louis XIV in 1681, and had settled in Switzerland, Holland, Germany, and Great Britain. Two families of these Huguenots, the Bonners and the Corneigles, migrated to Ireland where they purchased an entire township on the shores of Loch Neagh. Here they skillfully farmed the land, established schools in which the Bible was taught, and faithfully indoctrinated their children in the forms and practices of the Presbyterian church.

Jane, only daughter of the Corneigle family, was seven months younger than Thomas, having been born in September, 1763. Her father had died when she was seven, but as the only daughter of a pious mother, she had been given a thorough religious training. Jane was at that time described as tall but well-proportioned, with dark brown hair and a fine complexion. She carried herself with dignity but was modest in manner. Thomas was at about the same time described as being of medium stature, compactly built, and of good appearance. He had a prominent forehead and soft gray eyes and gave the impression of possessing a quiet and kindly disposition. They were well-suited to one another. The exact date of their marriage is unknown as family records were later lost but the date usually accepted is sometime in June, 1787, when she was twenty-four and he was twenty-five. When their first child, a son, was born, September 12, 1788, Thomas and Jane Campbell were still living near Ballymena, in the parish of Broughshane, in County Antrim. They named their first-born Alexander. Their house was doubtless a humble cottage, surrounded by only a few acres of land, but it was a Christian home. Thomas had already dedicated himself to the ministry, but in the interval of preparation he continued to teach school to provide for the needs of his family.

Shortly after Thomas Campbell completed his work at Whitburn in 1791, he and his family moved from Ballymena, returning to the vicinity of his father's home near Sheephridge, where he resumed teaching school and preaching for the Seceder congregations in the nearby area. After some years in the neighborhood of Sheepbridge, Thomas and Jane moved to Market Hill, a village in County Armagh. Thomas was still a probationer in the Seceder church and apparently the move was made to supply the needs of the weaker churches in the district around Market Hill. He supplemented his income by tutoring the children of families in the area, finally starting a small school. During this period Thomas' own family was enlarged by a daughter, Dorothea, born, July 27, 1793, and a second daughter, Nancy, born September 18, 1795. Another son, James, died in infancy.

About 1798 Campbell accepted a call to become the pastor of a church recently established at Ahorey, in the open country four miles from the city of Armagh. He and the family moved to a small farm near Rich Hill, a rather substantial town only a few miles from the church. Campbell continued the school at Market Hill for a short time, but eventually gave it up.

The Rich Hill vicinity was considered one of the most beautiful sections of Ireland. The soil was rich and the farms of that area were highly improved. The town of Newry was only ten miles distant and Belfast was thirty-five miles to the southwest. It was in this charming and relatively prosperous region that Thomas Campbell now determined to make his home. From a high hill near his farm Campbell would have been able to see several counties, and in the distance Loch Neagh. After getting settled in this home and when he had had opportunity of becoming acquainted with his new field of work, he was ordained as the pastor of the church. The family was happy at last to be settled on a fairly permanent basis.

Thomas Campbell was determined that his eldest child should have the advantage of a good education and when the family removed to Ahorey, Alexander was left behind at an elementary school in Market Hill, where he boarded with the family of a local merchant. Later Alexander spent two or three years in the academy which his uncles, Archibald and Enos, had opened in Newry.

The time came when Campbell decided to continue his son's education under his personal supervision, but he found Alexander more devoted to sport and physical exercises than to anything else. Alexander was about twelve years old at this time and study had become more and more a drudgery. Thomas decided to put young Alexander to work on the farm along with the laborers, in order, as he said, "to break him to his books." For several years Alexander continued to work and to increase in health and vigor but finally he turned back to his studies again, determined to achieve literary distinction. Whether in sports or in studies he had a burning compulsion to be the best. As Alexander grew older, his father introduced him to the works of John Locke, whose *Letters Concerning Toleration* made a lasting impression on him and whose *Essay Concerning Human Understanding* was read under the father's direction. Thomas was anxious that his son should be prepared to enter the university if ever opportunity presented itself and to this end he instructed Alexander in Latin and Greek, and as time went on, even anticipated the usual college course.

Anxious as he was about the secular education of his children, Thomas Campbell was by no means negligent of their religious training. It was not only a personal wish but also the instruction of the Anti-Burgher Synod that the minister should worship God in his family regularly by singing, and by reading and prayer, both morning and evening, and that he should catechize and instruct his children in religion at least once a week. In this the mother, Jane Campbell, concurred.

It was understood that during the day every member of the family should memorize some portion of the Bible to be given at evening worship. Even the small children participated by reciting a simple Bible verse. Attention was usually called to the truth presented and questions were asked in regard to the passages recited and always the Sabbath was faithfully kept. Every member of the household was expected to go to the meeting and to give an account not only of the text, but of the sermon itself, when he returned home. On Sunday evening the Scriptures memorized during the week were reviewed as a part of the evening worship. In carrying out this program of religious instruction, Thomas Campbell was both punctual and methodical. He was by no means exacting but appealed to the heart and conscience of each member of the family. When he was called away to assist other ministers in their duties, as often happened, his wife kept up the regular order of worship and religious instruction.

The father's influence on the character of his children was highly important. He set a good example in all things, but there was nothing austere and forbidding about him. His conversation was usually serious and on the subject of religion, but he was good-humored and both family and parishioners found his company most agreeable.

He knew the interests of the members of his congregation and sympathized with them in all their cares and sorrows. It was the unanimous testimony of those who were familiar with his ministry that, as a pastor, no one could have been more faithful and diligent. In addition to his ordinary visits and in company with one or two of the ruling elders, he made calls in every home regularly twice a year, inquired into the state of religion in the family, catechized the children, examined the older members on their Bible readings, prayed with them, and gave such advice and counsel as seemed appropriate.

Years afterward Alexander Campbell had this to say of his father's ministry at Ahorey:

> We only express a prevailing public opinion when we say that he was the most earnest, indefatigable, and devoted minister in the presbytery and synod to which he belonged.... His family training and discipline were peculiarly didactic, biblical and strict. The Bible, with Brown's catechism, was, during the minority of his family, a daily study and a daily recitation. He instituted these customs in all the families of his congregation.[7]

It is apparent that during the early years of his settled ministry Thomas Campbell was much given to self-examination. The portion of his diary for the year 1800 that is preserved for us is almost wholly devoted to an analysis of his own spiritual condition. Typical of this are the following excerpts:

Sabbath, June 1st, 1800.—This day very weak, both in body and mind. Slept long this morning. Very dull and heavy in prayer, both in secret and public . . . I have reason to bless God I have not felt so much concern for public approbation, nor such strong emotions of self-conceit as formerly; but alas! what weakness and timidity in publicly reproving the violators of the holy Sabbath.

Sunday and Monday, June 8th and 9th.—These days employed in public services.

Notwithstanding many interruptions, and much imbecility of mind and body, enabled to go through with the work with some degree or propriety of composure, and, I hope, of spiritual advantage, both to myself and to others. Glory to God!

I see, more and more, the necessity of self-denial, holy vigilance, of devotedness to God, of deep humility, of relying always as a worthless, helpless, guilty sinner, upon the free sovereign mercy of God in Christ, for pardon, acceptance, and assistance in everything.

Sunday, June 15th.—This day much as usual; weak and sickly in the morning. Mercifully assisted, I hope, this day in enduring the fatigue of the public work, as well as in speaking upon the different subjects, though with very little preparation. . . . I think I received some help and encouragement from an evening conversation with a few of the elders.

Tuesday, July 1st.—Lost, in a great measure, to any real purpose of improvement or preparation for public use. This destruction of much precious time has proceeded from a bad or imprudent arrangement of my own business; or rather, from a vain, restless curiosity in running after those things where my real business did not call me; or if it did, in not observing a proper punctuality in beginning and ending my engagements; and in giving way to every trivial inducement, either to delay or exceed due bounds.

Resolved, for the future, to abridge my intendments and purposes to matters of real obligation or very urgent expediency, and not lightly to follow the first impulse of a restless curiosity; but in all undertakings to proceed with cautious deliberations. A good man will guide his affairs with discretion unto the end.[8]

During this period of his life Thomas Campbell centered his personal study and development almost entirely on the Bible. In later years Alexander recalled the many times he had entered his father's study, with its large and well-selected library, to see his father studying with only his Bible, concordance, and writing materials before him. His reverence for the authority of the Bible was so great that when he found some of the children of the congregation confusing the language of the catechism with that of Scripture, he began to put aside the catechism, fearing that they might think the catechism of equal authority with the Bible.

A favorite comparison of the elder Campbell at this time was: "A man may enter a garden for three purposes: First, to learn the art of gardening; second, for pleasure; third, to gather fruit. So may a man read the Bible for three things: First, to learn to read it or dispute about it; second, read the historical parts for pleasure; third, to gather fruit; this last is the true way."

Prayer was regarded by Campbell as a sacred privilege to be exercised with a strict regard to the circumstances of the occasion. Neither Thomas, nor Alexander after him, would offer up special petitions for any who at the time united in the prayer. Thomas' prayers were given in detail and his thoughts as well as his sentences were sometimes involved. He inclined toward an abundant use of adjectives in his prayers. At the close of his prayer he would sometimes use the "Lord's Prayer," but instead of the simple words, "Thy will be done," he would say, "Thy *blessed* and *holy* will be done." On other occasions instead of asking for "mercy" and "grace," he would pray for "*sin-pardoning* mercy and *sanctifying* grace." As a contemporary said, the prayers of Thomas Campbell were characterized by "fluency, solemnity, fervency, and sincerity."

An event, which indicates the elder Campbell's response to personal sorrow and his complete trust in the divine will, occurred in 1804, while he was at Ahorey. One Sunday, just as he was ready to enter the meeting-house for the morning worship, a messenger arrived from Newry to inform him that his youngest brother, Enos, had been killed, having fallen into an open excavation. Though deeply moved, Campbell humbly resigned himself to God's will and proceeded to carry out the services of the day. When the services were completed, he immediately set out for Newry where he sought to comfort his eighty-five-year-old father.

As a preacher, Thomas Campbell was popular with the Seceder denomination and carried his fine teaching ability into the pulpit. He was good in defining terms and usually covered the subject fully. He made his sermons bright with many homely illustrations, and was able to hold the congregation's attention fully. At the same time he spoke sincerely and with conviction.

The following outline, made for a sermon preached at Ahorey on Sunday, June 22, 1800, is indicative of the elder Campbell's method and manner of preaching:

Text: What doth it profit, my brethren, though a man say he hath faith, and have not works? Can faith save him?— James ii:14.

Head I.

1. Introduction from the general scope of the Epistle, and the early corruption of Christianity.
2. Then, endeavor to catch the train of the apostle's reasoning in the context.
3. Show the consistency between James and Paul.

Assumption: *Faith without works will by no means save a man.*

Head II.
1. He may have a national faith or opinion.
2. He may have a professional faith.
3. He may have an imaginary faith.

Head III.
The genuine effects of a true saving faith are:
1. Sorrow for sin.
2. Application to the Divine mercy, as revealed.
3. Reliance upon the Divine love through the merits of Christ.
4. Conformity to the Divine will in all manner of conversation, viz., in piety, purity, justice, charity, and universal benevolence.

Why Can Not Faith Alone Justify?
1. A lonely faith can not justify, because it is deficient in itself.
2. It can not justify, because it can not reconcile.
3. It can not justify, because it can not sanctify.
4. It can not justify, because it can not glorify God.
N.B.—It has the direct contrary tendency.

Inferences
1. Mistakes about faith are most dangerous.
2. A person may suppose he has faith when he has not.
3. The sure way to prevent this self-deceit is to walk in the steps of those that are approved ensamples of faith.

Concluding Address
To the poor, to the rich, and to those in a middle station.
1. A reflection upon the conduct of the poor in time past.
2. A reflection upon that of the rich at present with the moral tendencies.*

Alexander testifies to the fact that this was his father's usual method of approaching a subject. It was in keeping with the style of sermonizing popular at the time.

Thomas Campbell's ministry in Ireland extended through troublous years of civil commotion. The first regular lodges of the Society of Orangemen were founded in 1795 in County Armagh, although the order had existed earlier. This organization had as its object the driving of all Roman Catholics from the country and this objective was sought by threats and attacks in the night. Great numbers of Roman Catholics were molested but could obtain no justice from the magistrates. Unidentified individuals went about in the night searching houses for arms. This was taken advantage of by common robbers who plundered the people of their property. Another group whose purpose was to "protect" the Protestants was the "Peep-o'-Day Boys" who gained their name from the dawn hour chosen for their raids on Catholic villages. The Roman Catholics in return formed the society of "The Defenders."

In the midst of this turmoil an organization of Protestants and Catholics, known as the United Irishmen, was formed under the leadership of Theobald Wolfe Tone, a Protestant lawyer in Dublin. Each member of the organization was bound by a solemn oath to work for the objectives of the group. The Catholics united with it to obtain protection against the Orangemen and the Protestants supported it because they earnestly desired to secure a reform from Parliament which would permit equal taxation and representation. Many Presbyterians became connected with this organization and gave the movement much of its strength and support. The original purpose of this society was no more than the formation of a political union between Roman Catholics and Protestants, but later the majority of the members conspired to establish an Irish republic by armed rebellion.

All these disturbances culminated in the rebellion of 1798. Discontent in Ireland was now rapidly becoming dangerous, and was finding its focus in the Society of the United Irishmen. French revolutionary doctrines had become ominously popular. Help for the rebellion was anticipated from France if there were a popular uprising. The leader, valuable for his social position more than his ability, was Lord Edward Fitzgerald of Dublin. The date of May 23 was fixed for the general rising, but plans miscarried. Fitzgerald was arrested and died in prison, thus ending the abortive "Rebellion of 1798."

After 1801 peace was partially restored by a new agreement with England, but many Irishmen were still restive. Among them was Robert Emmet, who, while traveling in Europe, came into contact with Theobald Wolfe Tone and other leaders of the United Irishmen, exiled since the rebellion of 1798. These men planned a fresh outbreak in Ireland, and again expected support from France. Emmet met Napoleon who convinced him that a French invasion of England might be looked for in August, 1803. Emmet therefore made plans to lead an uprising in Ireland which, lacking popular support, ended in a street brawl. Emmet was hanged for treason.

One important feature of the Society of United Irishmen was that it was a secret organization. In the six northern counties of Ireland, where most of the population was Protestant, the organization was most powerful but Thomas Campbell refused to have anything to do with it. He had strong convictions in regard to secret societies, and did not hesitate to speak out against them. This brought him into immediate disfavor with many of his congregation, but he continued his conscientious opposition to such associations.

In the midst of the heated discussion on this subject, he was requested by the leading men of the fraternity to deliver a sermon on the scriptural lawfulness of oaths and of secret societies. Campbell agreed to do so. On the appointed day he appeared in their lodge hall where the members had assembled in ceremonial regalia. Campbell proceeded to present his views so earnestly and so frankly that a large part of the audience became angered and some in the group suggested aloud that he be stopped. At this point, however, one of the leaders of the organization, fearing for his safety, courteously took him by the arm and conducted him safely through the crowd.

On another occasion during these difficult times, when Campbell was preaching to his congregation, the meetinghouse was suddenly surrounded by a troop of Welch horsemen. The captain of the troop, thinking that in this remote place he had discovered a meeting of rebels, dismounted and marched into the church. It was a moment of great suspense. Everyone was panic-stricken, and expected at any moment to be attacked by the soldiers. Just at this crisis, as the officer stalked up the aisle, an elder sitting near Campbell whispered, "Pray, sir!" Whereupon, in a deep and unfaltering voice Mr. Campbell began in the language of the Forty-sixth Psalm: "Thou, O God, art our refuge and strength, a very present help in trouble." No sooner was the first verse uttered than the captain paused, and apparently impressed, bent his head, listened to the close, then bowed reverently and left.

So great was Thomas Campbell's reputation for piety and fair-mindedness, that through all the troubles of this period he remained entirely unmolested and retained the confidence of the community. The Presbyterians who had become active in the United Irishmen began themselves to fear they would become a minority and that, if a rebellion should ever be successful, they would be unable to obtain liberty and toleration. Soon the entire community began to see Campbell's wisdom in opposing political agitation and secret societies, and the unhappy results of the uprisings of 1798 and 1803 vindicated the correctness of his principle. Thomas' stand in regard to secret associations made a deep impression on his son, Alexander, and together they continued throughout life to oppose everything of this nature as inconsistent with the Christian profession.

By virtue of his stand on secret societies Thomas Campbell came to the attention of the Governor-General, Lord Gosforth, who had been concerned with keeping order. Gosforth was so impressed with the position taken by Campbell, and with the excellence of his character and reputation, that he urged Campbell to become the tutor of his family. Gosforth offered him a large salary and a residence on his estate; but Campbell refused the position, fearing that his family would be influenced adversely by the frivolous and gay life of the nobility. He preferred to continue his plain life as a minister, with its comparative poverty.

While Thomas Campbell was thus in the midst of civil commotions, devoting himself to the care of his congregation and to the education of his children, his family continued to increase. Mention has been made already of the two daughters, Dorothea and Nancy, born before the move to Ahorey. A third daughter, Jane, was born on June 25, 1800. To these were added a son, Thomas, born May 1, 1802, another son, Archibald, born April 4, 1804, and finally Alicia, born April, 1806. This made seven living children: three sons and four daughters.

The salary of Seceder preachers was usually from fifty to sixty pounds per year at this time. Finding his expenses greatly increased as the family grew larger and the farm he had leased unprofitable as he had little knowledge of farming, Campbell found it necessary to adopt some other method of adding to his meagre ministerial income. His own time was considerably occupied in teaching his family, so he decided it would be profitable to open a public academy in which others might study as well. As his oldest son, Alexander, was now in his seventeenth year and had by this time become proficient in the ordinary subjects, Thomas thought his son competent to act as assistant. These matters were arranged and when a suitable house was found in nearby Rich Hill, the family moved there from the farm.

Rich Hill commands a sweeping view of all the surrounding countryside. In 1805 it was a small town with a neat public square around which, on three sides, the houses of the village were built. On the northeastern side of the public square was the manor house of the local lord whose house and grounds were separated from the square by an iron railing. Large shade trees filled the square. On the opposite side of the square, at the corner, Campbell found a plain two-story house, which served as a residence for the family and as schoolroom for the academy.

Thomas Campbell's character, ability, and reputation as a teacher were so well known that in a short while there was a flourishing school. To conduct a school in addition to his usual pastoral duties was no small task, but with the assistance of Alexander, he managed to keep things going. The school brought to the family an additional income of approximately two hundred pounds annually, making it possible for the family to have a few luxuries as well as necessities. In the meanwhile, Thomas continued to tutor Alexander in a special course of studies, preparing him for the university and encouraging him to consider the ministry as a life vocation. The days went by quickly. There were sermons to prepare, calls to be made, classes to meet, and always morning and evening devotions.

Influences at Rich Hill

There were not only political and economic disturbances in Ireland at the beginning of the nineteenth century, but religious ones as well. Presbyterianism had been established as the state church of Scotland under William and Mary in 1690. In 1712, under Queen Anne, an attempt had been made on the part of the established church to enforce the existing laws of patronage. This permitted "patrons," usually the crown or the great landlords, to force appointments of Presbyterian ministers to hostile parishioners. This deprived congregations of the privilege of choosing their pastors and produced great dissatisfaction on the part of some. Controversies were soon disrupting the Scottish church. In 1718 an anonymous seventeenth-century work, *The Marrow of Divinity,* was republished at the instigation of Thomas Boston, a zealous preacher and himself author of a popular book, *The Four-fold State.* One of the followers of Boston, Ebenezer Erskine of Stirling, a preacher of power, denounced all limitations on the power of the congregation to choose its ministers in 1733. He was disciplined by his synod, and he and several associates were deposed by the General Assembly in 1740. Before these censures were completed Erskine and his followers had founded the first Scottish free church. They formed themselves into a separate group, taking the name "Associate Presbytery," and were known ultimately as the Secession church or as "Seceders."

The Secession church itself divided into two parties in 1747 over the question whether the burgesses of the Scottish cities could properly swear to support "the true religion ... authorized by the laws" of Scotland. Those who claimed the oath unlawful were called *Anti-Burghers,* the other party being known as *Burghers.* This division spread at once through the churches in Scotland and Ireland, and continued with much bitterness for many years.

In 1795 a question arose among the Burghers over the power of civil magistrates in religion as it was asserted in the twenty-third chapter of the Westminster Confession and also in regard to the perpetual obligation of the "Solemn League and Covenant." This had the effect of producing two parties, distinguished from each other by the terms "Original" or "Old-Light" Burghers and

"New-Light" Burghers. The same controversy spread among the Anti-Burghers. The "Old-Light" party was headed by Archibald Bruce, Thomas Campbell's former teacher of theology. In August, 1806, Bruce organized a new Presbytery. There were thus at this time no less than four different bodies of Seceders, each adhering to its own "testimony" and all professing to adopt the Westminster Confession.

When he had joined the Seceder church as a youth, Thomas Campbell had become affiliated with the Anti-Burgher sect of the Secession church. It was in the Anti-Burgher theological school he had been trained. When in 1806 the Anti-Burgher's divided into "New-Lights" and "Old-Lights," Campbell found himself a member and minister of the Old-Light Anti-Burgher Seceder Presbyterian Church.

Even though he was a member of a strict Seceder sect, Campbell always displayed a surprising independence of mind. This could be seen at an early age in his stand against his father on the question of entering the Seceder ministry. It could be seen again in his withdrawal of the catechism from the children of his parish when he felt the authority of the Bible endangered, and again in his opposition to secret societies.

This independence of mind was balanced by a catholicity of spirit. His quiet nature was disturbed by the bitterness of sectarian strife and he was harassed by the triviality of the differences which were thought to exist. In his personality he was opposed to all that disrupted peace and harmony between Christians. In conjunction with these characteristics three influences began to operate and to produce in Thomas Campbell a variation of the normal type of Scotch-Irish Presbyterian minister of the time.

The first influence, and probably the most important, was that of the congregation of Independents which he found when he moved his residence to Rich Hill. He was on friendly terms with the pastor, a Mr. Gibson, and many members of the congregation and it was not unusual for Thomas Campbell, after his return from the services of the country church of Ahorey two miles distant, to attend the evening meeting of this Independent (Scottish Congregational) congregation. Among the Seceders it was required that all members must attend the services of their own church. If there were no Seceder meeting within reach at the same hour, however, it was permitted that they might go to other meetings. This was called the privilege of "occasional hearing." It was a privilege much appreciated and frequently used by Mr. Campbell.

The Independents were liberal in granting the use of their meetinghouse to preachers representing many points of view. This provided an opportunity for the residents of Rich Hill from time to time to hear persons distinguished in the religious world. On such occasions Campbell was one of the most attentive listeners. In this way his thinking on the religious questions of his day was tremendously stimulated.

On one such occasion Campbell heard the celebrated Rowland Hill. Born in 1744, Hill had entered St. John's College, Cambridge, at the close of 1764 and two years later became personally acquainted with George Whitefield, the great evangelist, who exercised great influence on him. Hill had been denied ordination because of his persistence in itinerant evangelism. He had great loyalty to the Church of England, but the influence of Whitefield and the evangelical movement was too great to resist and he finally built with his own money the independent Surrey Chapel, London, which was opened in 1783. He continued his itinerant preaching and it was as a traveling evangelist that his influence was greatest. It was on such a mission that Hill came to Rich Hill.

Hill's tours were financed partly by two Scottish Independents, the Haldane brothers. James Alexander Haldane, the younger of the two brothers, also visited Rich Hill and preached during Thomas Campbell's residence there. James Haldane and his older brother, Robert, were two wealthy seamen who had a profound religious experience, and as a consequence, had given leadership to the Independent movement in Scotland, a direct outgrowth of the current evangelical revival. Frustrated in missionary endeavor, the brothers opened tabernacle churches in Edinburgh and Glasgow. These societies, like those of Wesley in England, were not intended to detract from the established church, but antagonism arose which resulted in an independent movement which was practical and evangelical. Its aim was to approximate the ideal model of primitive Christianity and accordingly, the Lord's Supper was introduced as a weekly institution. The final conflict came when James Haldane announced to his congregation that he could no longer conscientiously administer infant baptism, and was immersed. The Haldane influence is seen in Thomas Campbell's later positions in regard to church organization.

Alexander Carson who left the Presbyterians and joined the Independents in 1803 preached about this time at Rich Hill; so did the eccentric John Walker, another Independent who had separated from Presbyterianism. Walker had been a professor in Trinity College and minister of Bethesda Chapel in Dublin. Alienated by the worldliness within the church, he resigned his positions in 1804, threw aside his Anglican clerical garb, and formed an independent society, a forerunner of the Plymouth Brethren. He taught that there should be no minister, that all members should preach. Baptism he considered unnecessary except for those who had never before professed Christianity. He was Calvinistic in doctrine and practiced closed communion, not only of the

Lord's Supper, but of all acts of Christian worship. He sold his carriage and traveled on foot through Ireland and England to dramatize his message. Walker was accustomed at his meetings to invite all who were interested to call on him the next day at his room for religious conversation. As he was extremely affable, these interviews were usually very agreeable. During Walker's visit to Rich Hill, Thomas Campbell, in company with one of his elders, called on him and spent several stimulating hours in deep religious discussion.

The right of every person to judge for himself as to the meaning of the Scriptures, and independence of the local congregation were the distinguishing features of the Scottish Congregational movement. These principles and the tolerant attitude which was evidenced in the Rich Hill congregation impressed Campbell very much. The natural tendency of his mind was to search for truth wherever it was to be found. By his very nature he could not limit himself to the confines of Old-Light Anti-Burgher Seceder Presbyterianism. Yet, while interested in the congregation at Rich Hill, he continued to hold essentially Presbyterian views. None of those who have been mentioned advocated explicitly the union of the churches, or of all Christians in one church; but they were opposed to ecclesiastical authority and emphasized an evangelical faith.

While under such independent influences Campbell had only a general knowledge of the Independent movement. There is little evidence that he was ever directly influenced by the ideas of such Independents as Glas and Sandeman. John Glas had been one of the first of the Scottish Independents. He had left the established church in 1728, adopted Independent views, and formed churches in most of the large towns in Scotland, where his followers were called "Glassites." Glas distinguished between the Old and New Testaments: in the former he held the state and the church to be identical, while in the latter he saw the church as purely a spiritual community. The aim of his movement was to restore primitive New Testament practices. About 1755 Robert Sandeman, Glas's son-in-law, had developed and sustained these views.

Sandeman gave the movement its theological content. He was an upholder of the doctrine of justification by faith, but he saw faith as limited largely to its intellectual element. Sandeman's beliefs were that faith is merely a simple assent to the testimony concerning Christ; that the word faith means nothing more than it does in common discourse, a persuasion of the truth of any proposition; and that there is no difference between believing any common testimony and believing apostolic testimony. He advocated the weekly observance of the Lord's Supper, the kiss of charity, love feasts, weekly contributions for the poor, mutual exhortation of members, and a limited community of goods. He would place church government in the hands of bishops, elders, and teachers. He approved of theaters and public entertainment, when not connected with circumstances really sinful. He afterward came to America and founded societies in New England.

The Independents of Rich Hill, though in connection with the Scottish movements, were mainly Haldanean in sentiment, and did not adopt many of the views of Glas or Sandeman. The Haldane brothers, while admiring many of the teachings of Glas and Sandeman, were much opposed to the bitter spirit which their followers manifested. The Rich Hill congregation observed the Lord's Supper weekly and made contributions to the poor, but were opposed to theaters and public entertainment and to the doctrine of the community of goods and foot washing as advocated by Sandeman. This congregation seemed to be free from the dogmatic and bitter controversial spirit so characteristic of Scottish Independents of the time.

The second influence operating at this time in the life of Thomas Campbell was that of the "evangelical" style of preaching which had been introduced by Whitefield and Wesley earlier in the eighteenth century. By their earnestness and zeal, by the introduction of the custom of field preaching, as well as by the Wesleyan system of lay preaching and itineracy, the churches had been roused from their apathy.

In 1797 James A. Haldane and others established a nonsectarian organization for tract distribution and lay preaching called the "Society for the Propagation of the Gospel at Home." The funds for the operation of the society were supplied chiefly by Robert Haldane. The main purpose of the society was evangelical, seeking to win converts to Christianity. Among those sent out as preachers were Ballantine, Cleghorn, and Rate who had been Seceder Presbyterians. Thomas Campbell warmly sympathized in the objects of the society, became a member, and took great pleasure in aiding its operations. Many earnest preachers were sent out by this society throughout the country. They would gather the people in the most public places in towns or wherever they could obtain an audience, and preach to them. These different movements by their emphasis on simple New Testament Christianity, increased Campbell's reverence for the Scriptures as the only true guide in religion. They deepened his conviction that the existence of sects and parties was a hindrance to the success of the gospel.

The third influence on Campbell was the very pronounced sectarian spirit in Ireland at this time. Not only was there a bitter feeling among the different denominations, but also there was a spirit of conflict among the various branches of the Presbyterian church. The differences which had occasioned the divisions were magnified, and all the branches were characterized by a spirit of narrowness and bitterness. In addition to the main divisions there were lesser parties which had developed in the heat of the controversy. The sectarian spirit is indicated by the fact that in 1798 the Anti-Burgher Synod forbade its members to attend or to recognize public preaching by any not of its ministry. In 1799 one of its ministers was deposed and excommunicated for having heard Rowland Hill and James Haldane preach. The Burghers were equally intolerant. The process of dissolution seemed to be going on before Campbell's own eyes.

Thomas Campbell was tolerant in spirit and was troubled in conscience by the narrowness and intolerance of the Christians of his day. He realized that this was contrary to the command of the Scriptures that Christians should love one another and he felt these divisions were unnecessary. It is not surprising that a man of his amiable disposition, catholic spirit, and deeply spiritual nature should find himself troubled by the divisions of the church by which he was surrounded.

Campbell was disturbed not only by the division of the church, but also because he sincerely felt that such a spirit was a hindrance to many individuals in accepting the gospel. His study and ministry thus far had presented him with the picture of a divided church. He was all too keenly aware of the trivial differences existing between the Burgher and Anti-Burgher churches in Ireland. The disputed oath was not required in Ireland, thus the original reason for the division did not exist. This so concerned Thomas Campbell that he urged reunion between the Burgher and Anti-Burgher Seceders in northern Ireland at every opportunity.

Under his leadership an effort was made to bring together those who felt as he did about the matter. A "Committee on Consultation" met at Rich Hill in October, 1804, to discuss the possibility of uniting the

Burgher and Anti-Burgher groups in Ireland. A report, with propositions of union, was prepared by Thomas Campbell and presented to the Anti-Burgher Synod of Ireland when it met at Belfast sometime after October, 1804, and was favorably received. In his address to the synod, Campbell stated that "the evil nature and tendencies of our unhappy division occupied, for some time, the serious consideration of the Committee." His report continued:

> It appeared to us, indeed, a matter truly deplorable, that, in the circumstances in which the Lord has placed us, there should not exist the most perfect harmony among all the sincere friends and lovers of truth as it is in Jesus; and that all such were not united in one common, energetic co-operation in the grand cause of truth and righteousness, under the banner of one common, comprehensive, and faithful testimony. More especially that a respectable body of professing Christians, in a declared secession from the surrounding Churches, on account of their heterodoxy, and other prevailing enormities, should be divided among ourselves; while, at the same time, there exists no real difference between them in doctrine, worship, discipline, or government.

Thus Thomas Campbell came to the heart of the matter. The sentences immediately following in the report were to be echoed and re-echoed by Thomas in the years ahead:

> This, our unhappy division, appeared to us an evil of no small magnitude, whether abstractly considered as inconsistent with the genius and spirit of the Christian religion, which has union, unity, and communion in faith, hope and love, for its grand object upon earth, or whether considered in its hurtful tendencies, as marring and embarrassing the cause which it was thus the grand object of the secession to promote.[10]

The report next makes inquiry into the means whereby reunion might be established. On behalf of the committee he submitted a plan for the review and criticism of the other members of the synod, "That so collecting all the information we could, we might, at our next meeting, revise, alter, or remodel the whole question, as we could understand the wish and views of our sincerely-esteemed and much respected brethren."

The following propositions were then submitted:

Proposition 1. That it is the opinion of this Committee that a union of both denominations of Seceders in this kingdom would, through the Divine blessing, contribute much to the edification of the Church, and to the credit of religion.

Proposition 2. That while we recollect with sorrow the melancholy consequences of our unhappy divisions, which have alienated affections on both sides, and tended rather to exaggerate our mutual infirmities than to heal and cover them, being heartily desirous that these evils may proceed no further, we are of opinion that, in existing circumstances, it is our incumbent duty to avoid all animadversions, or all direct or indirect criminations of either party, with regard to past ground of differences, which might tend rather to gender strife than to edify one another in love.

Proposition 3. That the circumstances in which the Lord has placed the secession Church in this kingdom do not render a judicial decision concerning oaths, disputed in Scotland, a necessary part of the testimony-bearing in this land.

Proposition 4. That seeing both denominations of Seceders in Ireland are of one sentiment in the grand abstract or covenanted system of doctrine, worship, discipline, and government contained in the Westminster Confession of Faith and Catechisms, Presbyterian Form of Church Government, and Directory for Worship; and seeing that the judicial decision about oaths in Scotland can be no actual subject of testimony-bearing here, much less a term of communion among us; therefore, it appears that there is nothing to prevent the two bodies of Seceders in this land to unite in a bond of a common testimony adapted to their local situation.

Proposition 5. That such a testimony should be emitted and adapted to our circumstances, as a branch of the secession Church in this part of the United Kingdom, as would, at the same time, preserve every article in the original testimony emitted by the Associate Presbytery, in so far as said articles may appear in any wise effective of the grand object of testimony-bearing among us.[11]

In March of the following year a meeting was held between representatives of the Burghers and Anti-

Burghers at Lurgan, in County Armagh. There was a unanimous desire on both sides for a union, and since the oath of the burgesses had never been required in Ireland, there was nothing to warrant the continued separation of the two groups there. In the meanwhile, the General Associate Synod in Scotland, hearing of a movement toward uniting the two denominations, expressed disapproval even before any application for union was received. Consequently, the effort failed for the time being.

In 1805 formal application was made to the General Associate Synod in Scotland, by members of the Synod of Ulster in Ireland, requesting them to consider whether or not it would be advisable to allow the brethren in Ireland to transact their own business without being in subordination to the General Synod. Thomas Campbell was selected as the spokesman for the Irish ministers and journeyed to Scotland to lay the matter before the higher court. He proceeded to Glasgow and presented the case to the synod with great earnestness and force. As one present at the meeting later declared: "In my opinion he out-argued them, but they out-voted him." The General Synod decided there was nothing to be gained by such a proposal and matters were left very much as they were before. These efforts were not without effect, however, for it brought the question to general attention, discussion was encouraged, and the sensibleness of union was made more and more evident. On September 5, 1820, in the same church in Edinburgh where the division had occurred seventy-three years before, the Burgher and Anti-Burgher Synods united.

Thomas Campbell was no less a Calvinist or a Presbyterian for his initial experiences in the uniting of two divisions of the church. His good standing with the ministry of his own church was shown by his being sent to Glasgow as their representative. He was deeply concerned that the church's witness be unimpaired by strife from within. Loyal to his church as he was, he could not have helped contrasting the lack of concern and the rigid thought patterns of the Scottish synod with the freedom of government and opinion enjoyed by the Independents. It is important to note that he was led to this position by the need for a united witness to the gospel, not by conscious convictions on Christian union. He was simply a pious minister seeking to convert a sinful world. The divisive tendencies in his own church first revealed to him the evils of sectarianism, and this limited project became his first adventure in uniting the divided church. His effort in 1805 failed, but his experience with this specific manifestation of the sectarian spirit—"fraught with the awful consequences of distracting, disturbing, and dividing the flock of the Lord's heritage, and of sowing discord among the brethren" as Campbell said in his address to the Anti-Burgher Synod of Ireland—made him more conscious than ever before of the need for a basis on which the church could unite.

Removal to America

With what mixed motives the decision to journey to America was made will never be known fully. We are told that the excessive strain of Campbell's double labors as preacher and teacher began to impair his health. He grew pale and was increasingly bothered by a stomach ailment. Undoubtedly his concern over the excessive sectarianism of the day played its part. Many remedies were tried but to no avail. His physician urged him to lighten his labors and, if possible, to seek a change of environment, perhaps a sea voyage, as an aid to his recovery. Some of his friends urged a visit to America. Friends and neighbors had been migrating there, and this would be an opportunity to visit them and to see the new country. But the trip did not appeal to him, for he found it difficult to leave his position and family and to undertake such a voyage.

Seeing the critical state of his father's health young Alexander resolved to urge the American trip. He agreed to look after the school and suggested that his father leave at once. Apparently there were family discussions as to the possibility of joining the steady stream of migrants to the new world. Alexander told his father that it was his purpose to go to the United States as soon as he came of age. If they should consider seriously removing to America, the father's trip would make it possible to seek a suitable location for the family.

There were many reasons why Thomas Campbell might wish to consider moving to America. At this time there was a large and constant migration of Scotch-Irish families to the United States. The political troubles, the religious dissensions, the oppressive tyranny of landed proprietors over tenants, and the almost hopeless prospects of those with large families for success in life, led great numbers to seek a happier home in the new world. Several families of Campbell's acquaintance in the vicinity of Rich Hill had made their arrangements to set out for the United States. Others had already left.

After careful and prayerful consideration Thomas Campbell finally gave his consent to take the long voyage. The decision was made that he should visit America, a land conjuring up visions of a rich and virgin country, a land of unlimited resources and opportunities. America might mean not only renewed health, but also the possibility of new opportunity for the family. It was, therefore, not only with sorrow but also with high hope that Thomas decided to visit the new world from which he would either write the family to join him or return to Ireland.

Among those who urged the American visit was the Acheson family. Members of the family had already gone to America and others were planning to leave. A young lady of Campbell's Ahorey congregation, Hannah Acheson, wished to go to her relatives who had previously migrated and settled in Washington, Pennsylvania, on the Western frontier, and Campbell agreed to escort her to her destination. He could thus perform a useful service and at the same time learn to know the country.

It was so arranged. Leaving the family and school in charge of Alexander, now a promising youth of eighteen, Thomas Campbell left for Londonderry on April 1, 1807, after bidding his congregation, family, and friends farewell.

At Londonderry arrangements were completed for passage to Philadelphia on the sailing-vessel *Brutus*, Captain Craig, master. While waiting for the ship's departure, he addressed a letter to his family. It reveals the thoughts of a deeply spiritual man, now in his forty-fourth year, about to leave family and friends for an unknown destination. What adventures and dangers were ahead? The letter made such an impression on young Alexander that he copied it in his notebook. Its advice was as follows:

Live to God; be devoted to him in heart, and in all your undertakings. Be a sincere Christian—i.e., imbibe the doctrines, obey the precepts, copy the example, and believe the promise of the gospel. And that you may do so, read it, study it, pray over it, embrace it as your heritage, your portion. . . . Live by faith in the Lord Jesus Christ, both "for wisdom, righteousness, sanctification and redemption." Above all things, attend to this, for without him you can do nothing, either to the glory of God or your own good.[12]

On the 8th of April, 1807, the wind being favorable, the ship *Brutus* set sail toward the West. Thomas Campbell carried with him only a statement of his ministerial standing, his Bible, and possibly a few books and other possessions. As he sailed from Londonderry, passed out of Loch Foyle, and rounded Malin Head, the most northern point of Ireland, Thomas gazed for the last time on his native land. Ireland was behind him. Before him was a voyage of many days, and then, America.

CHAPTER TWO

EXPERIENCES ON THE FRONTIER

The American Frontier—1790-1807

IN THE years during which Thomas Campbell had established himself in northern Ireland as an Anti-Burgher Seceder Presbyterian minister, a nation was struggling to come into being on the opposite side of the Atlantic. Something new in political and social life was developing in America, and in the vast expanse of land which lay across the Alleghenies, known only as "the West," the common man saw unlimited opportunity. Here was his hope for the future, however poor the past may have been.

The treaty which had closed the Revolutionary War had fixed the western boundary of the United States at the Mississippi River. This seemed to all contemporary viewpoints to take in as much territory as would be likely to be settled for many years to come. This vast area was sparsely populated except along the eastern seaboard and the first general census taken in 1790 revealed that there were approximately 4,000,000 people in the United States. An analysis of this figure shows that five per cent, or only 200,000 of the total population, was already living west of the Allegheny Mountains. The Ohio River was a part of the Pennsylvania gateway to the West. People went down the river in great flatboats loaded with supplies and personal possessions. Nothing like this westward migration was ever seen before. The roads west swarmed with wagonloads of settlers and their livestock.

During this period the United States was bound by close commercial ties to Europe and particularly to England. The era of American self-sufficiency had not yet arrived, and the great majority of manufactured articles still had to be imported. Cheap lands were the main motivation for the westward movement that was so upsetting the balance of the Union against the original thirteen states, and to move West was the poor man's opportunity to better himself.

The pioneers of the West had been, at first, too busy clearing away the forests and subduing the ruggedness of a wild, uncultivated region to devote much time to intellectual improvement. This caused them to develop a bold and self-reliant spirit but tended to impart roughness as well as awkwardness to manners. Life was often lived dangerously and boisterously. There was little time for reading and few books to be read. In the country, schools were opened only for a short while during the winter. Frontier education was usually poor and was largely supported privately. Marriages, as in colonial days, took place at an earlier age than in eastern cities and Europe. Courtship, as one frontier historian pointed out, was brief and to the point. Widowhood lasted briefly, and children became a prime economic asset.

Incessant physical labor was demanded of every member of the household in order to pay for a newly purchased farm or to extend the limits of an older one. The men and boys labored in the fields while the mother and girls looked after the household affairs, which usually included making clothes (and often the cloth) for the entire family. Indeed, in some seasons of the year, the women even assisted in the fields. Out of the conditions and struggles of the American frontier something unique emerged. Henry Steele Commager describes it by saying that

The American character was the product of an interplay of inheritance and environment, both varied and complex. . . . But the inheritance was highly selective and the impact of environment uneven. Institutions—notably those of a political and judicial character—suffered only minor modifications, but the modification of social organization was so profound as to suggest a departure from the normal course of evolution, while the psychological modification was nothing less than revolutionary.

It was not, in short, particular environments that determined the American character or created the American type but the whole of the American environment—the sense of spaciousness, the invitation to mobility, the atmosphere of independence, the encouragement to enterprise and to optimism.[1]

The American exhibited an intense practicality in almost every area of life: whether in business, politics, culture, science, or religion. He was resourceful, always ready to meet situations with ingenious solutions. Theories and speculations disturbed him, and he avoided difficult philosophies of government or conduct. In general, no philosophy that got much beyond common sense commanded his interest. His religion, too, was practical. Along with the doctrine of salvation by faith he instinctively placed faith in salvation by works. Frontier conditions both opposed and favored the spread of Christianity. On the one hand, many persons, removed from the influence of more stable communities, tended to leave behind all religious and moral practices taught by Christianity. On the other hand, the very fact of the newness of the country and the feeling that men could have a fresh start gave opportunity for building the church into the emerging frontier community.

The period immediately following the Revolutionary War was an epoch of great spiritual decline. During the latter part of the eighteenth century, religion was perhaps at its lowest ebb in the history of America. French and English rationalism, culminating in the "Age of Reason" reached its peak early in the first decade of the nineteenth century. Baptist and Methodist membership along the eastern seaboard fell off. In Virginia, Chief Justice John Marshall thought that the Episcopal Church was "too far gone to be revived." Nevertheless, without the aid of any single outstanding personality, like that of George Whitefield in the Great Awakening of the 1740's, there was a strong reawakening of religious interest. It began in New England about 1792, within the next four years was strongly manifested in the Middle States, and from there swept through the South. By the dawn of the nineteenth century it had come even to the new West beyond the Alleghenies.

To the isolated families along the frontier the birth of the camp meeting or revival, through the Second Awakening, became a much-needed social outlet and a new form of excitement as well as a religious experience. Two such camp meetings were those held in Logan County, Kentucky, about 1800 led by James McGready, a Scotch-Irish Presbyterian from North Carolina and the famous Cane Ridge meeting of 1801 in Bourbon County, Kentucky, where ten to twenty-five thousand people met for several weeks. Men of different denominations took turns at preaching and sometimes several spoke at once in different parts of the grounds. Hysterical, spasmodic laughs, spasms, jerks, fainting, dancing, and even barking by the possessed who "treed the devil," accompanied these meetings.

As a whole, this new revival period was far less marked than earlier revivals by these symptoms of overwrought excitement. Its effect was none the less profound, and the new religious interest with its uniquely American form of evangelism transformed the church on the frontier. The over-all effects of the Awakening were good. Moral life improved and infidelity received a permanent setback. Under the impulse of the new religious spirit, American Christian life blossomed with activities. The Sunday school, first introduced from England into Philadelphia in 1791, now flourished everywhere. The prayer meeting, heretofore only sporadic, became general. Foreign mission boards were begun. The progress of home missionary effort in the United States was no less remarkable. The circuit rider and the pastor kept pace with the progress of the population westward, and state and national organizations in the larger communions energetically supported the work.

The denominational picture in America at the beginning of the nineteenth century was little less confusing than it was in northern Ireland. When America was colonized, the religious conditions of Europe were transferred to the new world. These conditions were modified by life on the frontier, but nevertheless, persistently maintained their former sectarian spirit. There was no communion or sect common to the thirteen colonies. The Congregational church was strong in New England with the exception of Rhode Island where the Baptists predominated, the Episcopal church led in the southern colonies and a mixture of communions in the middle colonies. The Dutch Reformed church was prominent in New York, the Lutheran church in Delaware, and the Friends or Quakers in New Jersey and Pennsylvania. Baptists and Presbyterians were scattered throughout the middle colonies, but were especially numerous in Pennsylvania because of that state's policy of welcoming all communions.

The Treaty of Paris, which concluded the war between France and England in 1763, the same year in which Thomas Campbell was born, opened the western part of Pennsylvania to settlement by the British. Scotch-Irish immigrants poured across the Alleghenies into this new section. They were largely Presbyterians, who brought their faith with them and established churches in their new home. In 1781 the Redstone Presbytery, in western Pennsylvania, was established by the Synod of New York and Philadelphia at a time when there were only four preachers in the Presbytery. The first house of worship was erected in 1790, the meetings having been held in groves and private houses before that time.

The Presbyterians and Congregationalists made the largest contributions to the education and cultural life of the frontier, though they did not succeed in gaining large numbers for their churches. The Presbyterians were a particularly rigid body in both doctrine and polity, and every innovation to meet the peculiar needs or problems of the new country was always strongly opposed. Unlike the Methodist circuit rider and the Baptist farmer-preacher, to whom all frontier communities were alike, the Presbyterian preacher ministered primarily to people of Presbyterian background. The usual Presbyterian preacher on the frontier went forth seeking other Presbyterians and Presbyterian settlements made up of people of Scottish and Scotch-Irish descent. This was the pattern followed by Thomas Campbell on his removal to America.

With few exceptions, such as the co-operation between the Presbyterians and the Congregationalists in the "plan of union" of 1801, denominational rivalries were keen and controversy harsh. The very success of the revivals and camp meetings on the frontier led to hard feelings and deep-seated jealousies. Organized Christianity in America became far more bitterly divided and more intensive in its sectarian rivalries than even in Ireland or Scotland. In the isolated districts of the frontier, the party spirit waxed strong and each man felt himself competent in theology and his own judge in religious matters.

Calvinism was the prevailing system of theology throughout much of America. Parents objected to their children being lectured on their personal salvation, for it was felt God would save them in his own good time. One minister declared that he could not hope that God would be so partial to him as to foreordain all his eight children to be of the elect, so he did not pray for any of them for fear he might seem to be presuming against the plans and purposes of God. According to the Calvinistic interpretations of the day, some cataclysmic experience came to everyone truly led by the Holy Spirit and most individuals interested in religion sought such an experience.

There was a marked rebellion, however, against this overemphasis on Calvinism and the extreme sectarian bitterness. James O'Kelly of Virginia, who in 1792 left the Methodist church in protest against the power of the bishops, and organized the Republican Methodists to exemplify a democratic church government, two years later adopted the name "Christian" for the group and accepted the Bible alone as his authority.

Abner Jones, of Vermont, as early as 1800 had withdrawn from the Baptist church on account of the Calvinistic creed. Probably influenced by the Scottish Independents, he declared that church creeds were not sound authority for a Christian, that all should follow Christ alone, and should bear only the name of Christian.

About 1804 a Presbyterian minister in Kentucky, Barton W. Stone, was greatly disturbed by the religious conventions and creeds of his day, until he revolted and founded a group whose members called themselves simply "Christians," and preached that the Bible alone was authority for the church.

The first task of the American churches after the Revolution was to follow the ever-increasing stream of migration over the Alleghenies and into the Ohio and Mississippi basins, and throughout this whole period the churches were in contact with frontier conditions and frontier needs. Frontier liberalism was constantly contending against the narrow control of the older settled regions.

It was into this high adventure that Thomas Campbell was thrust on his arrival in America in 1807. He was to become a part of the westward migration—one of those most determined to take the church to the frontier. As a result of his experiences on the frontier, he was increasingly aware of the church's divided condition and rebelled against the bitterness of sectarian spirit. He was determined to become a part of the creative force then at work establishing the church firmly in a new land, and was to be subject to all the complex and varied influences of inheritance and environment then at work on the American frontier. Thomas Campbell never quite understood the frontier but he did have certain deep convictions about the Christian faith that were to be influential in the future of the church in America.

Arrival and Settlement in Washington, Pennsylvania

Thomas Campbell was a part of the steady stream of Presbyterians from Scotland and northern Ireland seeking a new life in America. The destination of most of these groups was the state of Pennsylvania, for in the central and western parts of the state the Presbyterians were the largest communion. There were, in fact, so many Scotch-Irish Presbyterians in this area that one of them called this region "an American Ulster." Most of those who came were regular Presbyterians, who had been members of the established church in Scotland or in northern Ireland. Toward the end of the eighteenth century the regular Presbyterians had four synods and sixteen presbyteries throughout the colonies and on the frontier. The organization of the General Assembly in 1788 gave them the character of a nation-wide movement and made them the strongest body of Presbyterians in the United States.

The Presbyterian immigrants were not all from the established church, however, for some of those who came were from the Secession churches. In addition to the General Assembly of the Presbyterian church there was the Associate Synod of North America. This was in reality the organization of the Anti-Burgher Seceder Presbyterians as the Burghers never had a distinct organization in America. This group later joined with other Presbyterian sects to create what is known today as the United Presbyterian church. The annual meeting of the Associate Synod for 1807 was held in Philadelphia.

In fact, the Associate Synod of North America was in session in May when the ship *Brutus,* from Londonderry, sailed into the harbor at Philadelphia after thirty-five days at sea. On Wednesday, May 13, 1807, Thomas Campbell and Hannah Acheson, his charge, stepped from the boat and touched foot on American soil for the first time. It had been a speedy trip for those days and they looked forward to the experiences that lay ahead. After two days, which were probably used to recover from the fatigue of their journey and during which he learned of the synod's meeting, Campbell sought the fellowship of his religious brethren and presented his credentials and the letters of introduction brought from Ireland. Among them was the following testimonial from the Presbytery of Market Hill:

We, the remainent members of the Presbytery at Market Hill, March 24th, A.D. 1807, do hereby certify that the bearer, Thomas Campbell, has been for about nine years minister of the Gospel in the seceding congregation of Ahorey, and co-presbyter with us, during which time he has maintained an irreproachable moral character; and, in the discharge of the duties of his sacred functions has conducted himself as a faithful minister of Christ; and is now released from his pastoral charge over said congregation at his own request, upon good and sufficient reasons for his resignation of said charge, particularly his intention of going to America. Given under our hands at our presbyterial meeting, the day and year above written.

The above, by order of the Presbytery, is subscribed by,

David Arrott, *Moderator.*[2]

Campbell was cordially received into the fellowship of the Anti-Burghers. Then, as now, there was the need for qualified ministers and the synod was probably delighted to receive one so highly recommended. In the minutes of the session held on Saturday afternoon, May 16, we read:

> Mr. Thomas Campbell, minister from Associate Presbytery of Market Hill, Ireland, presented a certificate subscribed by Mr. David Arrott as Mod'r of said Presb'y. He was received into Christian and ministerial communion; and his name being added to the roll, was admitted to a seat in the Synod.[3]

On Monday, May 18, he was appointed, along with John Dickie, to serve in the Presbytery of Chartiers, in southwestern Pennsylvania, until the next meeting. Campbell specifically requested assignment to Chartiers Presbytery since it included Washington, Pennsylvania, where many of his friends and acquaintances were already located and which was the destination of Hannah Acheson. The synod allowed Thomas fifty dollars for the necessary equipment and provisions for the journey. The minutes of Chartiers Presbytery show that Campbell had preaching appointments at Pittsburgh and at points between that town and Washington, Pennsylvania, beginning July 1, 1807.

As he prepared to leave Philadelphia for his assignments in the Chartiers Presbytery, Campbell addressed a letter, dated May 27, 1807, to this family in Ireland. The letter told of the thirty-five-day voyage across the Atlantic, of having found the Associate Synod in session on his arrival, and of his kind reception into fellowship and communion. A portion of the letter preserved for us continues at length as follows:

> What a debtor am I to the grace of God! . . . for these kindnesses conferred upon me are also for your sakes, that, through his mercy, we may yet praise him together in the congregation of his people. . . . My dear children, let me address you together: . . . see that you follow the directions I gave you at my parting, whether by word or writing. Be a comfort to your mother; love, cherish and pity one another. Love the Lord your God;

love his Son, Jesus Christ, and pray to the Lord constantly and ardently for me your poor father, who longs after you all, and who cannot rest, if the Lord will, till he has prepared a place of residence for you all, where I trust we shall spend the rest of our days together in his service.[4]

At the close of the synod's annual meeting, and after two weeks or more with the Seceder ministers and other acquaintances he had met in Philadelphia, Thomas Campbell and Hannah Acheson left for Washington, Pennsylvania. They either traveled by stagecoach or secured a ride on one of the numerous wagons which were then filling the roads west in increasing number. At best the three-hundred-and-fifty-mile journey from Philadelphia to Washington, by way of Pittsburgh, would have taken approximately two weeks.

Washington at that time contained only about five hundred inhabitants, and many of the houses, like those in the country around, were built of logs, notched and fitted near the ends with the chinks filled with mortar and small stones. There were some frame buildings and one or two were built of stone. It was, in short, a typical town of the then western frontier. The town stood on rising ground at the upper part of the valley of Chartiers. A good water supply was available since the town was located near the sources of several streams. The hills around the town were comparatively low and the country was gently sloping. It was described as having many fertile farms, orchards and grazing lands surrounding it; and on the steeper sides of the valleys, virgin forests of oak, ash, walnut, and hickory still stood. Already it was a prosperous and rapidly developing community.

The meeting of the Chartiers Presbytery held at the Harmony meetinghouse, June 30 and July 1, 1807, gave Thomas Campbell the following assignments:

Mr. Campbell at Buffaloe on the 2d and 3d sab. of July, at Mt. Pleasant on the 4th, at Pittsburgh on 1st sab. of August;

at Squire McKees on the 2d; at Cannamaugh on the 3rd and 4th, at Squire Smith's on 5th, at John Templeton's on the 1st sab. of Sept'r, at Upper Piney Creek in John Sloane's on the 2d, at Mercer's on the 3rd and 4th, at John Hammel's on the 1st of Oct'r, at Breakneck on the 2nd and at Buffaloe on the 3rd and 4th.[5]

On his arrival at Washington, Thomas Campbell was welcomed by a number of old friends who had previously migrated from Ireland. He renewed his acquaintance with the Acheson family, who were glad to receive Hannah into their midst after a safe journey from Ireland. Others who had heard of him in Ireland made themselves known. Typical was the visit of a woman who had come from Ireland with her husband and family in 1805. She called one day at the house where Campbell was staying and introduced herself. Immediately recognizing him, she told of walking six miles in Ireland to attend a communion service in the Seceder church in which he was one of the officiating clergymen. This woman and her husband, James Hanen, were later two of the first seven persons immersed by Thomas Campbell on a profession of faith. Only a few weeks after Campbell's arrival in Washington, Thomas Hodgens and James Foster, with their families, arrived and settled on a farm near Mt. Pleasant, a small village about ten miles north of Washington. Hodgens had known Campbell as the teacher of some of his children. Foster was a quiet but influential young man, who had been a member of the Independent congregation at Rich Hill and had known Thomas Campbell there.

Thomas thus found himself in the midst of friends and acquaintances who knew his worth and greatly respected his ministerial standing. They were anxious to have him lead them and were quick to advertise their high estimate of him to the people of the community. Campbell became increasingly popular, especially as his ability and relatively tolerant spirit became generally known. The Seceder congregations, not very numerous in the area, were pleased to have such a man as their pastor and as they knew him better and recognized more fully his earnestness and piety, they came to regard him as their most outstanding minister.

Trouble in the Chartiers Presbytery

It must have been exceedingly difficult for Thomas Campbell, reared in the stable environment of village life in northern Ireland, educated at one of Scotland's leading universities, and a respected leader of an established community, to adjust himself readily to the rudeness and lack of culture manifested in this typical section of the American frontier. Undoubtedly his sensitive nature was offended at many of the accepted customs and standards of the new West.

Certainly Campbell was soon disappointed in the religious conditions he found in southwestern Pennsylvania. He had been troubled over the divisions of the church in northern Ireland, but if he had hoped that the spirit of liberty in America would cultivate a closer fellowship among the churches, he was to be quickly disillusioned. The Anti-Burghers were among the first Presbyterians to arrive in this part of Pennsylvania, and many of the Burghers who came took membership with them. This did not broaden their vision, for the church in the western wilderness became more exclusive and intolerant than the church in either Ireland or Scotland. In 1796 the Associate Synod had passed an act prohibiting "occasional communion," or communion with other bodies of Christians. There was every attempt to maintain doctrinal soundness based on the standard of the Calvinistic theology of the Westminster Confession. At the 1807 meeting of the Associate Synod in Philadelphia, perhaps in the hearing of the recently arrived Campbell, a memorial had been presented which indicated there had already been trouble in one of the congregations of the Chartiers Presbytery between elders and a minister whose services had been refused.

The members of the Seceder church were widely scattered in this newly settled country, and in their midst were members of other denominations who were without church affiliation. There were members of other branches of the Presbyterian church without pastoral oversight. Usually they did not seek membership in the Anti-Burgher congregations, but unless they did this and were formally admitted to membership, they were treated as outside of the fold. It was naturally not long then before members of other parties and denominations, as well as friends and acquaintances from Ireland, sought fellowship with Campbell in this new land. He, of course, welcomed them and extended to them the ministrations of the church, even though they did not take formal membership, since it was his desire to be of service to all Christians.

Campbell, therefore, had not been long in the fellowship of the Chartiers Presbytery before suspicions began to arise in the minds of some of his fellow ministers as to whether he was as sound in doctrine and polity as they thought he should be. They looked askance at his friendship and fellowship with those of other communions. James Foster later suggested that these ministers were jealous or envious of his popularity and the real leadership he showed both as a scholar and as a preacher. Whatever the reason, there was evidence that all was not harmonious in Chartiers Presbytery.

Not long after his admittance into the Presbytery of Chartiers, Campbell was asked to visit a few scattered members of the Anti-Burgher Presbyterians who lived up the Allegheny River above Pittsburgh, at a community named Cannamaugh, and to hold a "sacramental" celebration among them. The trip there was probably made by boat and required two or three days. He was accompanied by William Wilson, a fellow minister of the Seceder church. This part of the country was thinly settled and religious services were held infrequently. Seldom did the neighboring families have the opportunity of enjoying the Lord's Supper.

On this occasion, Thomas' sympathies were strongly aroused in behalf of the many who belonged to other branches of the Presbyterian family who had not observed the Lord's Supper for a long time, and who were in attendance at his service. In the sermon of preparation, Campbell felt it his duty to express regret at the existing divisions in the church and to suggest to all present, who felt so disposed and were duly prepared, that they feel free to partake of the elements when they were offered, regardless of presbyterial connection. Wilson, the Seceder minister who was with him, said nothing at the time, but was surprised and shocked that Campbell would open the sacrament to all Presbyterians present. The story of this heresy circulated rapidly, for not long afterward a Rev. Mr. Anderson refused to keep an appointment assigned by the presbytery for Anderson and Campbell jointly, and gave as his excuse Campbell's supposed deviation from orthodoxy. At the next meeting of the presbytery real trouble began for Thomas Campbell.

The regular session of the presbytery was held at Mt. Hope meetinghouse October 27-29, 1807. Campbell's name is listed as among those present and the case against him is revealed by the following excerpt from the minutes of that same meeting:

Enquiry having been made concerning the fulfillment of appointments, Mr. Anderson acknowledged that he had not fulfilled the appointment to assist Mr. Campbel in dispensing the sacrament of the Lord's Supper at Buffaloe, and gave as his excuse or reason, an account, which he had by such testimony as he judged sufficient for him to proceed upon, that Mr. Campbel had publicly taught the opinions expressed in the two following propositions, viz.: "That there is an appropriation of Christ to ourselves in the essence of saving faith, such appropiation belonging to a high degree of that faith; and that we have nothing but human authority or agreement for confessions of faith, testimonies, covenanting and fast days before the dispensation of the Lord's Supper," and as Mr. Anderson judged that these propositions were inconsistent with some articles of our testimony, it appeared upon consideration most proper not to join with Mr. Campbel in the communion till the matter should be enquired into. After some consideration on this subject, it was agreed to put this question, Whether upon supposition that the testimony upon which Mr. Anderson proceeded was sufficient, his conduct in declining to fulfill his appointment was excusable? Which question being put, was carried in the affirmative.[6]

In this manner, within five months after his arrival in this country, Thomas Campbell was involved in controversy with his fellow Seceder ministers over questions of doctrine. He, who had served a congregation in northern Ireland successfully and without question for over nine years, had become in America an object of suspicion to such an extent that a fellow minister hesitated to officiate with him on a "sacramental" occasion.

The presbytery inquired into Anderson's evidence for Campbell's alleged deviation from Seceder testimony. At that point Wilson, who had accompanied Thomas to Cannamaugh, testified that he had heard Campbell declare unorthodox propositions in a sermon before the observance of the Lord's Supper on that occasion. The members of the presbytery were then asked whether this was sufficient reason for Mr. Anderson to decline to fulfill his appointment. It was agreed that this was sufficient evidence and Anderson's excuse was accepted.

The next morning, October 28, Thomas Campbell made a motion, which was seconded, asking the presbytery to reconsider Anderson's excuse for not fulfilling his appointment at Buffalo. The motion was lost. This apparently angered Thomas since after entering a verbal protest he left the meeting, saying "that he would not sit any longer in this Presbytery." On the following day the presbytery agreed to appoint a committee of five, four ministers and a ruling elder, to inquire into the reports concerning Campbell's orthodoxy. If the committee thought it necessary, a libel was to be drawn against him and in the meantime he was not to be given preaching appointments because of walking out of the meeting the day before. During the same day's session, October 29, the presbytery received a letter from Campbell containing a protest to them regarding Anderson's excuse. The presbytery asked Ramsay and Anderson to draft a reply to this letter, which was approved by the presbytery and sent to Campbell. We are entirely in the dark as to the contents of either Campbell's letter or the reply.

John Anderson with whom Campbell was engaged in controversy had the degree of Doctor of Divinity and had been the professor of theology for the Associate churches since April, 1794. He was ordained *sine titulo* in Philadelphia and had itinerated for some time. In 1792 he had been installed as pastor at Mill Creek and Harmon's Creek, in Beaver County, Pennsylvania, in the Chartiers Presbytery. He wrote a book, published in 1793, entitled *The Appropriation Which is in The Nature of Saving Faith*. Anderson lectured several hours each day in his seminary and while known for meekness and humility, had a hasty temper and was very impatient of contradiction on matters of principle. He was considered able and faithful to duty but somewhat tedious. Anderson was one of the four ministers appointed by the presbytery to investigate Thomas Campbell. The other three men, William Wilson, Thomas Alison, and James Ramsay, had all been students of Dr. Anderson's and had been ordained to serve as pastors of the Associate churches of Chartiers Presbytery. As former students of Anderson's, it is not surprising they had a oneness of mind in regard to Campbell's digressions from Seceder doctrines.

This fact also helps us to understand Thomas' feeling that he had not been treated justly.

Between the October and January meetings of the presbytery, Campbell endeavored to inform his family of events and happenings at Washington. But communication at best was slow in those days and letters required from eighty to ninety days to reach their destination and left long weeks when there was no news. It is not surprising then to learn that letters written in November, 1807, which told of the October meeting of the presbytery, failed to reach their destination.

The opposition which he encountered in the presbytery seems to have taken away any doubt left in his mind as to whether he would stay in America and made Campbell more determined than ever to have his family join him. In a letter dated January 1, 1808, written at Washington, Pennsylvania, Campbell urged his family to make preparations for immediate departure for America and in this letter he referred to the November letters and gave a summary of the news in them. The portion of this letter preserved for us reveals something of the consecration and devotion of Campbell, and in its tedious style, is typical of his writing:

> I have been encompassed with mercies from the day I left you until this day—not the slightest accident by sea or land has befallen me. . . . My confidence toward God in behalf of you all, to whose gracious providence and merciful protection I have heartily resigned you, keeps my mind in perfect peace. . . . I do not know but that I have felt more solemn, elevated pleasure in this grateful exercise, since I set my foot in this land of peace, liberty, and prosperity, than I could have done in the same time had I remained in the midst of you, all things considered. . . . Be of good comfort through his grace, and cautiously avoid danger. Omit no opportunity of removing, as the Lord may graciously permit. The merciful providence of the Lord be with you. Wishing you a happy new year under his gracious auspices, adieu.
>
> THOMAS CAMPBELL[7]

On January 5, 1808, the Chartiers Presbytery was in session at Monteur's Run meetinghouse. Campbell, who was present, sought to correct the minutes of the October meeting to state that he had asked permission to present his grievances to the presbytery. The presbytery refused the correction, stating "that Mr. Campbel made only one motion at the time, not two." On the evening of January 6, at a meeting in the home of John Hay, the ruling elder appointed to investigate Campbell along with the ministers, the presbytery heard the report of the committee appointed at the October meeting to investigate Thomas Campbell's public declarations. The committee presented its report in the form of a seven-point "libel" or written statement of charges usually presented in an ecclesiastical court. It is important to examine the specific charges leveled at Campbell and to consider his reply to them. The libel charged that the accused:

1. Taught that a person's appropriation of Christ to himself as his own Savior, does not belong to the essence of saving faith; but only to a high degree of it.
2. Asserted that a church has no divine warrant for holding Confessions of Faith as terms of communion.
3. Asserted that it is the duty of ruling elders to pray and exhort publicly in vacant congregations.
4. Asserted that it is permissable to hear ministers that are in stated opposition to our testimony.
5. Asserted that our Lord Jesus Christ was not subject to the precept as well as the penalty of the law in the stead of his people or as their surety.
6. Asserted that man is able in this life to live without sin in thought, word and deed.
7. Preached in a congregation where a minister was settled, without any regular call or appointment.⁰

When it is remembered that Dr. Anderson's one effort in the field of writing was entitled *The Appropriation Which is in The Nature of Saving Faith,* it is not difficult to understand the reason for the first charge. The second item apparently grew out of the trip to Cannamaugh in company with Wilson for the observance of the Lord's Supper. The last article indicates that Campbell had preached to congregations and communities without appointment, but at the request of the people, and this despite his suspension by the presbytery in October.

In the original minutes six of the seven articles begin with the ominous statement: "It is erroneous or contrary to the Holy Scriptures and our subordinate standards to assert that...." In the seventh article the phrase is modified to read: "It is contrary to the Holy Scriptures and to the Rules of the Presbyterian Church Government...." In each instance numerous quotations are given from several sources supposedly pointing out the error. References are given to *The Bible, The Westminster Confession of Faith, The Larger Catechism, The Shorter Catechism,* and *The Declaration and Testimony* (i.e., of the Secession Church). The libel is almost ponderous in the sevenfold recurrence of the refrain which concludes each article with "But you, the Rev'd Thomas Campbell, have publickly taught the above mentioned error...."

The articles of the libel were read and Campbell was given an opportunity to speak informally to each one. After some discussion it was agreed to give him a copy of the articles and to delay further discussion until the next meeting of the presbytery on the second Tuesday of February. The meeting was to be held at Buffalo to hear the testimony of such witnesses as might be there. It was hoped to bring the affair to a close at that meeting.

The presbytery met at Buffalo as scheduled on Tuesday, February 9, 1808, but it was not until the following day at ten o'clock that the presbytery proceeded to hear Thomas Campbell's answer to each of the charges brought against him. The charges and Campbell's written answer to them were read one by one and were heard distinctly by all present. In Campbell's defense or explanation on each of the seven charges is seen his developing thought on the state of the divided church, therefore, it is well to examine his answers carefully. Here is found the first expression of principles enlarged upon at a later date. To the first article, concerning "saving faith," Campbell's answer in part was:

> With respect to faith I believe that the soul of man is the subject of it; the Divine Spirit is the author of it; the Divine Word the rule and reason of it; Christ and him crucified the object of it; the Divine pardon, acceptance and assistance, or grace here and glory hereafter, the direct, proper and formal end of it. That it is an act of the whole soul intensively looking to, embracing and leaning upon Jesus Christ for complete salvation—for with the heart man believeth unto righteousness—that it is the right of all that hear the gospel so to believe upon the bare declaration, invitation and promise of God, holden forth equally and indiscriminately unto all that hear it, without restriction or exception of any kind; though at the same time none can do this, except it be given him of god.

The main point of difference between orthodox Seceder Presbyterian theology and Campbell was that Campbell refused to include any sort of mystical experience as an essential element in saving faith. He said that it may or may not accompany a high degree of faith and a man's faith does not depend on it. He considered faith as an intelligent response of the mind to evidence rather than a Spirit-given emotional experience. In all other respects he affirmed Seceder testimony.

To the second article, concerning Confessions of Faith as terms of communion, Campbell's answer was:

> With respect to Confessions of Faith and Testimonies I believe that the church has all the Divine warrant for such exhibitions of the truth, that our Confession and Testimony adduce for that purpose; and that it is lawful and warrantable to use them as terms of communion insofar as our testimony requires; in which sense I have never opposed them.

In his answer to this charge Campbell sought to be diplomatic by stating that he had never opposed Confessions of Faith as terms of communion "insofar as our testimony requires." But apparently the Confession and Testimony did not, in fact, allege any divine warrant for using them as terms of communion. The minutes record that after Campbell gave his answer to this charge he was further questioned as to what he had meant in the former meeting at Monteur's Run "that we have neither precept nor example in Scripture for Confessions of Faith and Testimonies." He answered "that there was no formal nor express precept to that purpose." It was the decision of the presbytery that it was not satisfied with Campbell's answer to the first and second articles.

To the third article, concerning the duty of elders to pray and exhort, Campbell's answer was:

> With respect to Elders, it appears to me that it is their duty as ordained overseers and rulers of the house of God to see that all his ordinances be duly observed by those over whom the Holy Ghost hath made them overseers; and that, of course, in the absence or want of the teaching elder, the others should do what is competent to them to prevent the objects of their charge from forsaking the assembling of themselves together.

He confessed without argument that he thought elders should pray and exhort in public worship when no minister was at hand. In this answer he reveals his belief that there should be little distinction between clergy and laity, that the minister is the teaching elder and that all elders should feel their responsibility to care for the congregation.

To the fourth article, concerning "occasional hearing," Campbell's answer was:

> I believe that in the present broken and divided state of the church, when Christians have not an opportunity of hearing those of their own party, it is lawful for them to hear other ministers preach the gospel where the publick worship is not corrupted with matters of human invention.

This was an honest statement of his belief on the subject of "occasional hearing." In Ireland he had been accustomed to avail himself of the opportunity and saw no reason to change his conviction in the new country in which he found himself. Since Campbell so frankly stated his views on the third and fourth charges it was to be expected that the presbytery found him guilty of teaching the beliefs with which he is charged in those articles.

To the fifth article, concerning the doctrine of substitutionary atonement, Campbell's answer was:

That our Lord Jesus Christ was subject both to the precept and penalty of the law for his people; that if he had not been subject to the former he could not have been subject to the latter as their surety; and that by his one obedience unto the death he hath wrought out for them a complete deliverance from the curse of the law, being made a curse for them; which obedience is embraced and rested upon by all that believe for their justification; and is actually imputed to them for righteousness, as if they had wrought it out in their own persons.

It is clearly seen in his answer to this charge that Campbell was but affirming the orthodox belief of Calvinists in the doctrine of the substitutionary atonement. After some explanation, the presbytery admitted his answer to the fifth article of the libel to be satisfactory.

To the sixth article, concerning a "sinless" man, Campbell's answer was:

I believe that no mere man since the fall, is able in this life to keep the commandments of God, but doth daily break them in thought, word, or deed, either by actual transgression or want of conformity in some degree or other; and that our very best actions are so imperfect that they could not be acceptable to God without a Mediator. These are my sentiments respecting the matters alleged against me, and which I constantly believe and teach.

THOMAS CAMPBELL

Again, Campbell had been charged with a deviation from accepted doctrine, that of the sinfulness of man, and again he denied the charge. His answer in this instance is as orthodox as his answer to the charge regarding his beliefs on substitutionary atonement. The minutes indicate that Campbell turned in to the clerk his written statement after the sixth charge and his answers were read. The seventh charge was concerning his supposed invasion of Mr. Ramsay's parish, and he answered this charge separately, as follows:

> As to the 7th charge, I acknowledge that I preached at Cannonsburg, but not in a congregation where any of our ministers is settled, nor yet without a regular call, as I conceive I have appointment to preach the gospel and the call of some of the most regular and respectable people of that vicinity to preach, thereof which I can produce sufficient testimonials if required.
>
> THOMAS CAMPBELL[9]

This was considered a flouting of the presbytery's authority and was therefore declared unsatisfactory. Thus Campbell answered the charges made against him. Except for his answer to the first article, Campbell's replies indicate a complete orthodoxy in matters of doctrine and theology. Even in his reply to the first charge Campbell's only deviation from orthodoxy is in matter of degree and not in principle. The main differences between Campbell and the presbytery prove to be matters of church order and government. Campbell was in revolt against the authority of the presbytery and its limitation of fellowship to those who belong to their particular sect. In these charges and in Campbell's answers clear evidence is presented of Campbell's growing impatience with the sectarian spirit so apparent in his section of the American frontier.

On Friday, February 11, the session received the testimony of various witnesses. Saturday, February 12, was devoted to evaluating the evidence presented to the presbytery the day before. It was the presbytery's decision that articles one and two were clearly proved, three and four were acknowledged by Campbell, the fifth article was found not sufficiently proved, six was satisfactory, while he had personally acknowledged seven. In short, the presbytery censured Thomas Campbell for not adhering to "Secession testimony," when in reality he was objecting only to its assumed authority in matters of discipline.

At the next meeting of the presbytery, held at Mt. Hope, March 8-11, Campbell was present but not included in the list of those participating in the meeting. He presented a request asking the presbytery to reconsider its action and spoke in favor of his request. The request was refused. On March 11, after the presbytery had been adjourned and Campbell had left the meeting, it was reconstituted for the sole purpose of making his suspension from preaching "indefinite *sine die.*" According to the minutes, the only ministers present for this action were Anderson, Wilson, and Alison.

The April, 1808, meeting of the presbytery was given over to preparation for the annual meeting of the Associate Synod of North America, which was to be convened in Philadelphia in May. It had been this group to which Campbell had presented his papers on his arrival in America the previous May. It was to the synod Thomas Campbell now decided to take his case.

Appeal to the Associate Synod

Thomas Campbell was present when the Associate Synod was called to order on Wednesday, May 18, 1808, at Philadelphia. The first day was given over to general matters of business, but on the second day of the meeting, Thursday, May 19, as the fourth matter for the consideration of the synod we read:

> Reasons of protest and appeal by Mr. Thomas Campbell against the Presb'y of Chartiers, in his case and particularly proceedings of a deed of said Presb'y suspending him from the office of the ministry and Answer by Presb'y.[10]

As the fifth item of business there is listed "Petitions from Buffaloe, Chartiers, Mt. Pleasant and Burgettstown in favour of Mr. Campbell." We see Campbell's friends rallying to his defense.

At the following day's meeting the synod entered into a discussion of the dispute between Campbell and the Chartiers Presbytery. The minutes of the presbytery which related to the case, and the remonstrance which Campbell had sent to the presbytery in March, were read. The synod next read Campbell's "Reasons of Protest and Appeal" and the presbytery's answer. In the "Protest and Appeal," Thomas Campbell makes unmistakable declaration of a principle from which he will not be moved. This appeal sets forth in clear and sincere words his determination to accept the Bible as the basis of all his beliefs and practices, for in reality, this was the issue involved in the charges on which the presbytery had decided against him. It is the "Protest and Appeal" which is of most importance in revealing Campbell's thinking at the time and thus it deserves attentive study.

It is also important because it is the first document written by Campbell which reveals the germ thought of principles more fully worked out at a later date. From this time forward he felt himself called on to defend the thesis stated in this document: namely, that the union of all Christians rests on the authority of Scripture alone. Here we find phrases which echo and re-echo through Campbell's later ministry:

Honored Brethren:
Before you come to a final issue in the present business, let me entreat you to pause a moment, and seriously to consider ... how great the injustice, how highly aggravated the injury will appear to thrust out from communion a Christian brother, a fellow-minister, for saying and doing none other things than those which our Divine Lord and his holy apostles have taught and enjoined to be spoken and done by his minis-

tering servants, and to be received and observed by all his people. ... It is therefore, because I have no confidence, either in my own infallibility, or in that of others, that I absolutely refuse, as inadmissable and schismatic, the introduction of human opinions and human inventions into the faith and worship of the Church. Is it, therefore, because I plead the cause of the Scriptural and apostolic worship of the church, in opposition to the various errors and schisms which have so awfully corrupted and divided it, that the brethren of the Union should feel it difficult to admit me as their fellow-laborer in that blessed work? ... Nor do I presume to dictate to them or to Others how they should proceed for the glorious purpose of promoting the unity and purity of the Church; but only beg leave, for my own part, to walk upon that sure and peaceable ground, that I may have nothing to do with human controversy, about the right or wrong side of any opinion whatsoever, by simply acquiescing in what is written, as quite sufficient for every purpose of faith and duty, and thereby to influence as many as possible to depart from human controversy, to betake themselves to the Scriptures, and, in so doing, to the study and practice of faith, holiness and love.

And all this without any intention on my part, to judge or despise my Christian brethren who may not see with my eyes in those things, which, to me, appear indispensably necessary to promote and secure the unity, peace, and purity of the Church. ... For what error or immorality ought I to be rejected, except it be that I refuse to acknowledge as obligatory upon myself, or to impose upon others, anything as of Divine obligation, for which I cannot produce a "Thus saith the Lord?" ... As to human authority in matters of religion, I absolutely reject it—as that grievous yoke of antichristian bondage which neither we nor our fathers were able to bear.

Surely, brethren, from my steadfast adherence to the Divine standard—my absolute and entire rejection of human authority in matters of religion—my professed and sincere willingness to walk in all good understanding, communion, and fellowship with sincere, humble Christian brethren who may not see with me in these things ... you will do me the justice to believe, that if I did not sincerely desire a union with you, I would not have once and again made application for that purpose. ... I am therefore, through his grace ready to forbear with you; at the same time, hoping that you possess the same gracious spirit, and therefore will not reject me for the lack of those fifty forms which might probably bring me up to your measure, and to which, if necessary, I also, through grace, may yet attain, for I have not set myself down as perfect.

May the Lord direct you in all things. Amen.

Thomas Campbell.[11]

After hearing these words the synod proceeded to read the articles of libel on which Campbell had been tried, the answers which he had given them, and also the depositions of the witnesses at Buffalo. After the reading, verbal comments were allowed, but further consideration was postponed until the next session.

On Saturday, May 21, the consideration of Thomas Campbell's case was resumed. An order of procedure was agreed on. The clerk was to read the articles of the libel over again, one by one, with Campbell's replies. After the first article and the answer were read, and before any decision was reached as to whether the article was proved, several of the members insisted that they should be allowed to judge whether the presbytery had properly handled the case. Finally, after heated discussion the session was adjourned until the following Monday.

The discussion was resumed at three o'clock on Monday afternoon, May 23. After some consideration the synod decided to read again the "Reasons of Protest and Appeal" and the presbytery's answer, to take the judgment of the synod on them item by item, then to decide on the articles of the libel, and afterwards, if necessary, to appoint a committee to bring in a finding on the case. The fact that Dr. Anderson had declined to fill his appointment because of reports he had heard concerning Thomas Campbell's orthodoxy, and that the presbytery sustained his excuse, was then brought into the open. The synod condemned Dr. Anderson's conduct because he had not first written Campbell on the subject or sought an interview with him and then voted to disapprove the presbytery for sustaining such an excuse. So the discussion proceeded all afternoon alternating between the claims of the presbytery and those of Campbell.

On Tuesday, May 24, a motion was made and seconded that first, in consideration of the synod's judgment that the proceedings of the Chartiers Presbytery in the trial of Thomas Campbell had been irregular, they lay aside any further consideration of the case as it had been brought before them, and that secondly, they reverse the sentence of suspension passed by the presbytery on Campbell, and either order a new trial or deal with Campbell directly. The motion, conciliatory in tone to both parties, was adopted and the sentence was reversed. This reproof to the presbytery shows the "informality" of the presbytery's action.

The synod resolved further to handle Thomas Campbell directly and agreed to consider his written answers to the articles of libel presented by the presbytery. After reading and considering each of the articles, a committee was appointed to meet and bring in a statement on behalf of the synod in regard to the matter. The committee reported on Wednesday, May 25. They had some difficulty coming to an agreement, but finally submitted the following report:

> Upon the whole the committee are of opinion that Mr. Campbell's answer to the first two articles of charge are so evasive and unsatisfactory, and highly equivocal upon great and important articles of revealed religion, as to give ground to conclude, that he has expressed sentiments very different upon these articles, and from the sentiments held and professed by this Church, and are sufficient ground to infer censure.
>
> Signed, David Acheson,
> Philadelphia, A.D. 1808.[12]

On Thursday afternoon the synod resumed the consideration of Campbell's case. After some discussion of what censure was appropriate for Campbell on the basis of what was decided against him, a motion was made that he be rebuked and admonished, and that if further satisfaction was not received by the synod, he should be suspended from office. An amendment was made that he should be admonished only. When the question was put it was voted that he should be both rebuked and admonished. Campbell requested that the synod delay passing censure and the moderator agreed to delay until the next day. The synod adjourned to meet that evening to care for other matters.

At eight thirty on the evening of May 26 when the synod met, Thomas Campbell turned in a paper, called a "Remonstrance," stating that he could not submit to the censure as it was proposed because he could not acknowledge the charges found against him. He added, however, that he would be willing to submit to an admonition on the score of imprudence. One can almost sense the struggle taking place within the mind and spirit of Thomas Campbell. He was angered by the synod's action, yet could not bring himself to break connection with the fellowship he had known since youth. He requested the synod to reconsider its decision and after some discussion, the synod agreed.

The next session opened on Friday morning, May 27, at the early hour of six o'clock. At that time a letter from Campbell to the moderator was received and read, leveling charges against the synod for its judgment of him as guilty of evasion and equivocation, accusing it of partiality and injustice, and informing the body that he declined their authority. The synod then summoned him to appear immediately to answer for such impertinence. When he appeared, the synod demanded that he retract the charges he had made and submit to its authority. He agreed to withdraw the letter, acknowledge his rashness in bringing such charges and in declining the authority of the synod. The session then adjourned until 9:30 A.M.

At half past nine the synod reconsidered their judgment in the case of Campbell. They again found his answers in the first two articles evasive, unsatisfactory, and highly equivocal. A motion was made to strike out the word "evasive" and it was so agreed. The question was then put whether to adhere to the synod's original decision to rebuke and admonish and it was voted to adhere. Campbell was then asked if he was ready to submit to censure. After a few remarks he agreed to submit, handing in at the same time a statement that "his submission should be understood to mean no more, on his part, than an act of deference to the judgment of the court, that, by so doing, he might not give offence to his brethren by manifesting a refractory spirit."[13] After a season of prayer he was accordingly rebuked and admonished by the moderator.

It was evident that the synod, while it could not justify the method of the presbytery, felt called on to pass censure on Thomas Campbell's actions, and so virtually sustained the spirit and purpose of the charges originally brought against him. It is just as obvious that Campbell must have been somewhat petulant and that his sense of right was outraged. Furthermore, he may have been poorly advised at times during the trial. From the minutes it may be concluded, however, that the synod was doing its best to reach a decision satisfactory to all parties.

At the same time it should be pointed out that the synod was quite justly suspicious of Campbell's views, and its analysis of his position was, in the main, correct. Campbell himself at this time was feeling his way, and no doubt, failed to appreciate the full implications of his teaching. The final judgment of the synod seems a little ambiguous. As one writer put it, it was as if it had said: "You are not guilty, but don't do it again!" Campbell had progressed rapidly from a vague fraternal attitude toward those Christians who held opinions differing from his own to a conviction that the creed he had previously confessed consisted largely of opinions that did not matter much in comparison with the essentials presented in the New Testament.

Before the synod finished its work, it made the appointments to the various presbyteries for the coming year. Last on the list is the notation, "Mr. Th. Campbell in Phil'a., Jun., July, then in Chartiers till next meeting." We have no word of Thomas Campbell's activities in Philadelphia during these two months of 1808. He may have been trying to decide if he should return to Ireland and forget the frontier and its quarrels. It is more probable he was anticipating the arrival of his family, whom he had written on January 1 to come to America. If this was his purpose, he was disappointed, for they did not come.

Withdrawal from Presbytery and Synod

Even after the stormy sessions of the Associate Synod in Philadelphia, Campbell still hoped that friendly relations would be restored between himself and the other members of Chartiers Presbytery and that he would be permitted to work among the churches in peace. He was extremely reluctant to separate himself from the Seceders, for many of whom, both ministers and people, he had the highest regard. He must indeed have been greatly disturbed at the outcome of his trial and of his appeal to the synod. He was sure his motives were of the best and found it difficult to understand the spirit of those who he considered were sincerely working for the same goals as himself.

Although the synod had released him from censure with a "rebuke and admonition" he was still under a cloud of suspicion and some of those who opposed him did everything in their power to undermine his influence. Their hostility was only intensified by the meeting at Philadelphia. They frequently misrepresented him and sent different persons to attend his meetings and to make notes on his sermons in order to secure fresh evidence of his disloyalty to Seceder doctrines. His desire for peace and harmony was not to be realized. Campbell himself soon concluded that he could no longer continue as a minister of the gospel with the Seceder church.

The Chartiers Presbytery met on August 2, 1808, and read an extract of the minutes of the synod which had met in Philadelphia in May. The members of the presbytery dissented from some of the findings of the synod and especially from the action of the synod in removing suspension from Campbell.

In the meanwhile, Campbell returned to Washington after his two-month assignment in Philadelphia to find that the presbytery had made no assignments for him to preach. At the next meeting of the presbytery, held at Burgettstown on September 13, 1808, Campbell asked the reason why and the presbytery replied lamely that it was not sure that he would be within the bounds of Chartiers since he had indicated his intention to serve in Philadelphia. Besides, they said, he had not taken care to inform anyone of the time when he would be returning. At this point, Campbell said that he wished to know on what basis the presbytery considered him as one of its members. The presbytery was then forced to admit that he was a member only because of the action of the synod and the fact that he was within the limits of its jurisdiction.

Considerable controversy developed relative to the extracts which had been read from the minutes of the Philadelphia meeting. Apparently there was some variance in the copy of the minutes which the presbytery possessed and the copy in the hands of Campbell. Sharp words, and possibly charges of falsehood, must have passed between Campbell and the presbytery, with the result that he took from the hands of the clerk the paper that he had presented as a copy of the minutes of the synod concerning his case. He then publicly and heatedly refused to acknowledge the authority of the presbytery, the authority of the Associate Synod of North America, and "all the courts subordinate thereto." He refused all further communion with them. After this, he offered to read another paper, which he said, contained reasons for his leaving the Seceder fellowship. The presbytery directed him to lay this paper on the clerk's desk, but he refused. He was then told that unless he did so, it would be deemed improper to permit the reading of it. On further questioning it developed that this paper was the letter given to the synod at Philadelphia, at the May meeting, but later withdrawn. Before the matter was settled, the lateness of the hour brought an adjournment.

On the next day, September 14, 1808, Campbell was not present, but a paper was reported received from him. This was probably the following document:

Taking into my most serious consideration, the present state of matters between the reverend Synod and myself, upon a review of the whole process and issue as commenced and conducted, first by the Presbytery of Chartiers, and as now issued by this reverent court, I cannot help thinking myself greatly aggrieved . . . this Synod, after examining my written declarations to said Presbytery upon the articles of libel, and also after a long and close examination of my principles relative to said articles; and not being able to point out a single error in the former, and declaring themselves satisfied with the latter . . . yet proceeded to find me guilty of evasion and equivocation, in my written declarations, upon great and important articles of revealed religion; and thence infer that I had expressed sentiments upon these articles very different from the sentiments held and professed by this Church, and upon these presumptions proceed to judge me worthy of a solemn rebuke . . . while, no notice is taken of the Presbytery's breach of faith and avowed dissimulation and flagrant injustice toward me. . . .

It is with sincere reluctance, and, at the same time, with all due respect and esteem for the brethren of this reverend Synod who have presided in the trial of my case, that I find myself in duty bound to refuse submission to their decision as *unjust* and *partial;* and also *finally to decline their authority,* while they continue thus to overlook the grievous and *flagrant maladministration of the Presbytery of Chartiers.* And I hereby do decline all ministerial connection with, or subjection to, the Associate Synod of North America, on account of the aforesaid corruptions and grievances. . . . I will distinctly state that, while especial reference is had to the corruptions of *the Presbytery* of Chartiers, which constitute only a part of this Synod, *the corruptions of that Presbytery now become also the corruptions of the whole Synod; because when laid open to this Synod, and protested against, the Synod pass them over without due inquiry, and without animadversion.*

Thomas Campbell.[14]

After reading this paper from Campbell, the presbytery was unanimously of the opinion that his conduct demanded censure. Action was taken to suspend him immediately from ministerial office and to cite him to attend the next meeting of the presbytery to be further dealt with. Moreover, all congregations belonging to the presbytery were to be informed of his suspension, along with all the other presbyteries belonging to the synod.

At the next meeting of the presbytery, Campbell was again cited to appear before the group, but he ignored all such communications. It is not until May of the following year, 1809, that we learn of any further action on the part of the presbytery in regard to Thomas Campbell. In preparation for the annual meeting a committee drew up a protest to present to the synod against the actions of the preceding year. A transcript of procedure in Campbell's case since the last meeting of the synod also was prepared.

The synod met in Philadelphia on May 17, 1809, but it was not until May 19 that a paper entitled "Declaration and Address to the Associate Synod" prepared by Thomas Campbell was received and referred to a committee appointed to study the case. The committee reported the same afternoon and suggested that Campbell be permitted to withdraw his paper since in it he declined subjection to the synod, reflected on the presbytery of Chartiers, and offered proposals inconsistent with Seceder doctrine. The paper itself was read and the report of the committee accepted.

In the *Minutes of the Synod of the Associate Churches* for Tuesday, May 23, 1809, occurs the notation: "A letter inclosing a Fifty Dollar note, refunding a like sum given him by the Synod in May, 1807, was re'd from Mr. Th. Campbell. The clerk was directed to give him a receipt." Campbell's prompt return of the money advanced to him for his work as a missionary is typical evidence of his integrity. In this manner Thomas Campbell brought to an end his relations with the Associate Synod of North America, almost two years from the date he first entered into fellowship with it, May 16, 1807.

Formation of the Christian Association of Washington

We can be sure that the decision to withdraw from the presbytery and the Associate Synod caused Thomas Campbell no little concern. All his deepest convictions were opposed to sectarianism and when he realized that he was cut off from the brethren with whom he was associated, although feeling that he had done nothing for which he should be censured, he must have had many misgivings. He doubtless found comfort in the fact that he had acted to the best of his ability and, according to his belief, in harmony with the Word of God. It must have been doubly difficult to face the disapproval of his fellow-ministers alone. Now in his forty-sixth year, after eleven years or more as an ordained minister of the Anti-Burgher Seceder church, Campbell found himself without formal ministerial connection. He was alone in a comparatively strange country, still waiting for his family to join him and whatever feeling of freedom such a step may have given him must have been mixed with a sense of confusion and doubt as to what step to take next. Jane, his wife, would have been a great comfort to him and his son, Alexander, could have helped him.

His withdrawal from the presbytery and synod, however, meant no interruption to his ministerial labors. It is evident that from Campbell's first difficulty with the presbytery in October, 1807, he had continued to meet groups of friends and acquaintances in religious services and had preached and administered the Lord's Supper without interruption. In fact, this was the content of one of the articles in the libel placed against him by the presbytery. For over a year and a half, then, Thomas Campbell had continued to preach in the vicinity of Washington, Pennsylvania, whenever he was given the opportunity.

Campbell had great personal influence in the various sections of Washington and Allegheny counties. Those who heard him were intrigued by the constantly recurring theme of his sermons: a plea for the union of the divided church on the basis of the Bible. In his sermons he deplored the partisan divisions of the church, set forth the Bible as a sufficient rule for faith and practice, and pleaded for Christians to cooperate with one another. Large numbers still attended whenever he announced a religious service. Summer meetings were held out of doors under the trees, although the usual places of meeting were in the houses and barns of his old neighbors from northern Ireland.

After several months of such meetings it became apparent that a permanent organization must be made. Many of those who heard Campbell were from the regular and Associate Presbyterian churches; some were from other communions, and others had never belonged to any church but were in agreement with the principles which he taught. Thomas Campbell proposed to several of the leading individuals among those who regularly heard him that a special meeting be called to consider giving more order, definiteness, and permanency to their efforts. They had met so far without special agreement, and were held together only by a vague sentiment of Christian union and by the personal influence of Campbell. Such loose arrangements could not be continued indefinitely. Accordingly plans were made for all interested persons to gather at the house of Abraham Altars, who lived between Mt. Pleasant and Washington. Altars was not a member of any church but was interested in what Campbell and his friends were attempting. The call for the meeting was issued without any conscious intention of forming a new religious group. Actually its purpose was to try to influence all Christians to unite together on the basis of the Bible and to get them to cease petty controversies over matters of opinion and the day-to-day affairs of the church. Campbell was not attacking confessions of faith and historical creeds as such. There was scarcely anything in the Westminster Confession of Faith with which he personally disagreed. At this time, and long after, Thomas Campbell was a sound Calvinist. As a Protestant who believed that the Bible was the only rule of faith and practice, he felt that he had a right to urge all Christians to adopt the Bible as the basis of belief and that it alone should be accepted as the basis of Christian co-operation. To Campbell the evidence of the validity of his position was the large number of people surrounding him who were dissatisfied with the divided church of their day.

The exact date of the meeting at Abraham Altar's farm is unknown. We do know that some time in the early summer of 1809 a large group gathered to discuss plans for future organization and that all present felt the importance of the occasion. The assembly grew quiet as Thomas Campbell led the group in prayer, earnestly seeking divine guidance, and then proceeded to review the reasons for their gathering. He dwelt at length on the evils resulting from divisions within the church—divisions that were unnecessary for God had provided, in his sacred Word, an infallible standard which was all-sufficient and alone sufficient, as a basis of union and cooperation among Christians. He insisted on a return to the simple teachings of the Scriptures, and the abandonment of everything in religion not found in the Bible. At long last, after reviewing again and again the need for returning to the Bible as a basis for belief and practice, he brought his message to a close, putting into simple terms the principle he understood the group to be acting on, and on which he trusted they would continue to act. "That rule, my highly respected hearers," said he in conclusion, "is this, that where the Scriptures speak, we speak; and where the Scriptures are silent, we are silent."

It was some time after Campbell sat down before anyone dared to break the silence. At length, a Seceder from Scotland, Andrew Munro, bookseller and postmaster at Cannonsburg, arose and said: "Mr. Campbell, if we adopt *that* as a basis, then there is an end of infant baptism." This created some discussion. "Of course," said Campbell, "if infant baptism be not found in Scripture, we can have nothing to do with it." This greatly excited Thomas Acheson of Washington, and an old and trusted friend of Campbell's, who said: "I hope I may never see the day when my heart will renounce that blessed saying of the Scripture, 'Suffer little children to come unto me, and forbid them not, for of such is the kingdom of heaven.' "[15] With this he burst into tears and was about to leave the room, when James Foster, realizing the misapplication of Scripture, cried out, "Mr. Acheson, I would remark that in the portion of Scripture you have quoted there is no reference, whatever, to infant baptism." This incident did nothing to destroy the confidence which the majority had in the principle presented to them and after further discussion and conference the rule was adopted with apparent unanimity.

This meeting was important for several reasons. Most importantly, it defined clearly for the first time the exact position which the group held and, as a result, some withdrew when they saw the direction in which the majority was going. With some the troublous question was, "Where will it lead us?" With others the question of infant baptism was the issue most widely discussed. James Foster, who had become convinced while in Ireland that there was no scriptural foundation for infant baptism, was very decided in his views on the subject. Campbell was by no means prepared to admit that the principle adopted would necessarily involve any direct opposition to infant baptism but he insisted that the question should be made a matter of forbearance. He did not favor hastily abandoning a custom of such long standing, and urged that this question and others of a similar character might be left to private judgment. He was convinced that some concessions were needed if Christian union was to come about.

One day as he was riding with Foster, Thomas Campbell presented his convictions on infant baptism and Foster, turning to him, asked: "Father Campbell, how could you, in the absence of any authority in the Word of God, baptize a child in the name of the Father, and of the Son, and of the Holy Spirit?" Campbell, somewhat confused and irritated, replied: "Sir, you are the most intractable person I ever met."

Even with such differences of opinion, however, most of those in attendance at the weekly meetings felt themselves united in the great object of promoting Christian union on the Bible. Campbell more than anyone else realized the need of guiding principles and of some organized effort to give them practical effect. He conceived the idea of forming a Christian Association, which would not be a church, but an agency for helping propagate the ideas of Christian cooperation. It is probable that he got his idea from the Haldanean societies and from the evangelical society to which he had belonged while minister at Ahorey in Ireland.

A second meeting was held on August 17, 1809, at the headwaters of Buffalo Creek composed of those from the community, regardless of denominational affiliation, who believed in the principles of Christian union generally agreed upon. It was decided to name the organization "The Christian Association of Washington"—after the county in which the association proposed to be active. A committee of twenty-one members was appointed (probably the approximate number in attendance) whose first action was to agree on the need for a published statement of the purposes and objectives of the organization. Thomas Campbell was to write such a document.

As it was inconvenient to hold the weekly meetings for worship and preaching in private homes, it was decided to build a meetinghouse. The neighbors, in true frontier fashion, assembled and erected a log building on the Sinclair farm, about three miles from Mt. Pleasant, on the road from Mt. Pleasant to Washington at the point where it was crossed by the road from Middletown to Cannonsburg. The building was also to be used as a community school and after it was completed, Campbell preached here regularly.

During this time, Campbell made his home with a Dr. Welch, whose farm was not far from the meetinghouse and who was a friend of the Association. Thomas was assigned a room upstairs for his use. In this room he spent most of the week in study and in writing, only occasionally visiting Washington, which he still regarded as his postoffice and place of residence. Campbell was engaged at the time in writing a brief "Declaration" and an extended "Address" to express more fully the statement of principles and objectives requested by the Christian Association. When the *Declaration and Address* was completed, he read it at a special meeting of the leaders in the Association at the home of Jacob Donoldson and on September 7, 1809, they unanimously approved it.

The Family Arrives in America

After the Christian Association had approved his *Declaration and Address,* Thomas Campbell, at the direction of the organization, set about having it printed. His time was spent in editing, proofreading, and correcting the copy which the printer supplied. During the first days of October, 1809, in the midst of these labors, Thomas received word that his family had arrived safely in New York from Scotland on September 29 after a voyage of fifty-four days. He learned further that the family had proceeded by stagecoach to Philadelphia and that from there they had made arrangements with a wagoner to be conveyed to Washington, leaving Monday, October 9.

As soon as adequate preparations could be made for the reception of his family, Thomas left Washington with a friend, John McElroy, and two lead horses equipped with sidesaddles. Thomas knew that his wife and daughters would probably be tired of the wagon and wanted to give them relief from the long and difficult journey. On October 19 on the road from Philadelphia, about three days out of Washington, he and his friend met the wagon with his wife Jane and the family. Having been separated for over two years, they were now united on the American frontier. How Thomas' eyes must have feasted on each of them! First, his wife, Jane, his companion of the years, and then the children. How they had grown! Alexander was well into his twenty-first year. He was tall, athletic and well built. There was about him an air of frankness and of self-reliance. The next in age, his sister Dorothea, now in her sixteenth year, was somewhat tall and slender, resembling her brother Alexander more than any member of the family. There was Nancy, about thirteen, more like her father in figure and disposition, and Jane, now nine years old. Thomas, a boy of over six, was extremely active and restless. Nearby the mother were the two younger children, Archibald, four and Alicia, two years old.

Thomas introduced his friend, John McElroy, who had been kind enough to lend the horses, and after spending a little time visiting, they proceeded on the way westward. On the third day they reached Washington, where Thomas had secured a house in a field adjoining the town. Here, at last, the family once more formed an unbroken circle. They were together and that was the important thing. They were in a new country and unlimited opportunity lay before them.

During the three days since their meeting on the Philadelphia road, Jane and the children had related to Thomas the various incidents of the two years since his departure from Londonderry. At first everything had gone well with them, but in the spring of 1808, on receipt of Thomas' New Year's letter and in the midst of preparations for the trip to America, an epidemic of smallpox had broken out in Rich Hill. Several of the Campbell children had taken ill. This and other things had delayed them until late summer before they were ready to leave. At Londonderry they had taken passage on an ill-fated ship which was wrecked off the coast of Scotland. For various reasons, but especially because it would permit Alexander to take courses at the university, the family decided to winter in Glasgow. They had stayed in Glasgow and vicinity until August, 1809, when they had taken ship for New York.

Thomas, in turn, gave the family a detailed account of his pleasure with America, of what had happened to him, and especially of his difficulties with the presbytery and synod. Alexander was particularly interested when his father told him that all his ties with the Seceder church were broken. This was surprising to Alexander because by a somewhat different route he had been brought to practically the same conclusions as his father. While in Glasgow he had come under the influence of Greville Ewing, a Scottish Independent, with Haldanean connections. The opposition to Ewing among the clergy had raised questions in Alexander's mind about ecclesiastical organizations, and he came more and more to favor the principles of congregationalism. He was thus in an unsettled state of mind when the semiannual communion of the Seceder's came around. He had many misgivings and at the last minute felt that he could not partake of the Seceder communion. Wishing to be free to follow the dictates of his conscience, he broke with the Seceder church. In addition, Alexander had decided finally to dedicate his life to the Christian ministry.

Thus, father and son, three thousand miles apart, with no knowledge of what the other was doing, came to similar decisions regarding the sectarian spirit of the day. They both determined to find a basis for Christian faith in the Bible and from this foundation eventually to see the union of all Christians.

The father told his family of the recent organization of the "Christian Association of Washington." In their brief time together since their reunion Thomas already sensed the development of Alexander's mind, keener and more inquiring even than when they were together in Ireland. Thomas was interested in sharing his literary efforts with Alexander and wanted him to read and to examine the *Declaration and Address,* now at the printers. Alexander read the proof sheets of the *Declaration and Address* as they came from the press and was greatly impressed with the importance of the ideas expressed by his father. In this document Thomas had more fully stated and developed the principles he believed, and had answered at length, the various objections which were likely to be offered. It is to the pages of this document we must turn to learn of the elder Campbell's thinking on the subject of Christian union. Others held Christian union as something to be desired, but Thomas Campbell made a definite effort to realize the ideal.

CHAPTER THREE

THE DECLARATION AND ADDRESS

Background and Description

THE DECLARATION AND ADDRESS is the major literary accomplishment of Thomas Campbell and reveals more fully than anything else the spirit and genius of the man. An understanding of the character of Campbell is the principal key to an explanation of the document since it represents the culmination of all his ideas and experiences to this point. It is an unpretentious document, the work of a man who wrote down in simple and honest words the thoughts that had grown up in his soul. The sentences are unnecessarily long, the thought is often too involved, but the ideas presented are Campbell's "heart thoughts," as one writer has called them, and reveal his very soul. The presupposition of the *Declaration and Address,* and of the "Christian Association of Washington" for that matter, was that the Christian faith of the various communions was valid enough; the only objection was that the different parties held as essential many features which were nonessential and that these nonessential features caused divisions. One fundamental principle is apparent throughout the document and that is Thomas Campbell's emphasis on the authority and importance of the Word of God which was apparent in all his teachings in Ireland and in America. This emphasis had been revealed at the meeting held at the home of Abraham Altars. As James Foster reported many years later:

... having taken it for granted that the holy Scriptures were all-sufficient and alone-sufficient, as the subject-matter of faith and rule of conduct; that as the Old Testament was all-sufficient for the Old Testament worshipers, so the New Testament Scriptures were all-sufficient for the New Testament worshipers; therefore, we conclude that where the holy Scriptures speak, we speak; and where they are silent, we are silent.... He held several meetings for the purpose of knowing wherein we were deficient, or superfluous, either in faith or practice, that in all things we might be regulated by the Divine testimony.[1]

The importance and authority of the Scriptures are as prominent in the document, if not more so, than the appeal to Christian unity.

The final statement of Thomas Campbell's thinking and writing came from the press at Washington, Pennsylvania, some time during the last two weeks of 1809. The full title of the document was *Declaration and Address of the Christian Association of Washington*. Printed at the office of the local newspaper, it was a pamphlet or small book of fifty-six closely spaced pages containing four sections: first, a Declaration (three pages) stating briefly the reasons, purposes, and form of organization of the Christian Association; secondly, an Address (eighteen pages) amplifying the argument for the unity of all Christians and developing in detail the proposals for attaining this goal; thirdly, an Appendix (thirty pages) answering actual or anticipated criticisms and explaining several points in the Address; fourthly, a Postscript (three pages) suggesting two steps to be taken immediately. Aside from the main divisions, the book is without subheadings, has no topical arrangement, and the paragraphs are long and involved.

In the original edition of the work, the following prefatory statement precedes the Declaration:

At a meeting held at Buffaloe, August 17, 1809, consisting of persons of different religious denominations; most of them in an unsettled state as to a fixed gospel ministry; it was unanimously agreed upon the considerations, and for the purposes herein after declared, to form themselves into a religious association, titled as above—which they accordingly did, and appointed twenty-one of their number to meet and confer together; and, with the assistance of Mr. Thomas Campbell, minister of the gospel, to determine upon the proper means to carry into effect the important ends of their association: the result of which conference was the following declaration and address, agreed upon and ordered to be printed at the expense and for the benefit of the society, September 7, 1809.[2]

The Postscript, written after a meeting of the standing committee of twenty-one members, held December 14, 1809, reveals that the three-month delay in publication was caused by the difficulty in securing paper of the right quality. If any of the twenty-one committee members actually aided Campbell in the writing is unknown, but it seems certain that he was the sole author.[3]

The Declaration

The brief but important Declaration sets forth at least four principles underlying the Christian Association and lists nine articles pertaining to the methods and organization of the society. The Declaration was intended only for introductory purposes and as a justification for the main section, the Address, which followed. The four principles worthy of note are as follows:

First, the right of private judgment is boldly asserted.

From the series of events which has taken place in the churches for many years past, especially in this western country, as well as from what we know in general of the present state of things in the Christian world; we are persuaded that it is high time for us not only to think, but also to act, for ourselves; to see with our own eyes, and to take all our measures directly and immediately from the Divine Standard. . . .

Secondly, the sole authority of the Scriptures is established.

We are also of opinion that as the divine word is equally binding upon all, so all lie under an equal obligation to be bound by it, and it alone, and not by any human interpretation of it and that therefore no man has a right to judge his brother, except in so far as he manifestly violates the express letter of the law.

Thirdly, the evil inherent in sectarian spirit is pointed out.

Moreover, being well aware, from sad experience, of the heinous nature, and pernicious tendency of religious controversy among Christians, tired and sick of the bitter jarrings and janglings of a party spirit, we would desire to be at rest; and, were it possible, we would also desire to adopt and recommend such measures, as would give rest to our brethren throughout all the churches;—as would restore unity, peace, and purity, to the whole church of God.

Fourthly, the way to a Christian union based on exact conformity to the Bible is set forth.

This desirable rest, however, we utterly despair either to find for ourselves, or to be able to recommend to our brethren, by continuing amidst the diversity and rancour of party contentions, the veering uncertainty and clashings of human opinions: nor, indeed, can we reasonably expect to find it any where, but in Christ and his simple word. ... Our desire, therefore, for ourselves and our brethren would be, that rejecting human opinions and the inventions of men, as of any authority, or as having any place in the church of God, we might forever cease from farther contentions about such things; returning to, and holding fast by, the original standard; taking the divine word alone for our rule: The Holy Spirit for our teacher and guide, to lead us into all truth; and Christ alone as exhibited in the word for our salvation. ...[4]

Immediately following the introductory principles are found nine resolutions which were intended to serve as a constitution for the Christian Association and to enable all interested individuals to carry out the principles developed in the Address. The resolutions made provision for the promotion of simple evangelical Christianity, the voluntary support of a ministry, and the encouragement of the formation of similar associations. The organization was pledged to support such ministers, and such only, as exhibited a conformity to the supposed pattern of the New Testament. A standing committee of twenty-one members, to be chosen annually, was to guide the work of the association and look after its interests. The entire society was to meet twice a year, each meeting to be opened by a sermon, the constitution read, an offering for the work of the society taken, and any necessary business transacted.

The program clearly presented in the Declaration is that of an organization optimistically hopeful of attracting ministers and people committed to its program. The Association would support these ministers and send them forth to preach the principles of "simple evangelical christianity," by which all Christians might be united. It is obvious that the Christian Association hoped that it could become a means for the reformation of all the churches while at the same time it continued to be, not a church, but only a voluntary society of individuals.

The Association was to be disappointed in all of its aims. No other ministers joined the association, no missionaries went forth, and no similar societies were formed. It was, in fact, not to remain long an association, although the constitution expressly denied any thought of church organization. Its objective was to work among the churches but not to assume the name or functions of a church. Thomas Campbell was insistent upon this point and only reluctantly gave it up when the logic of events later forced him to revise his views. Campbell's objectives are fairly obvious, but the great problem that arose was where those called out of the various churches were to go? It should have been apparent to him that it would be difficult for men and women to belong to such an association and remain long in their denominational church, yet, he provided no church for them to enter. Campbell's general fear of founding another sect kept him from seeing that it would be impossible to organize outside the communions and still not become a church. Nevertheless, that is precisely what he was trying to do.

The assumption underlying and harmonizing the proposals of the Declaration is that it is possible to define a simple evangelical Christianity, with a definite body of doctrines and a definite program of ordinances, worship, and government for the church, and have them all derived from the Scriptures and completely without the "inventions of men." The doctrine of universal reason as it is set forth by John Locke was accepted and indeed underlies the whole of the Declaration, as well as the Address. Since Campbell believed the final authority for all men was revelation interpreted by reason, the Scriptures must be regarded as the ultimate authority in religion. More will be said of this later.

The Address

The Address, eighteen pages in length, amplifies the argument for the unity of all Christians on the basis of Scriptural authority and develops in detail the proposals for attaining the goal. The author makes a full statement of his position and advances arguments to support his conclusions. It is, for the most part, a tract on Christian unity but always with the Bible put forward as the only acceptable basis for such a union. The first ten pages and the last five pages are devoted to a discussion of Christian union and the three pages that come between are devoted to the presentation of thirteen numbered propositions, all concerned with the subject of Christian unity.

The heading of the section containing the Address in the original edition is interesting:

ADDRESS &c.

To all that love our Lord Jesus Christ, in sincerity, throughout all the churches, the following address is most respectfully submitted.

Dearly Beloved Brethren,
That it is the grand design, and native tendency, of our holy religion, to reconcile and unite men to God, and to each other, in truth and love, to the glory of God, and their own present and eternal good, will not, we presume be denied, by any of the genuine subjects of christianity.[5]

With these words Thomas Campbell opens the major division of his work on New Testament Christian unity. Intended for the ministers of all churches and especially those of the Presbyterian church, it is interesting to note that he addressed his words specifically "to all that love our Lord Jesus Christ, in sincerity, throughout all the Churches." The first point which he makes is that fellowship with God and with man is the "grand design" and "native tendency" of the Christian religion. It is a Christian's duty to seek to reconcile and unite men to God; a fact often forgotten in the consideration of the problem of Christian union. The reasons for the proposals of the Christian Association are announced as Campbell continues:

. . . The whole tenor of that divine book which contains its institutes, in all its gracious declarations, precepts, ordinances, and holy examples, most expressly and powerfully inculcates this. . . . Impressed with those sentiments, and at the same time grievously affected with those sad divisions which have so awfully interfered with the benign and gracious intention of our holy religion, by exciting its professed subjects to bite and devour one another; we cannot suppose ourselves justifiable, in withholding the mite of our sincere and humble endeavours, to heal and remove them.[6]

There follows a lengthy section describing the baleful effects of divisions in such a new and thinly settled area:

congregations are divided, party spirit keeps individuals away from church, there is infrequency of participation in the Lord's Supper, and discipline is relaxed. There is nothing academic or theoretical about the language which Campbell uses, for he speaks from personal experience when he speaks of "large tracts of country entirely destitute of a gospel ministry." Campbell is vitally concerned with the moral conditions of the American frontier and the ineffectiveness of the church because of its sectarian divisions. It will be remembered that the period of moral and religious decline following the Revolutionary War had reached its lowest level shortly before Campbell came to America. Campbell comes to the point and asks if a minister's ordained duty is not plain:

... Is it not then your incumbent duty to endeavour, by all scriptural means, to have those evils remedied? Who will say, that it is not? ... The favorable opportunity which Divine Providence has put into your hands, in this happy country, for the accomplishment of so great a good, is in itself, a consideration of no small encouragement. A country happily exempted from the baneful influence of a civil establishment of any peculiar form of christianity—from under the direct influence of the anti-christian hierarchy—and, at the same time, from any formal connexion with the devoted nations, ... Can the Lord expect, or require, any thing less, from a people in such unhampered circumstances—from a people so liberally furnished with all the means and mercies, than a thorough reformation, in all things civil and religious, according to his word?[7]

In the above statement Campbell recognized a factor in the American frontier which had seldom, if ever before, been present in history: namely, that religious liberty was present in America in a way and to a degree in which it had never before existed.

While there is little direct reference to the subject, there can be no question as to whether Campbell intended to give a premillenarian cast to his appeal for Christian union on a biblical basis. He appears quite clearly to have identified current events with the predictions of the Apocalypse. This was the period of the Napoleonic wars and Napoleon, at the height of his power, was widely identified as the beast spoken of in Revelation. The premillenarian mood is well illustrated in the following:

... Is it not the day of the Lord's vengeance upon the antichristian world; the year of recompenses for the controversy of Zion? Surely then the time to favour her is come; even the set time. And is it not said that Zion shall be built in troublous times? Have not greater efforts been made, and more done, for the promulgation of the gospel among the nations, since the commencement of the French revolution, than had been done for many centuries prior to that event? ... Should we not, then, be excited, by these considerations, to concur with all our might, to help forward this good work; that what yet remains to be done, may be fully accomplished. ...[8]

With all humility Campbell discusses the right and competency of any group of individuals to set forth the proposals that the Christian Association was making:

... as for authority, it can have no place in this business; for surely none can suppose themselves invested with a divine right, as to anything peculiarly belonging to them, to call the attention of their brethren to this dutiful and important undertaking. For our part, we entertain no such arrogant presumption; nor are we inclined to impute the thought to any of our brethren, that this good work should be let alone, till such time as they may think proper to come forward, and sanction the attempt, by their invitation and example. It is an open field, an extensive work, to which all are equally welcome, equally invited.[9]

Campbell takes pains to emphasize the universal possibilities of his plea for Christian union and disclaims any desire to assume leadership. He affirms that he is not seeking prominence or glory of any kind, but is trying to discharge, on his part, an obligation which rests equally on all Christians. The call to a restoration of the simple New Testament church is sounded in the following quotation:

Dearly beloved brethren, why should we deem it a thing incredible, that the church of Christ, in this highly favored country, should resume that original unity, peace, and purity, which belongs to its constitution, and constitutes its glory? Or, is there any thing that can be justly deemed necessary for this desirable purpose, but to conform to the model, and adopt the practice, of the primitive church, expressly exhibited in the New Testament.[10]

Again Campbell, in his idealism, sees all Christians united if only they will conform to a clear pattern supposedly presented in the New Testament. He forgets that there are many ways of interpreting the Scriptures and that what appears plain to one is obscure to another. The vision is a worthy one, but the bringing of it to reality has been exceedingly difficult and has been attended, not by unity, but by actual further division within the church.

Campbell expresses the essence of his plea, and at the same time, gets at the heart of the problem of Christian unity, when he says:

It is, to us, a pleasing consideration that all the churches of Christ, which mutually acknowledge each other as such, are not only agreed in the great doctrines of faith and holiness; but are also materially agreed, as to the positive ordinances of Gospel institution; so that our differences, at most, are about the things in which the kingdom of God does not consist, that is, about matters of private opinion, or human invention. What a pity, that the kingdom of God should be divided about such things! ... Our dear brethren, of all denominations, will please to consider, that we have our educational prejudices, and particular customs to struggle with as well as they. But this we do sincerely declare, that there is nothing we have hither to received as matter of faith or practice, which is not expressly taught and enjoined in the word of God, either in express terms, or approved precedent, that we would not heartily relinquish, that so we might return to the original constitutional unity of the christian church....[11]

In this statement Campbell reveals not only his difficulties in coming to a decision to return to the practice of the New Testament, but also his determination to do so. He asks that others follow him in taking such a step, a return to "an entire christian unity," with Christ as the head and his word as the rule: "More than this," he says, "you will not require of us; and less we cannot require of you." This is Christian union reduced to its least common denominator. By Campbell's frequent reference to "our brethren of all denominations," it is clear that he looked on members of various sects and parties as Christians and brothers, and was not proposing an exclusive group. Indeed, if he had not regarded them as Christians, he would not have been interested in seeing them united.

He refuses however, to distinguish between "essentials" and "non-essentials":

... We dare neither assume, nor propose, the trite indefinite distinction between essentials, and non-essentials, in matters of revealed truth and duty; firmly persuaded, that, whatever may be their comparative importance, simply considered, the high obligation of the Divine Authority revealing, or enjoining them, renders the belief, or performance of them, absolutely essential to us, in so far as we know them.[12]

Finally, in closing this section of his argument, he places the will of God at the center of the undertaking:

... whatever is to be done, must begin—sometime—somewhere; and no matter where, nor by whom, if the Lord puts his hand to the work, it must surely prosper. And has he not been graciously pleased, upon many signal occasions, to bring to pass the greatest events from very small beginnings, and even by means the most unlikely. Duty then is ours: but events belong to God.[13]

The following lengthy paragraph discusses the timeliness and the reasonableness of the proposals of the Christian Association and at the same time reviews once more the divisions of the church and the partisan religious spirit of the country. So certain is Campbell of the validity of the principles that he has come to accept that he discusses only incidentally the possibility of their being erroneous.

The next paragraph reflects the thoughts of many on the frontier, where death was ever present and inspired concern with the consequences of the grave and of life after death. There are no divisions in the grave, says Campbell. This is followed by another appeal to the urgency and obvious duty of all Christians to unite. Campbell was sensitive in the extreme about the assumption of leadership. Over and over again, he echoes and re-echoes his unwillingness to be regarded as a leader.

With some hesitancy he proceeds to introduce the thirteen numbered propositions which are the heart of the Address and to suggest that Christians go back to the New Testament to restore a "pure" church:

> ... As the first fruits of our efforts for this blessed purpose we respectfully present to their consideration the following propositions—relying upon their charity and candour that they will neither despise, nor misconstrue, our humble and adventurous attempt. . . . They are merely designed for opening up the way, that we may come fairly and firmly to original grounds upon clear and certain premises: and take up things just as the Apostles left them.—That thus disentangled from the accruing embarrassments of intervening ages, we may stand with evidence upon the same ground on which the church stood at the beginning—Having said so much to solicit attention and prevent mistakes, we submit as follows:[14]

The thirteen propositions are presented to stimulate thinking about common ground on which to build a united church. After his experience with the presbytery and synod Campbell was most careful to insist that these propositions were not to be used as a term of communion. The first proposition is perhaps the most famous sentence about unity that Thomas Campbell ever wrote, and all the other propositions seek to expand and implement it:

> Prop. 1. THAT the church of Christ upon earth is essentially, intentionally, and constitutionally one; consisting of all those in every place that profess their faith in Christ and obedience

to him in all things according to the scriptures, and that manifest the same by their tempers and conduct, and of none else, as none else can be truly and properly called christians.

It is from this basic premise that all else is developed. The first proposition not only asserts the necessity of the unity of the church but also defines who are and who are not Christians. The need for obedience to Christ in all things "according to the scriptures," is clearly stated. The comprehensiveness of Campbell's definition is indicated by the three adverbs—essentially, intentionally, and constitutionally, and affirms that Christian union is not a matter of indifference, accident, or choice.

The second proposition again discusses the church of Christ "upon earth" as it should be constituted:

2. That although the church of Christ upon earth must necessarily exist in particular and distinct societies, locally separate one from another; yet there ought to be no schisms, no uncharitable divisions among them. They ought to receive each other as Christ Jesus hath also received them to the glory of God. And for this purpose . . . to be perfectly joined together in the same mind, and in the same judgment.

This proposition suggests that although there is one church of Christ, there are of necessity many local churches or congregations. These groups are united in the common bond of brotherhood and love, and in rational agreement on essentials, "perfectly joined together in the same mind, and in the same judgment." In other words, Campbell is saying that true Christian union is not mere co-operation.

The third proposition proceeds immediately to establish the basis of authority for Christians:

3. That in order to this, nothing ought to be inculcated upon christians as articles of faith; nor required of them as terms of communion; but what is expressly taught, and enjoined upon them, in the word of God. Nor ought any thing be admitted, as of divine obligation, in their church constitution and managements, but what is expressly enjoined by the

authority of our Lord Jesus Christ and his Apostles upon the New Testament church; either in express terms, or by approved precedent.

Here is Campbell's fundamental doctrine—a doctrine stating that the only authority for Christians and for the church is the Scriptures. There is a hint of the return to original ground (the beginnings of the early church) which was promised in the introduction to the propositions. Campbell wished to sweep aside all the "accruing embarrassments of intervening ages" in the firm belief that if Christians returned to the Bible, and the Bible alone, they would be united.

The fourth proposition seeks to establish the relative importance of the Old and New Testaments for Christians:

4. That although the scriptures of the Old and New Testament are inseparable connected, making together but one perfect and entire revelation of the Divine will . . . the New Testament is as perfect a constitution for the worship, discipline and government of the New Testament church . . . as the Old Testament was for the worship, discipline and government of the Old Testament church. . . .

After establishing the basic authority of the Scriptures in proposition three, Campbell, in proposition four, points to the primacy of the New Testament as the foundation of the church of Christ. While generally accepted today, this was a radical position at the time it was first advocated. Campbell is careful again to assert, however, the complete authority and inspiration of both the Old and New Testaments.

The fifth proposition has to do with the commands and ordinances of Christ:

5. That with respect to the commands and ordinances of our Lord Jesus Christ, where the scriptures are silent . . . no human authority has power to interfere, in order to supply the supposed deficiency. . . . Much less has any human authority power to impose new commands or ordinances upon the church,

which our Lord Jesus Christ has not enjoined. Nothing ought to be received into the faith or worship of the church; or be made a term of communion amongst christians, that is not as old as the New Testament.

This proposition is specifically aimed at the traditions and requirements fixed on Christians through the centuries by both Roman Catholic and Protestant groups. In the light of Campbell's well-known emphasis on the need for scriptural evidence to guide the Christian, the acceptance of this principle would seem to replace the freedom of the individual by what is written in the New Testament.

The sixth and seventh propositions are highly involved, but form one of the most important sections of Campbell's platform for Christian union:

6. That although inferences and deductions from scripture premises, when fairly inferred, may be truly called the doctrine of God's holy word; yet are they not formally binding upon the consciences of christians farther than they perceive the connexion, and evidently see that they are so; for their faith must not stand in the wisdom of men; but in the power and veracity of God—therefore no such deductions can be made terms of communion, but do properly belong to the after and progressive edification of the church. . . .

7. That although doctrinal exhibitions of the great system of divine truths, and defensive testimonies in opposition to prevailing errors, be highly expedient . . . yet, as these must be in a great measure the effect of human reasoning, and of course must contain many inferential truths, they ought not to be made terms of christian communion: unless we suppose, what is contrary to fact, that none have a right to the communion of the church, but such as possess a very clear and decisive judgment . . . whereas the church from the beginning did, and ever will, consist of little children and young men, as well as fathers.

In these two propositions Campbell discusses the proper place and the positive value of theology in the church but maintains that theological findings and conclusions should not be a test of fellowship among Christians. He recognizes the usefulness of theology in developing the higher intellectual life of the Christian but insists that credal statements are useless as a test of fellowship since human reasoning enters into them. He suggests further that the church needs a simpler statement of faith than most creeds provide.

The eighth proposition sets forth the terms of admission to the church:

> 8. That as it is not necessary that persons should have a particular knowledge or distinct apprehension of all divinely revealed truths in order to entitle them to a place in the church; neither should they, for this purpose, be required to make a profession more extensive than their knowledge; but that, on the contrary, their having a due measure of scriptural self-knowledge respecting their lost and perishing condition by nature and practice; and of the way of salvation thro' Jesus Christ, accompanied with a profession of their faith in, and obedience to him, in all things according to his word, is all that is absolutely necessary to qualify them for admission into his church.

This proposition outlines the essentials of church membership: consciousness of sin, acceptance of Jesus Christ, and willing obedience to him in harmony with the teaching of God's word. The phrase, "to make a profession more extensive than his knowledge," may be taken to mean the relation of an experience of conversion which Campbell had known in his youth and which was required by many of the churches in America at that time. When in proposition eight Campbell speaks of the "lost and perishing condition" of those who are sinners "by nature and practice," he reveals a belief in the doctrine of original sin which he is later to give up as a moral contradiction.

The ninth proposition insists on the universal brotherhood of Christians as a part of the family of God:

> 9. That all that are enabled, thro' grace, to make such a profession, . . . should consider each other as the precious

saints of God, should love each other as brethren, children of the same family and father. . . .

This is an idea found throughout the New Testament record of the early church, yet the failure to practice Christian brotherhood was at the very heart of the sectarian bitterness with which Campbell was surrounded. Campbell's Calvinistic theology reveals itself in the use of the phrase, "that are enabled, thro' grace." It was difficult for Campbell to accept the fact that those who had been foreordained by the grace of God to eternal salvation should be unwilling to live on terms of brotherhood.

The tenth proposition is a denunciation of the evils of a divided church:

> 10. That division among christians is a horrid evil, fraught with many evils. It is anti-christian . . . anti-scriptural . . . anti-natural. . . . In a word, it is productive of confusion, and of every evil work.

The divided church is denounced as (1) anti-Christian because it destroys the visible unity of Christ's body; (2) anti-Scriptural because Christ himself prayed that all his followers might be one; (3) antinatural because it excites Christians to condemn, to hate, and to oppose one another instead of loving one another as brethren, even as Christ has loved them.

The eleventh proposition places the blame for the divided church on those who neglected the will of God and made human inventions a term of communion:

> 11. That, (in some instances,) a partial neglect of the expressly revealed will of God; and, (in others,) an assumed authority for making the approbation of human opinions, and human inventions, a term of communion, by introducing them into the constitution, faith, or worship, of the church; are, and have been, the immediate, obvious, and universally acknowledged causes, of all the corruptions and divisions that ever have taken place in the church of God.

There can be no doubt but that the above-mentioned causes of the divisions in the church are valid, but that they entirely explain the lack of co-operation among all Christians or that they explain all the divisions of history may be questioned. Campbell may then be justly accused of exaggeration at this point. The causes of division he mentions may seem the reasons to him, but they do not satisfactorily explain all divisions among Christians. People do not always interpret "the revealed will of God" in the same way.

The twelfth proposition contains a summary of the church program outlined in the Address:

12. That all that is necessary to the highest state of perfection and purity of the church upon earth is, first, that none be received as members, but such as having that due measure of scriptural self-knowledge described above, do profess their faith in Christ and obedience to him in all things according to the scriptures; nor, 2dly, that any be retained in her communion longer than they continue to manifest the reality of their profession by their temper and conduct. 3dly, that her ministers, duly and scripturally qualified, inculcate none other things than those very articles of faith and holiness, expressly revealed and enjoined in the word of God. Lastly, that in all their administrations they keep close by the observance of all divine ordinances, after the example of the primitive church, exhibited in the New Testament; without any additions whatsoever of human opinions or inventions of men.

According to the twelfth proposition, the following terms of church membership should be required: (1) acceptance of Christ and the authority of the Scriptures, (2) a Christian spirit exhibited in the life and conduct of the member, (3) only those things taught in the Bible to be preached by the scripturally qualified ministry, and (4) the example of the early church as it is revealed in the New Testament to be followed.

The thirteenth proposition reluctantly permits human expedients:

13. Lastly. That if any circumstances indispensably necessary to the observance of divine ordinances be not found up-

on the page of express revelation, such, and such only, as are absolutely necessary for this purpose, should be adopted, under the title of human expedients, without any pretence to a more sacred origin—so that any subsequent alteration or difference in the observance of these things might produce no contention nor division in the church.[15]

Campbell is saying, in other words, that if it is absolutely necessary to add something to the practice of the church in promoting its work, let it be clearly understood that it is of human origin. If something of human invention is added and it is later found necessary to change the custom, a new cause for division will not be produced.

The fundamental principles enunciated in these thirteen propositions may be summed up as follows:

First, the essential unity of the Church of Christ.
Second, the supreme authority of the Scriptures.
Third, the special authority of the New Testament.
Fourth, the fallacy of human creeds.
Fifth, the essential brotherhood of all who love Christ and try to follow him.
Sixth, that if human innovations can be removed from the church, the followers of Christ will unite upon the scriptural platform.[16]

Phrases found in the propositions of the *Declaration and Address* sound familiar when we recall the "Protest and Appeal" submitted to the synod and the letter delining the authority of synod and presbytery. In his protest and in his letter submitted to the Chartiers Presbytery, Thomas Campbell was in process of working out the basis of his future course of action. Undoubtedly he incorporated into the larger document the phrases of the earlier documents and in the full *Declaration and Address* expanded and carried forward his ideas of Christian union on the authority of the Bible. The experiences and meetings of the intervening months doubtless contributed to the further development of his ideas.

These principles, stated so forthrightly and clearly in the *Declaration and Address,* show the uniqueness of Thomas Campbell's contribution to the concept of Christian union. He advocated the New Testament as a basis on which the divided church could unite and set forth a plan of action, however imperfect, which could be implemented. These propositions emphasize the importance of the individual Christian and lift up Christian faith as personal rather than doctrinal. They make a decided distinction between the personal faith of the believer and the theological faith of the creeds.

The importance of the propositions is reaffirmed in the succeeding section and with this the case is allowed to rest:

. . . To prepare the way for a permanent scriptural unity amongst christians, by calling up to their consideration fundamental truths, directing their attention to first principles, clearing the way before them by removing the stumbling blocks . . . is, at least, the sincere intention of the above propositions. It remains with our brethren, now to say, how far they go towards answering this intention.[17]

There is an appeal to join those who are seeking scriptural unity and a motto is stated which was later used by Campbell over and over again:

. . . Union in truth has been, and ever must be, the desire and prayer of all such—Union in Truth is our motto. The Divine Word is our Standard; in the Lord's name do we display our banners.

This ends the most important part of the document. The remaining pages of the Address are filled with an urgent appeal to join in the cause of promoting a scriptural church. The latter part reads like a sermon. Campbell exhorts, appeals, quotes Scripture, and beseeches those who read to join the cause. Those who are near are asked to join the local association, those who are at a distance are urged to form additional associations.

Campbell reviews again and again his conviction of the rational and logical position of the Christian Association, and urges all of similar mind to work with them. Thus he closes this significant document on Christian unity on the authority of the Bible by quoting relevant passages of Scripture:

... and "this is my commandment that ye love one another as I have loved you; that ye also love one another." And again, "Holy Father, keep through thine own name, those whom thou has given me that they may be one as we are," even "All that shall believe in me—that they all may be one; as thou Father are in me and I in thee, that they also may be one in us; that the world may believe that thou hast sent me. And the glory which thou gavest me, I have given them, that they may be one, even as we are one: I in them and them in me, that they may be made perfect in me; and that the world may know that thou hast sent me, and has loved them, as thou hast loved me." May the Lord hasten it in his time. Farewell.

Peace be with all them that love our Lord Jesus Christ in sincerity. Amen.

THOMAS CAMPBELL, Secretary.
THOMAS ACHESON, Treasurer.[18]

By use of Thomas Acheson's name as treasurer of the Christian Association it would appear that he had been reconciled on the question of infant baptism since the initial meeting at Abraham Altar's farm. It was quite likely that the use of his name was desired because he was a man of influence in and around Washington, Pennsylvania, and would add prestige to the enterprise.

Philosophical Background

In order to understand fully the *Declaration and Address* a brief review of Thomas Campbell's philosophical background is in order. The influence of Thomas Reid's philosophy on the University of Glasgow in the last half of the eighteenth century has already been indicated. This philosophy, it will be remembered, emphasized native powers of the human understanding—

powers which were considered the principles of common sense. In an age of skepticism Reid's philosophy gave support to orthodox Christian faith and the basis of Reid's thought is to be found in the empiricism of John Locke. It is to Locke we must ultimately turn.

Actually it is the philosophy of John Locke rather than that of Reid which is most apparent in the *Declaration and Address*. An explanation for this is difficult to find, since the only known contact between Thomas Campbell and Locke's philosophy was that which must have taken place at the University of Glasgow under Reid. But it is more than likely that Reid introduced his students to the writings of John Locke. It is known beyond question that Thomas Campbell was familiar with Locke's *Essay Concerning Human Understanding* and his first *Letter Concerning Toleration*, and that he guided his son in the study of these writings. A perfect familiarity with all of these writings must certainly have been among the resources which Thomas Campbell brought with him to America.

John Locke, the son of a Puritan, had been born in 1632 and was educated at Oxford, where he opposed the scholastic philosophy being taught there. He disliked both the intolerance of the Presbyterians and the overzealous nature of the Independents, and showed great sympathy with those seeking civil, religious, and philosophical liberty. He worked many years on his theory of knowledge which first appeared in print in 1690 entitled, *An Essay Concerning Human Understanding*. He was in exile in Holland during the period 1683 to 1689, and returned to England in 1689, with the exodus of the Stuart kings and the coming of William and Mary. His first *Letter Concerning Toleration* was written and published in Latin in Holland and also appeared in English after his return to England. He was writing a fourth

Letter Concerning Toleration at the time of his death in 1704, a little over one hundred years before Campbell wrote the *Declaration and Address*.

Locke's philosophy exerted a tremendous influence on human thought. It was especially influential in England, Scotland, and America all through the eighteenth century and the beginning of the nineteenth. It was from the *Essay Concerning Human Understanding* that the basic ideas concerning reason and faith were derived by Thomas Campbell. Locke was struggling with the "principles of morality and revealed religion," and was inquiring into the origin, certainty and extent of human knowledge, together with the grounds and degrees of belief, opinion, and assent. Locke held that the mind was passive in the process of knowing: that the mind began with nothing and that all knowledge came from without, in. He was a thorough-going empiricist.

A distinction was made between knowledge proper which gives certainty, and belief and opinion which give only probability. Locke called this whole process reason. Reason is the discovery of truth by the use of our natural faculties. But Locke took care not to stop before he marked out a large class of subject matter as an exception to this rule:

> Besides those we have hitherto mentioned there is one sort of propositions that challenge the highest degree of our assent, upon bare testimony, whether the things proposed agree or disagree with common experience, and the ordinary course of things, or no. The reason whereof is, because the testimony is of such an one as cannot deceive nor be deceived: and that is of God himself. This carries with it an assurance beyond doubt, evidence beyond exception. This is called by a peculiar name, *revelation*, and our assent to it, *faith* . . . and we may as well doubt of our own being, as we can whether any revelation from God be true.[19]

Thus faith is the assent to any proposition, not made by the deductions of reason, and it comes to men through revelation. Faith based on revelation is set in contradistinction to reason, and affirms a "duality of knowledge." The proper realm of faith is above that of reason. Reason is natural revelation but true revelation is reason enlarged.

It is interesting to note that Locke's successors, taking various portions of his philosophy, attained such different ends. Berkeley and Hume took the idea of intuitive knowledge in Locke to its logical conclusion, and ended in skepticism; the English Deists and Voltaire accepted the distinction between reason and faith but denied the reality of revelation. Yet Thomas Campbell, and later Alexander to a greater degree, used Lockean premises as the philosophical basis of Christian proofs.

It is in the *Declaration and Address* that this background of Lockean thought is first evidenced to any considerable degree in the writings of Thomas Campbell. Later articles written for his son's magazines reveal even more fully a knowledge of Locke's philosophy—a knowledge undoubtedly derived from his reading of the *Essay Concerning Human Understanding*. It was in the first *Letter Concerning Toleration*, however, that Campbell found an appeal for nonsectarian Christianity, though from a different approach. Many years later, in 1844, Thomas Campbell printed in the *Millennial Harbinger* over a period of months the entire first *Letter Concerning Toleration*. Locke wrote all four of these letters at the time of and immediately following England's peaceful revolution, when great issues of civil and religious liberty were in the balance. Paragraphs could be quoted, especially from the first letter, that could easily be mistaken for extracts from the *Declaration and Address*.

Locke's ideas on the function of the church are reflected in the *Declaration and Address* in Campbell's conception of a voluntary association of those interested in Christian union and in his assumption that individuals have the right to organize a church to worship God as they think proper. Locke says:

> Let us now consider what a church is. A church, then, I take to be a voluntary society of men, joining themselves together of their own accord in order to the public worshipping of God in such manner as they judge acceptable to Him, and effectual to the salvation of their souls.[20]

In Locke's discussion of the nature and authority of the church occurs a passage which might have been used in the *Declaration and Address,* since Campbell advocated this view so positively:

> But since men are so solicitous about the true church, I would only ask them here, by the way, if it be not more agreeable to the Church of Christ to make the conditions of her communion consist in such things, and such things only, as the Holy Spirit has in the Holy Scriptures declared, in express words, to be necessary to salvation; I ask, I say whether this be not more agreeable to the Church of Christ than for men to impose their own inventions and interpretations upon others as if they were of Divine authority, and to establish by ecclesiastical laws, as absolutely necessary to the profession of Christianity, such things as the Holy Scriptures do either not mention, or at least not expressly command? Whosoever requires those things in order to ecclesiastical communion, which Christ does not require in order to life eternal, he may, perhaps, indeed constitute a society accommodated to his own opinion and his own advantages; but how that can be called the *Church of Christ,* which is established upon laws that are not His, and which excludes such persons from its communion, as He will one day receive into the Kingdom of Heaven, I understand not.[21]

In the above quotation may be observed the emphasis on the sole authority of the Scriptures that occurred so frequently in the *Declaration and Address.* Locke may not have been the only source for Campbell's ideas on this subject, but certainly Campbell's knowledge of

Lockean thought must have been influential in the formulation of his basic principles. Even Campbell's observation in the *Declaration and Address* that members of the church may be dismissed for failure to use the right "temper and conduct" is to be found in Locke's statement:

And, first, I hold that no church is bound, by the duty of toleration, to retain any such person in her bosom as, after admonition, continues obstinately to offend against the laws of the society. For, these being the condition of communion and the bond of the society, if the breach of them were permitted without any animadversion the society would immediately be thereby dissolved.[22]

The duty and obligation of the ministry to teach the doctrine of peace and toleration is emphasized, even as Campbell emphasized it. Of this, Locke says:

I will not undertake to represent how happy and how great would be the fruit, both in Church and State, if the pulpits everywhere sounded with this doctrine of peace and toleration.... But this I say, that thus it ought to be. And if anyone that professes himself to be a minister of the Word of God, a preacher of the gospel of peace, teach otherwise, he either understands not or neglects the business of his calling and shall one day give account thereof unto the Prince of Peace.[23]

It is not difficult to see Campbell's idea of the supremacy of the New Testament for Christians and his feeling that the Old Testament was intended for the discipline and order of the Old Testament church in the following excerpt from Locke:

... But it may be urged farther that, by the law of Moses, idolaters were to be rooted out. True, indeed, by the law of Moses; but that is not obligatory to us Christians. Nobody pretends that everything generally enjoined by the law of Moses ought to be practiced by Christians....[24]

Locke has something to say in regard to the divisions within the church and the following words may have had something to do with Thomas Campbell's ideas on Christian union:

> Schism, then . . . is nothing else but a separation made in the communion of the Church upon account of something in divine worship or ecclesiastical discipline that is not any necessary part of it. Now, nothing in worship or discipline can be necessary to Christian communion but what Christ our legislator, or the Apostles by inspiration of the Holy Spirit, have commanded in express words.
>
> In a word, he that denies not anything that the Holy Scriptures teach in express words, nor makes a separation upon occasion of anything that is not manifestly contained in the sacred text . . . yet in deed and truth this man cannot be either a heretic or schismatic.[25]

Locke believed that when things went wrong it was good to go back to the beginning and seek to restore the original conditions. Campbell believed that churches had departed from the divine standard and that it was his duty to lead a revolt against the established sectarianism. Proper order could be established in the church only by going back beyond creeds and councils and restoring conditions as they were at the beginning. Locke advocated the reduction of doctrinal requirements for membership in the church so that many different factions could be brought together in harmonious relations in one body. Campbell similarly outlined the only permissible requirements for church membership in the propositions of the *Declaration and Address.*

Locke's system was fundamentally intellectual. He was opposed to emotionalism and traditionalism in the state as well as in the church and his aim was to get men to use their own minds, to shake off the bondage of the past, and to obtain liberty in rationality. The revelation which was made was confirmed by miracle and was made so plain that all should accept it. In summary, Thomas Campbell wrote the *Declaration and Address* well-grounded in the principles of Lockean thought, especially such of those principles as were worked out in the *Essay Concerning Human Understanding* and in the first *Letter Concerning Toleration.*

Importance of the Declaration and Address

The *Declaration and Address* merits particular attention, not only on its own account, but also because it laid the foundation for the religious movement, so uniquely American, known today as Disciples of Christ or Christian churches. Another movement known as the Church of Christ also traces its origin to this document. The *Declaration and Address* is considered one of the basic documents of the communion of Disciples of Christ and as such ranks along with *The Last Will and Testament of the Springfield Presbytery* as being of prime importance.

The significance of this document to the future development of Thomas Campbell's efforts to restore the New Testament church and promote Christian union cannot be overemphasized. It was the basis on which Alexander Campbell and others laid their labors. One scholar of the brotherhood has said:

> The Declaration and Address is, in its substance and spirit, as well as in its vigorous and scholarly style, the most notable document of the initiatory period of our reformatory movement. It is worthy of the perpetual remembrance and diligent study of our people. It, and the Appeal to the Synod, prove to us that this great enterprise to restore in spirit and form, in doctrine and life, apostolic Christianity, was conceived and projected in its principles by Thomas Campbell, in remarkable completeness and clearness, before his son Alexander had yet reached the shores of this Western world.[26]

The claim of the *Declaration and Address* to greatness can be made not only because of Campbell's influence on the history of the movement of Disciples of Christ, but also because of its intrinsic merit. The *Declaration and Address* is an important document in the history of the ecumenical church. It touches on one of the most important problems of the modern church, and until the problem of Christian union is settled it will always possess a direct and searching appeal. The evils of the church, outlined by Thomas Campbell, are still with us even though we might not agree on the solution.

The chief importance of the *Declaration and Address,* however, is that Thomas Campbell in this document has carefully thought through and set down in writing a statement of principles on which he and his group of friends proposed to act. The germ thoughts of all subsequent developments are in this document. It was the basis on which all who came later were to build, including Thomas Campbell's son, Alexander, who soon took leadership in the movement initiated by the father. The father and son were to elaborate, clarify, and follow to their logical conclusion, the fundamental principles stated in the *Declaration and Address,* especially the principle of putting the New Testament first in all religious matters. But always, without fail, they returned to the *Declaration and Address* as to a charter of religious freedom and as a guide for their cause.

The Appendix and Postscript

The Appendix, although its thirty pages constitute by far the longest section of the pamphlet, is looser in style than either of the preceding parts. It contains some interesting passages, but is, in the main, a reiteration and extension of the ideas expressed in the Declaration and in the Address. It is essentially a commentary on the positions already advanced and effort is made in it to anticipate possible objections. It explains and clarifies several points in the proposals of the Christian Association set forth in the *Declaration and Address.*

The purpose of the Appendix is indicated in the opening words of Campbell:

> To prevent mistakes, we beg leave to subjoin the following explanations. As to what we have done—our reasons for so

doing—and the grand object we would desire to see accomplished—all these, we presume, are sufficiently declared in the foregoing pages. As to what we intend to do in our associate capacity, and the ground we have taken in that capacity, tho' expressly and definitely declared; yet, these, perhaps, might be liable to some misconstruction.—[27]

In the very next sentence Campbell stresses the point that it is not intended to "proselyte":

. . . we beg leave to assure our brethren, that we have no intention to interfere, either directly, or indirectly, with the peace and order of the settled churches, by directing any ministerial assistance with which the Lord may please to favour us, to make inroads upon such; or, by endeavouring to erect churches out of churches—to distract and divide congregations.[28]

Campbell next emphasizes that he has nothing new to offer—nothing indeed which is not as old as the New Testament itself, and that the unity desired could be brought about only by a return to the faith, to that which a "thus saith the Lord" can be given, and not to opinions. The place of creeds and confessions is touched on; disavowal of any wish or plan to form a sect or denomination is stated, and the matter of the disciplining of members is discussed.

The largest amount of space is given in the Appendix to the attempt to show that the creedless condition of the Association did not make it a latitudinarian body or an advocate of weak doctrinal position. Campbell insists that it will never be possible for God's people to see alike on all things, or that it is necessary that they should do so on those things which are matters of opinion. He is firm in his belief that there is a core of assured Divine revelation which is so obviously divine and so clearly set forth that there should be universal agreement on it. This, and this alone, is essential for a basis or system on which unity might become a fact. The Appendix insists that the *Declaration and Address* is an appeal based on the facts of the gospel as distinct from theological opinions about these facts.

The Appendix closes with a most interesting quotation from a work entitled *Scott's Family Bible.* The quotation tells of the report made by a missionary to the American Indians who preached on Christianity as the one true religion and who was rebuked by the Indians because the white man was divided over this same religion. In the closing statements of the Appendix, Campbell addresses to the Indians words meant for his readers:

. . . Alas! poor people! how do our divisions and corruptions stand in your way? What a pity that you find us not upon original ground, such as the Apostles left the primitive churches! Had we but exhibited to you their unity and charity; their humble, honest, and affectionate deportment towards each other, and towards all men; you would not have had those evil and shameful things to object to our holy religion, and to prejudice your minds against it. But your conversion, it seems, awaits our reformation—awaits our return to primitive unity and love. To this may the God of mercy speedily restore us, both for your sakes and our own; that his way may be known upon earth, and his saving health among all nations. Let the people praise thee, O God; let all the people praise thee. Amen and Amen.[29]

The Postscript was written three months after the main body of the *Declaration and Address* had been submitted to the printer. On November 2 the Christian Association held its first meeting in Washington, Pennsylvania, at which a sermon was preached by Thomas Campbell, and the provisions of the seventh and eighth articles of the Declaration were put into effect. On December 14, 1809, the first meeting of the committee of twenty-one was held, and two steps for the promotion of the association's program were suggested.

The first of the two proposals was the preparation of:

. . . a catechetical exhibition of the fulness and precision of the holy scriptures upon the entire subject of christianity—

an exhibition of that complete system of faith and duty expressly contained in the sacred oracles; respecting the doctrine, worship, discipline, and government of the christian church. . . . a catechetical exhibition . . . would, if duly executed, demonstrably evince their perfect sufficiency independent of human inference . . . and would at the same time, inevitably lead the professing subject to learn every thing, respecting his faith and duty, at the mouth of God, without any reference to human authority . . . a performance of this nature might, with apparent propriety be called the Christian Catechism.[30]

It was proposed that there be affixed to the catechism a "dissertation," the purpose of which would be to outline the authority of the Scriptures and to "detect and expose" the reasoning by which others had twisted Scripture to human ends. The statement "to detect and expose" is not in keeping with the spirit of the main body of the *Declaration and Address,* and therefore, may have come from some other hand than that of Thomas Campbell. This proposal coming so soon after the rejection of creeds and the assertion that simple faith in Christ and obedience to him were the proper tests of fellowship, must be viewed in connection with the seventh proposition of the Address, which said that "doctrinal exhibitions" are "highly expedient" if not used as terms of communion. It is assumed that such a catechism as the one proposed would not be used as a test of fellowship, but doubtless would have been used to instruct and to serve as a proof that the Christian Association was not "latitudinarian." The proposal is evidence enough that the general belief was that a set of self-evident, expressly revealed Bible standards was available for reconstituting the New Testament church. In view of the difficulty and the seeming impossibility of such a task, it may well be that Winfred Ernest Garrison was right when he remarked: "Only one thing can be said in defense of the proposed 'catechetical exhibition.' It never was written."

The second proposal contained in the Postscript is the following:

> ... a periodical publication, for the express purpose of detecting and exposing the various anti-christian enormities, innovations and corruptions, which infect the christian church; which counteract and oppose the benign and gracious tendency of the gospel. . . . Such a publication from the nature and design of it, might with propriety be denominated *The Christian Monitor*.[31]

The magazine was to be a monthly, to begin in 1810, whenever five hundred subscribers could be secured, but since the proscribed number was not forthcoming the project was dropped. The proposal is significant, however, for its revelation of the fact that as early as 1809 the need for exposition and dissemination of the views expressed in the *Declaration and Address* was recognized.

CHAPTER FOUR

THE MOVEMENT IS LAUNCHED

Effect of the "Declaration and Address"

ON ITS publication the *Declaration and Address* was scarcely noticed by the religious leaders of western Pennyslvania. Campbell had seen to it that ministers of all communions received a copy and had personally asked them to consider the propositions of the Address. He had assured them that all written objections to the arguments set forth "... we shall thankfully receive, and seriously consider ... but verbal controversy we absolutely refuse."[1] But nothing further was heard of the matter. The ministers to whom Campbell sent the *Declaration and Address* with such eager expectation were unmoved by it and, if they brothered to read it, they said nothing about it.

Neither Thomas Campbell nor those associated with him had a full conception of all that was involved in the principles published in the *Declaration and Address*. Campbell was convinced, however, that he had discovered an infallible formula for Christian union and discussed only incidentally the possibility of its being erroneous. He was willing to stake his entire case for union on this platform and, as he said in the Address: "Indeed, if no such divine and adequate basis of union can be fairly exhibited ... then the accomplishment of this grand object must be forever impossible." Campbell felt also that the lack of an established church in America was good reason to expect success. All the members of the association shared this confidence more or less, and believed they were working to carry out God's commands. They did not consider themselves a distinct denomination with a theological system, but they were an association for the development of a movement which would lead to the union of the church on a scriptural basis.

Although little notice was given the *Declaration and Address,* the Christian Association itself was watched with considerable interest. Various persons in the community, some of them ministers and others close personal friends of Campbell, expressed their approval of the objects of the organization, but did not take part in its activities. There was, indeed, general respect for the members of the society and for its leader, Thomas Campbell, who was highly regarded for his moral and religious worth. Many of the members of the association were influential persons loosely connected with the religious denominations in the community and their community standing gave prestige to the association.

Thomas Campbell's son, Alexander, after his arrival in October, 1809, read and studied the *Declaration and Address* with great interest, and at once gave hearty approval to all its propositions—propositions which expressed clearly the convictions toward which he had been led by his experiences in Scotland. When Campbell asked his son about his plans for the future, Alexander responded immediately that he was determined to devote himself to the spreading of the principles and views presented in the *Declaration and Address.* Impressed by the example of the Haldanes in Scotland, Alexander further stated that he had resolved never to receive any compensation for his ministerial labors, to which his father replied: "Upon these principles, my son, I fear you will have to wear many a ragged coat." Campbell, was, of course, delighted at his son's decision, and urged Alexander to give up all other concerns and to study the Bible intently for at least six months.

About this time two other members of the Christian Association, James Foster and Abraham Altars, began a course of study under the direction of Thomas Campbell in order to prepare themselves for leadership in the work of the ministry and of the association. Methodical and economical in his use of time, Thomas gave only general direction to the course of study for the three ministerial students and left the details of their instruction to Alexander. Thomas himself spent much time in visiting the scattered families connected with the association and in endeavoring to promote the objects of the society. So passed the winter of 1809 and the spring of 1810.

Approach to the Synod of Pittsburgh

As spring turned into summer, it became increasingly evident to Thomas Campbell that the cause of Christian union on the principles he advocated was not progressing as he had hoped. The proposals of the *Declaration and Address* were not widely accepted and no apparent effort was being made anywhere to form societies similar to the Christian Association of Washington. On the contrary, the association seemed to be unconsciously assuming a somewhat different character than had been intended and was, under the ministrations of Thomas Campbell, gradually taking on the characteristics of a church. It was about this time that Campbell was joined in his labors by his son, Alexander, who preached his first sermon in July, 1810, at one of the weekly meetings.

This tendency of the association to become a church caused Thomas Campbell great concern. These were difficult days for Campbell, who saw his vision of a scripturally united church still unfulfilled. He began to hear himself reproached for adding one more to the number of sects instead of promoting union. The idea that he should be the instrument for the creation of a new sect was most abhorent to him. As he became more and more aware of the truth of these observations, he resolved to adopt any measures consistent with his principles to prevent such an occurrence. Some time during the summer of 1810 it was suggested to Thomas Campbell by different members and clergy of the regular Presbyterian church that the Christian Association form a union with them. The pastor of the Presbyterian church at Upper Buffalo, a close friend of Campbell's, expressed confidence that the synod would willingly receive the members of the Christian Association on the principles they advocated. Campbell was further encouraged to consider such a course by several considerations. All his former association had been with a Presbyterian body; he regarded his religious views, in the main, as substantially in agreement with the Westminster Confession; and furthermore, most of his followers were in some branch of the Presbyterian church. To Campbell the most potent argument in favor of such a proposal was the desire to avoid the appearance of forming a new sect. Campbell could not see the inconsistency of his position in advocating union on a purely scriptural basis with all its problems of interpretation and the attempt to work within an ecclesiastical organization. Alexander, however, did not anticipate any favorable results, and disapproved approaching the synod, but under the circumstances did not think it proper to make any direct opposition to his father's wishes. After much meditation and prayer the elder Campbell finally decided to apply to the Synod of Pittsburgh at its next meeting for membership of the Christian Association in the regular Presbyterian church. This synod was a unit of the main Presbyterian body, and had been authorized by the General Assembly of 1802.

The Synod of Pittsburgh met at Washington, Pennsylvania, October 2, 1810, and was opened with a sermon by Samuel Ralston of Ohio, the moderator of the previous meeting. The following entry appears in the minutes of the afternoon session for the third day of the meeting, October 4, 1810:

> Mr. Thomas Campbell, formerly a minister in connection with the associate synod, now representing himself as in some relation to a society called the Christian Society of Washington applied to this Synod to be taken into christian and ministeral communion.
>
> Upon hearing Mr. Campbell at length, and his answers to various questions proposed to him, the Synod unanimously resolved, that however specious the plan of the christian association, and however seducing its professions, as experience of the affects of similar projects, in other parts, has evinced their baneful tendency, and destructive operations on the whole interests of religion, by promoting division, instead of union, by degrading the ministerial character, by providing free admission to any errors in doctrine, and to any corruption in discipline, whilst a nominal approbation of the scriptures as the only standard of truth may be professed, the Synod are constrained by the most solemn considerations to disapprove the plan and its native effects.
>
> And farther, for the above and many other important reasons, it was resolved that Mr. Campbell's request to be received into christian and ministerial communion cannot be granted.[2]

Campbell requested and was granted a copy of the synod's decision in his case. On Friday afternoon Campbell again appeared before the synod and asked for an explanation of the "important reasons" respecting him mentioned in the former minute which prevented the synod from seeing fit to receive him into its fellowship. Apparently Campbell was concerned for fear that his moral character was in question. The synod carefully explained that

> It was not for any immorality in practice, but, in addition to the reasons before assigned, for expressing his belief that

there are some opinions taught in our Confession of Faith which are not founded in the Bible, and avoiding to designate them, for declaring that the administration of Baptism to infants is not authorized by scriptural precept or example, and is a matter of indifference, yet administering that ordinance while holding such an opinion; for encouraging or countenancing his son to preach the gospel without any regular authority; for opposing Creeds and confessions as injurious to the interests of religion; and also because it is not consistent with the regulations of the Presbyterian church, that Synod should form a connection with any ministers, churches or associations; that the Synod deemed it improper to grant his request.[3]

When these reasons had been read to him, Campbell denied having said that infant baptism was a matter of indifference to him and affirmed that he accepted many truths drawn by inference from the Bible. He acknowledged that he opposed creeds and confessions when they contained any thing not expressly contained in the Bible and furthermore that there were some things in the Confession of Faith not expressly revealed in the Bible.

From the minutes of the synod it appears that Campbell made application as the representative of the Christian Association and that he laid before the synod a full statement of the plan and purpose of the society—plans and principles which he had no intention of giving up. No doubt he presented the synod with a copy of the *Declaration and Address*. He simply wished to "be taken into Christian and ministerial communion," while he went on with the work of his nonecclesiastical organization. In his address before the synod, Campbell was careful to define clearly the position of the society as simply an organization for the promotion of biblical Christian union and not a church and he gave no indication that the society intended to lose its identity or relinquish its aims. When all is considered the chief reason for the synod's rejection was, as the minutes record, that "it is not consistent with the regulations of the Presbyterian Church that Synod should form a connection with any ministers, churches or associations."

The refusal of the synod to admit his group to membership must have keenly disappointed Campbell and at first reading the statement of the synod as to the reasons for its action sound complacent and self-righteous, but with all their smugness they were aware, as was Alexander, of the impossibility of reconciling a plea for union based on biblical interpretation with a church coming out of traditional backgrounds. It was inevitable that Campbell's effort to join the Presbyterian church should fail. No minister holding his views about creeds, about the union of all Christians on a simple evangelical basis, and about the independence of the local congregation, could reasonably expect to be received into full fellowship by a Presbyterian synod. The religious-minded of the frontier had seen and heard many itinerant ministers with strange and often radical ideas. Thomas Campbell appeared to them to be but another such individual. Campbell's fear of creating a new sect kept him from seeing that no existing denomination could possibly shelter him or his followers. At the same time, the approach to the Synod of Pittsburgh shows how far he was from having worked out any definite system of doctrine or polity of his own at this time.

Alexander Emerges as a Strong Leader

Alexander, after his arrival in America, always attended his father's meetings. On determining to enter the ministry and give himself to the cause of promoting Christian union on a scriptural basis, he began at once to study under the direction of his father. After several months of such study Thomas suggested that his son take part in the meetings, but because Alexander was only twenty-two years old and inexperienced in public speaking, this was postponed. At last, however, Thomas felt the time was ripe to present his son to the public. At one of the meetings held at Jacob Donaldson's home in the spring of 1810, Campbell announced that following his sermon there would be a short intermission after which Alexander would speak. Accordingly, after the meeting resumed, Alexander arose and spoke for a short time. When he had finished, his father appeared very pleased, and remarked in a quiet voice, "Very well." This was Alexander's first attempt at public speaking.

Thomas Campbell and friends of the family urged Alexander to prepare and deliver a sermon and he finally agreed to do so. An appointment was made for July 15, 1810, for him to preach in a grove on the farm of a Major Templeton, eight miles from Washington, Pennsylvania. The interest in the Christian Association and the rumors concerning the promising abilities of Alexander, combined to produce a large congregation when the day arrived. His text was from Matthew 7:24-27, the story of the two foundations, one of sand and one of rock. Anxious to succeed in his first trial, Alexander had taken pains to write out the message in full and had then committed it to memory. There was nothing outstanding in the sermon itself but there was something commanding in the bearing and voice of the speaker. Indeed, after the gathering was dismissed nearly everyone commented on the excellence of the delivery. Some of the older members of the association even said to each other: "Why, he is a better preacher than his father!"

This judgment expressed by friends of both father and son symbolized the arrival of a new personality on the religious scene of the western frontier and the coming of a personality who had qualities of leadership sadly lacking in the older man. The effect of this first sermon was notable. Members of the Christian Association who were present were unanimous in agreeing that Alexander should have a formal call to the ministry. Alexander himself realized that he had found his true vocation. From that day forward his services were in continual demand and the first year he preached no less than one hundred and six sermons, delivered at the crossroads, at Washington, at Buffalo, at Middletown, and in private homes.

Alexander had received careful training from his father in the preparation of sermons. Thomas Campbell had carefully instructed Alexander on the proper sermon form, that form required by the strict rules of the Seceder church, and the father was never satisfied unless a sermon was composed and arranged according to these rules. The rules were founded on what were considered correct principles of both logic and rhetoric. It became an almost invariable custom that the father and son, after returning home from hearing each other's sermons, would examine and test them according to the established rules. Alexander probably learned as much through this criticism of his father's sermons as through being criticized himself. Thomas Campbell always made it a special point to ascertain first, whether or not the views or doctrines delivered were truly those of the text, taken in proper connection with what preceded and what followed it. He would not allow fanciful interpretations or farfetched applications, but insisted constantly on limiting the sermon to the range of ideas incorporated in the passage itself.

After the synod's rejection of his application in October, 1810, Thomas Campbell, still opposed to religious controversy, was willing to let matters rest as they were and to take no public notice of the rejection. Alexander, however, soon convinced the members of the Christian Association that some answer would have to be made to the statements of the synod. It was generally felt that only through such a public declaration would the nature and objects of the association be brought to the attention of the public. The essential difference between Thomas and his son is brought to the forefront in their attitude toward this matter. The son was to give evidence of an aggressive and disputatious nature in contrast to the indecisiveness and avoidance of conflict so apparent in the father. In fairness, however, it must be said that much of the difference in attitude was but that of a young and ambitious man in contrast to a man thrust in middle age into an unfamiliar environment.

The next semiannual meeting of the Christian Association was scheduled for November, and Alexander decided to make it the occasion of a public reply to the synod. To this end the following advertisement was inserted in the *Reporter* on October 22 and 29, 1810:

> The Christian Association of Washington holds its semiannual meeting at Washington on Thursday, the first of November next, at 11 o'clock. There will be delivered upon that occasion by Alexander Campbell, V.D.S., an appropriate discourse illustrative of the principles and design of the Association, and for the purpose of obviating certain mistakes and objections which ignorance or willful opposition has attached to the humble and wellmeant attempts of the Society to promote a thorough scriptural reformation, as testified in their address to the friends and lovers of peace and truth throughout all the Churches.[4]

In the above advertisement Alexander used the initials of the words *Verbi Divini Servus,* meaning "Servant of the Word of God." The idea came from Thomas Campbell, who, about this time, renounced the title "Reverend" but continued to use occasionally the initials "V.D.M." after his name, representing the words *Verbi Divini Minister,* or "Minister of the Word of God."

At the appointed time, Alexander addressed a large audience, using as his texts Isaiah 57:14 and Isaiah 62:10, and expounding the principles of the proposed reformation and replied to the synod's criticisms. From this address it is clear that Alexander and his father were in agreement: (1) that they regarded the religious denominations around them as having the substance of Christianity, but as having failed to preserve its original nature; therefore the chief object of the proposed reformation was to restore the true basis of union, (2) that they regarded each congregation as an independent organization, bound by fraternal relations, (3) that they considered "lay preaching" as authorized and denied the distinction between clergy and laity, (4) that they looked on infant baptism as without direct scriptural authority, but were willing to leave it as a matter of forbearance, (5) that they clearly anticipated the probability of having to resolve the Christian Association into a distinct congregation of the church in order to carry out for themselves the duties and obligations demanded in the Scriptures, and (6) that in depending solely on scriptural authority they foresaw that many things, considered important by others, must inevitably be excluded.

The vigor of Alexander's championship of the cause of scriptural union at this meeting of the Christian Association did much to win recognition for him as the most competent and energetic advocate of the movement. It is apparent that by the end of 1810 Alexander Campbell had rapidly emerged as a strong leader and preacher. Under the guidance and tutelage of Thomas Campbell, the tremendous potential of Alexander's mind began to be displayed and the community became increasingly aware of his dynamic personality, his aggressiveness and personal magnetism, and his burning conviction of the righteousness of the cause of Christian union on a scriptural basis.

The Association Becomes a Church

After the November meeting of the Christian Association, Thomas Campbell and his son continued to preach in and about Washington, Pennsylvania. Sometimes Thomas preached at the courthouse in Washington, sometimes at the crossroads meetinghouse, and occasionally at private homes such as Thomas Hodgen's or James McElroy's. Neither Thomas nor his son appears to have made their views on restoration and Christian union the particular subject of their sermons unless the text lent itself to the topic, but devoted themselves to explaining scriptural passages or to setting forth the duties of the Christian life.

Thomas Campbell's problem was how to have the Christian Association remain an agency promoting the restoration of the primitive church without allowing it to become a separate religious sect. He still considered himself a Christian minister even though officially he had been out of the Seceder connection for over a year. Alexander had left the Seceder church while in Scotland, and therefore did not actually belong to any church. Others in the Christian Association, while nominally members of one or another of the various religious groups in the community, were equally perplexed about their position. Its members were breaking away more and more from their previous church connections and it seemed that the Christian Association was inevitably to become a new religious party.

In the course of Thomas Campbell's visitation among the members of the Christian Association he had met John Brown, a carpenter and millwright, and a warm friendship had developed between them. The Browns lived on a farm located on Buffalo Creek, about sixteen miles west of Washington but only eight miles from the town of Charlestown (now Wellsburg), in Brooke County, Virginia (now West Virginia). John Brown, his only daughter Margaret, and her stepmother were members of the Presbyterian church at West Liberty, about four miles south of their farm. Sometime in the fall of 1810 Thomas asked Alexander to return some books to the Brown household and it was at this time that Alexander first met eighteen-year-old Margaret. The friendship ripened into love through the winter months and on March 11, 1811, Alexander Campbell and Margaret Brown were married. It was an event that was to be of great significance to the infant movement. The immediate result was that since Alexander and his bride made their home with his father-in-law, John Brown, on the family farm, Thomas Campbell decided to move from Washington to a small farm about a mile and a half from Mt. Pleasant, Pennsylvania, not far from his old friend John McElroy. Thomas felt that he could live with his remaining family more inexpensively there than in town, and his friends and neighbors would be nearby to assist in the management of the farm.

By the spring of 1811 the elder Campbell had come to feel that the Christian Association must become an independent church in order to carry out the functions and duties of a Christian fellowship. It was with great reluctance that he decided to take this step, but it was the logical thing to do. Therefore, at the next meeting of the association, held May 4, 1811, the group constituted itself a church and the congregational form of church government was adopted. Campbell betrayed his previous habit and training by insisting that each person present give some personal and public statement regarding the way of salvation and a satisfactory answer to the question: "What is the meritorious cause of a sinner's acceptance with God?" Only two failed to give a satisfactory answer. Their admission was postponed, and it was subsequently refused, but on other grounds.

James Foster happened to be absent from this meeting and later the question was asked: "Is James Foster a member, not having been present at the time the test question was asked?" Some thought not, but Alexander, who was not entirely convinced that there was scriptural authority for such a question, immediately arose and said: "Certainly, James Foster is a member, having been with us from the beginning, and his religious sentiments being perfectly well known to all." The test question was not put to Foster, or to anyone else after that time. Once again Alexander had taken the initiative. In suggesting this test question Thomas Campbell showed his ineptness at leadership and his lack of understanding as to what was actually taking place.

At this same meeting, Thomas was chosen elder and Alexander was licensed to preach the gospel. John Dawson, George Sharp, William Gilcrist, and James Foster were elected deacons, and after prayers were said, they united in singing the one hundred and eighteenth Psalm, in the metrical version some of them had been in the habit of using as Seceders. In forming an independent congregation the group was taking an important step, for if their relations with their former churches had been strained before, they were now broken. Contrary to their original desire, they had become a separate sect, although they consisted of only one small country church. On the next day, Sunday, May 5, 1811, the Lord's Supper was observed for the first time, and it was observed weekly thereafter. There is no record of any previous consideration of this point. It was not among the items of controversy between Thomas Campbell and the Seceder Presbyterians, nor was it mentioned specifically in the *Declaration and Address*, but as soon as the congregation was organized, the members were unanimous in reverting to the practice of the Haldanean churches. At this first service Alexander preached from John 6:48 ("I am that bread of life"), and following him, Thomas preached from Romans 8:32 ("He that spared not his own son, but delivered him up for us all, how shall he not with him also freely give us all things"). Thus the association became a distinct religious group, with the determination to be guided in all things solely by the Scriptures.

The Christian Association had been meeting in a log building at "crossroads," about three miles from Mt. Pleasant, Pennsylvania, but the newly organized church at once arranged for the erection of another meetinghouse. The site selected was on the farm of William Gilcrist, in the valley of Brush Run, about two miles above the junction of that stream with Buffalo Creek and two miles southeast of West Middletown. The location of the meetinghouse gave the congregation the name of the Brush Run Church, by which it is known in history. It was a simple frame structure, eighteen by thirty-six feet with rough seats provided for the congregation, and was soon ready for use. The first service was, in fact, held in it on June 16, 1811, with the interior still unfinished.

Adoption of Immersion

Even before the writing of the *Declaration and Address* the question of infant baptism had arisen among the followers of Thomas Campbell. Previous reference has been made to the meeting at the home of Abraham Altars where the elder Campbell enunciated his famous dictum that he would speak where the Scriptures speak. It will be recalled that Andrew Munro, bookseller and postmaster at Canonsburg, arose and said such a principle would do away with infant baptism. Such a statement inferred that the concern was not the form or purpose of baptism so much as the fact that infant baptism as such is not mentioned in the Scriptures, and therefore is not binding on Christians. It was more or less assumed that the alternative form of baptism was the immersion of adults. Apparently a number of the group had given considerable previous thought to the question.

At this time, however, Thomas Campbell felt strongly that the question was one of forbearance and was not the central issue which faced the group. One of Alexander's first reactions upon reading the proof sheets of the *Declaration and Address* in October, 1809, was to question whether or not these principles, if applied, would mean giving up infant baptism and other practices for which there was no express scriptural precept or example. Many years later he expressed his reaction as follows:

> I read to him the third proposition. . . . On reading this, I asked him in what passage or portion of the inspired oracles could we find a precept or an express precedent for the baptism or sprinkling of infants in the name of the Father, the Son, and the Holy Spirit? His response, in substance, was, "It was merely inferential."[5]

Alexander then proceeded to study in detail the arguments for infant baptism. He requested Andrew Munro, the bookseller, to furnish him with all the books he had in favor of infant baptism and the more he read the more convinced he became that the practice of infant baptism should be classed as a "human invention." He felt that the arguments of the pedobaptists were not well reasoned and, after reading all their arguments, turned to his Greek New Testament to see what he could find there.

At a later date Thomas was again questioned by his son on the subject of authority for infant baptism. Thomas readily admitted that there were neither "express terms" nor "precedent" to authorize the practice, and continued,

> But as for those who are already members of the church and participants of the Lord's Supper, I can see no propriety, even if the scriptural evidence for infant baptism be found deficient, in their unchurching or paganizing themselves, or

in putting off Christ, merely for the sake of making a new profession; thus going out of the Church merely for the sake of coming in again.[6]

Thomas took the position that they ought not to teach or practice infant baptism since it was not expressly mentioned in the Scriptures but that they should preach and practice immersion for all who were to make, for the first time, a profession of their faith. Alexander felt that this reasoning was fallacious and that his father had failed to apply his own principles, but in deference to his father's views, said nothing further. Once again Thomas failed to catch the full implication of the principle which he was advocating.

When the application was made for union with the Synod of Pittsburgh in October, 1810, it was recorded that a few of the members of the Christian Association "doubted and others denied, the validity of infant baptism, though they all seemed willing to make this a matter of forbearance." Thomas Campbell's views at this time were brought out in his answer to the synod's charge that he had said that infant baptism was a matter of indifference. He said: (1) infant baptism is not a matter of indifference but of forbearance (2) that he believed many things gained only inferentially from the Scriptures, and (3) that the Confession of Faith contained some things not expressly revealed in the Bible.

After the formation of the Brush Run Church in May, 1811, it was noticed that two or three of the members, who had given satisfactory answers to the test question asked by Thomas Campbell, did not partake of the Lord's Supper with the rest. On being questioned about this one of the members, Joseph Bryant, replied that he did not consider himself authorized to partake since he had never been baptized. Two other members, a Margaret Fullerton, whose father had been a Baptist and Abraham Altars, whose father had been a Deist, felt the same way. This raised the question of baptism in a new and more practical way. It particularly called for discussion of the question as to what was meant by baptism. There is record of Alexander's having preached June 5, 1811, on Christ's commission to the apostles as it is recorded in Mark 16:15-16. In this sermon Alexander revealed his stand on baptism at this time when he said: "As I am sure it is unscriptural to make this matter a term of communion, I let it *slip*. I wish to think and let think on these matters."

Thomas Campbell had serious scruples about whether or not to baptize those who had already been recognized as members of the church, but that question was not relevant to the present case, for none of the candidates had ever received baptism in any of its forms. He did not appear to have any objection to immersion as a form of baptism and admitted to one or two of the church members that he believed the New Testament practice was to have the candidates go down into the water and be symbolically buried in it. After due consideration, he agreed to do the immersing, and this took place on July 4, 1811, at a convenient place on Buffalo Creek where the water was deep enough to come just up to the shoulders of the candidates. Thomas Campbell, without going into the water, stood on a root that projected over the edge of the creek, and bent down the heads of the candidates until they were covered, and repeated in each case, "I now baptize thee, in the name of the Father, and the Son, and the Holy Spirit." James Foster, who was present, neither approved the manner of the baptism, nor thought it logical that one who had not been immersed himself should immerse others. There is a pathetic element in the picture of a middle-aged minister standing precariously on a root overhanging a stream and awkwardly administering the rite of baptism. He wished with all his heart to do that which was scripturally commanded but did not exactly know how. Thus it was that Thomas Campbell, who had been the first to seek to unite the churches on a scriptural basis, was the first to introduce immersion.

Six months later, on January 1, 1812, Alexander Campbell was ordained to the ministry. A certificate was later recorded in Brooke County, Virginia, which stated that "after a due course of trials preparatory to the work of the holy ministry," Alexander was "according to the principle of this church regularly chosen and ordained a minister thereof." The certificate was signed by Thomas Campbell as the "Senior Minister of the First Church of the Christian Association of Washington, meeting at cross-roads and Brush Run, Washington County, Pennsylvania."[77]

On March 13, 1812, Alexander's first child, Jane, was born, and with her birth he began to restudy the whole subject of baptism. His wife, and her father and stepmother, with whom they made their home, were still members of the Presbyterian church, and it may be safely assumed that the question of the child's baptism became immediately a matter of practical interest. Up to this point the unity of the church and the restoration of the authority of the Bible had been the principal concerns of Thomas Campbell and his son, and both of them had regarded baptism as of comparatively little importance. Now Alexander began to wonder if baptism was not a matter of much more importance than they had supposed. As a recent father he was concerned to know if there was direct authority in the Scriptures for infant baptism. Painstakingly he sought out the meaning of the word "baptize" in the Greek and became convinced it meant "to immerse." He became further convinced that the sprinkling to which he had been subjected in infancy was wholly unauthorized by Scripture, and that he was consequently an unbaptized person. Furthermore, he could not consistently preach immersion and remain unimmersed himself.

From March until June, 1812, the infant United States was disturbed politically by the increasing difficulties with Great Britain over maritime policy, and war seemed imminent. Such disturbances, however, were far removed from the western frontier and only indirectly affected the inhabitants of the trans-Allegheny region. Even the shadow of the War of 1812 was insufficient to distract the attention of Alexander from this question of immersion, for to him it was a question of far more personal concern.

Early in June, Alexander made his final decision and prepared to act at once. He knew a Matthias Luce, a Baptist preacher, who lived some miles from Washington and Alexander decided to ask Luce to immerse him. On his way to visit Luce he stopped to see his father and family who were then living on the little farm between Washington and Mt. Pleasant. His sister, Dorothea, had participated in the conversation and study that had been going on in Thomas' home and revealed to Alexander privately that she had come to the conclusion that she had not been scripturally baptized, and that she wished Alexander would present her case to their father. Alexander explained that he was on his way to arrange for his own immersion, and would lay her case along with his before their father. Thomas listened to Alexander's decisions and conclusions in silence, and to his son's surprise, offered no particular objections. Thomas spoke only of the position they had previously taken in regard to baptism, and concluded by saying: "I have no more to add. You must please yourself." Thomas Campbell had never interfered with Alexander's decisions and had perhaps fought as long as he could against what reason told him was the logical conclusion of his own principles. Before Alexander left for Mr. Luce's, however, Thomas suggested that in view of the public position they occupied as leaders of the church, Alexander's decision should be publicly announced among the people to whom they regularly preached. Thomas further requested that Luce call on him on his way to the baptismal service.

The day decided on for the service was Wednesday, June 12, 1812, and on the day before Matthias Luce and another man called at Thomas Campbell's on their way to the baptismal site, the spot used by Campbell for the first immersion. The two men spent the night, and the next morning, as they were setting out, Thomas Campbell simply remarked that Mrs. Campbell had prepared a change of clothing for herself and him. This was the first indication he had given to anyone that they intended to be immersed.

It was a clear and beautiful day, and when they arrived at a farmhouse near the place on Buffalo Creek chosen for the service, they found a large number of the community gathered, along with most of the members of the Brush Run Church. Thomas Campbell thought it proper to present in full the reasons that had determined his course of action. In a very long address he reviewed the entire history of his thought on baptism, the struggles through which he had gone, and his determination to settle the matter in such a manner that it might be no hindrance in the attainment of the Christian unity he desired to establish on the basis of the Bible alone. He admitted that he had overlooked the importance of baptism and the evident teachings of the Scriptures and had now come to submit to what he plainly saw as the express command of the Bible. After Thomas had finished, Alexander spoke concerning his reasons for submitting implicitly to all God's commands and tried to show that the baptism of believers only was the authorized Word of God. Between them father and son spoke for nearly seven hours. When the speeches were over, Alexander Campbell and his wife, Thomas Campbell and his wife, and their daughter, Dorothea, were immersed in Buffalo Creek. Mrs. Hanen, who had been one of the first to visit Thomas Campbell on his arrival in Washington, and her husband, James, were baptized at the same time and increased the number to seven persons. They were immersed after making a simple confession that "Jesus is the Son of God" and there was no account of a "religious experience" or other formality.

By this act Thomas Campbell made his first serious theological break with Calvinism. His previous differences with the Presbyterian church had been in the realm of church government and polity. In accepting immersion as the proper form of baptism he was leaving the pedobaptist tradition and creating a climate favorable to Baptist views. Undoubtedly Thomas Campbell reached this decision only after great mental struggle. He was torn not only by the conflict with his early training and the fact that he had been a Presbyterian minister for twenty-five years, but also by his concern not to do anything likely to frustrate his efforts to secure Christian union. It is obvious that he had no idea in the beginning that to take the Bible alone as authority would lead to the abandonment of infant baptism and that he continued to hope for some time the question of baptism might be a matter of forbearance. When the application of his own principles, however, pointed to the evident fact that the New Testament church had practiced immersion, and when his eldest son had come to the same conclusion, Thomas Campbell, with some heaviness of heart, consented to accept an immersionist position. It is useless to speculate on what the results would have been had he continued to hold pedobaptist views but it must be clearly understood that once he had made the change, however reluctantly, it was a permanent decision. From this time forward he believed and preached that immersion was the accepted biblical form of baptism and that only believers should be so baptized.

In the steps leading to this decision there had been no formal declaration of, no discussion of, the purpose of baptism. It was simply through common consent that Thomas and Alexander Campbell came to believe that baptism by immersion was the express teaching of the New Testament and therefore, it was no longer a matter of "human opinion." The adoption of immersion as an essential item in Thomas Campbell's plan of Christian union radically changed the direction which the movement was to take from this time forward. The movement had begun with the idea that all the various sects had a common enough core of belief and practice to form an adequate basis of union if they would discard the divisive "human inventions" which had grown up through the years. Thomas Campbell could no longer say, as he had said in the Address:

> It is, to us, a pleasing consideration that all the churches of Christ, which mutually acknowledge each other as such, are not only agreed in the great doctrines of faith and holiness; but are also materially agreed, as to the positive ordinances of Gospel institution; so that our differences, at most, are about the things in which the kingdom of God does not consist....[8]

Christian union, to Thomas Campbell, was no longer simply a matter of persuading churches to unite on the beliefs which Christians already held. Now it was felt necessary to persuade them also to accept the "positive ordinance" of baptism which at that time only the Baptists believed to be commanded in the New Testament. It now seemed most important to seek first the reformation of the church, the restoration of it to the purity it had known in New Testament days, and *then* to work for the union of Christianity.

At the next services of the Brush Run congregation following the baptism of Thomas Campbell, thirteen other members of the church (among them James

Foster) requested immersion, and this was administered by the elder Campbell, as each participant made a simple confession of his belief in Jesus as the Son of God. Within several weeks others asked for immersion and before long most of the congregation of approximately thirty members consisted of immersed believers. The other individuals in the church who did not wish to be immersed soon withdrew, and among these was Thomas Acheson. After this the little congregation held meetings alternately at the crossroads and at Brush Run, and became a single congregation with two meeting places.

Matters of Faith and Worship

One of the most important aspects of the acceptance of immersion by the Campbells was that they made a simple confession of faith in "Jesus as the Son of God." The essential fact of this profession of faith was that Christ was at the center of the Christian faith and the important question became not "what" but "in whom" one believed. This distinction had been recognized to some extent by Thomas Campbell at the outset. It was implied in the sixth proposition of the Address when he had written that inferences and deductions from Scripture may be true doctrine, but that they are not binding on the conscience of Christians further than they perceive them to be so. Again, in the eighth proposition of the Address, Campbell had stated that full knowledge of all revealed truth is not necessary to entitle persons to membership in the church, "neither should they, for this purpose, be required to make a profession more extensive than their knowledge." Realization of their need of salvation, faith in Christ as Savior, and obedience to him are all that is essential, said Campbell. The theological distinctions between a statement of faith and a belief in Christ, implied in the principles set forth by

Thomas Campbell in the *Declaration and Address* do not seem, however, to have been considered immediately. During the fall of 1811 and the winter of 1812, Thomas maintained an interesting correspondence with his son on various religious subjects, among which was the nature of faith. The father was still living on the farm between Washington and Mt. Pleasant, and Alexander and his wife were making their home on the Brown farm in Brooke County, Virginia. For some unknown reason in writing to one another the father used the pseudonym of "Philologus" and the son used "Philomanthes." Extracts from these letters help to show their thinking on questions of faith at this time. The first letter, dated October 7, 1811, from Alexander to his father, speaks of a work by Thomas Taylor, entitled *The Necessity and Efficacy of Faith in Prayer,* published in 1661, and quoted Taylor as saying that true faith is not always accompanied by certainty and that the prayer of faith is sometimes accompanied by doubt. Alexander agreed that this was correct and to this letter Thomas replied at length in the excellent handwriting for which he was known, that

> The subject you have introduced must, on all hands, be acknowledged to be one of leading importance. Next to the revelation of salvation for guilty men, that by which we are made partakers of it, and by which alone we must live, and be actuated while in this world, as legitimate expectants of the heavenly felicity, is to us of all things most important, for it is written, "The just by faith shall live."

With characteristic caution, Thomas Campbell next suggested to Alexander that always before turning to one's own or another's opinions:

> ... It behooves us to have immediate recourse to the Sacred Oracles, that we may stand upon sure ground; be the better educated in truth; have its impressions deepened in our minds, and behold it with still greater advantage....

From this beginning Thomas spoke of faith as being "the belief of the truth" and defined truth as comprehending everything that God has revealed of himself concerning his being and perfections, his work and will, and the present and future state of his creatures. He took the entire revelation of God as the subject matter of faith, the authority of God himself (who cannot lie) as the foundation or reason of our faith and "God in Christ the only proper and qualified object of it." Thus he continues:

> For as such he revealed himself from the beginning, and as such only is he the subject of supernatural revelation, and as such only can he be justly considered by all them that truly believe it; for, as such, is he held forth to have been "from everlasting," from the "beginning, or ever earth was," though not so revealed till after the fall, and then, at first, but obscurely. But no sooner did he reveal himself in relation to the redemption and recovery of fallen man, than he did so by the means or mediation of Jesus Christ. And, since then, in the process of the revelation with which he hath favored the Church, he hath declared himself acting or proceeding in and by Jesus Christ, in the creation of all things and in all his managements.

After interjecting several paragraphs of scriptural references, Thomas resumes:

> . . . But, God in Christ, or God, laying and executing all his purposes of creation, sustenation, gubernation, redemption and judgment, in and by Jesus Christ, is the adequate, comprehensive and adorable object of the Christian faith. . . .[9]

A second letter from Thomas Campbell on the nature of faith, dated November 29, 1811, entered minutely and somewhat philosophically into a consideration of the effects of faith. After some little discussion of these matters, he corrected himself and expressed his dislike of metaphysical distinctions and definitions. He concluded with some deductions from the whole discussion, among which are the following:

... he that would be saved should hearken diligently to the testimony of God, by the knowledge and belief of which alone, testified to all who hear it for their salvation, he may be delivered from the wrath to come. ... An effect this, which no systematic theory can either produce or promise, and of course makes no part of the preacher's business. ...

. . . .

I further infer that all the distinctions, directions and cautions about kinds and acts of faith, thrust upon the public attention by preachings and writings, polemical and practical, are little, if anything, better than fallacies, and amusive speculations, tending to divert and distract the mind from the truth —the great subject of salvation. ... The Scriptures exhibit no such theory. They consider the subject through a different medium. "Show me thy faith by thy works" is the Scripture test, to distinguish the true from the false. ...

Upon the whole, it is not theory, but a believing experience of the power of truth upon our own hearts, that will qualify us either to live or preach the gospel of a free, unconditional salvation through faith, and we may as well look to the north in December, for the warming breeze to dissolve the wintry ice, as to extract this believing experience of the power of truth out of the most refined and exquisite theory about the nature and properties of faith, or of justification, or of any other point of the Divine testimony. ... Let us, once for all, be convinced of this, that we may addict ourselves to study, believe and preach our Bibles, and then shall we study, live and preach to profit.[10]

These extracts from the correspondence between Thomas and Alexander Campbell during the fall of 1811 reveal views on faith held by Thomas, with which his son Alexander agreed. It may be observed that to Thomas the only source of spiritual truth is to be found in the Bible, which is essentially a record of the revelation of God in Christ reconciling a guilty world. Since Christ is "the way, the truth and the life," to believe on him and to trust in him, was to attain the purpose of divine revelation. The great work of salvation which Christ accomplished was embraced in a few comprehensive facts, adapted to the humblest understanding and a knowledge of these was deemed sufficient as the basis of faith, however these might be subsequently enlarged by an increased knowledge and experience. A simple confession of faith, said the elder Campbell, was all that was demanded in the apostolic age as a demonstration of discipleship.

One question after another, covering the whole range of Christian faith and worship, came up in succession. Alexander, during the winter of 1812, must have given much consideration to the question of religious fellowship, and in the correspondence with his father took opportunity to raise the question as to the position of the unbeliever in family or public worship. In a letter dated February 26, 1812, Alexander raised such questions as: (1) what is prayer and how many kinds are there? (2) is it scriptural and lawful for believers and unbelievers to join in prayer and worship? and (3) is there scriptural authority for making family worship a term of communion? He spoke of the corruptions of Christianity in the perversion of the ordinances of baptism, the Lord's Supper, the Lord's day, preaching, and inquired if it were not probable that prayer and worship have been misused as well. He also criticized contemporary preachers for emphasizing the Old rather than the New Testament.

To all these questions Thomas Campbell replied at considerable length in two letters, dated March 2 and March 12, 1812, in which he considered particularly the questions involved in religious fellowship. Thomas agreed with his son that Christianity as it was currently practiced was greatly corrupted and urged a return to the example of the New Testament and suggested that all worship looks to Christ for its authority. He said, speaking of the early Christians:

> ... their religious esteem and intercourse in all religious acts and exercises were precisely and necessarily limited to each other, and of course must of necessity still be the same, for there is still but one body, one Spirit, one Lord, one faith, one baptism, one God and Father of all, and of course but one law of love pervading and uniting all within the manifold limits of this unity and under its manifest influences....
>
> ... And now that the world has for a long time been misled about this baptism, and in the way of administering it to children, which are utterly incapable and always unqualified subjects—the one faith, manifested by an intelligent and consistent profession, is the immediate, proper, and formal reason of religious communion in all the instituted ordinances of gospel worship, beyond which it cannot be lawfully or profitably extended; and this instituted worship can be nowhere performed upon the Lord's day, where the Lord's supper is not administered. Wherever this is neglected, there New Testament Church-worship ceases....

Thomas insisted that all "gospel ordinances" are for Christians only and already had substituted "Lord's Day" for the term "Sabbath." Campbell proceeded to answer Alexander's next question about who our fellow Christians are and says that

> ... any fellow-sinner of the human race, how vile soever he may have been, who makes an intelligent profession of the truth as it is in Jesus, as comprehensively specified in the eighth proposition of the overture in our Address; and so long as he continues to manifest the reality of his profession by his temper and conduct, still to consider him in the same light....

He considered further those who are to be admitted to the communion table:

> ... Therefore, when any number of persons assemble on the Lord's day for the avowed purpose of public worship, there we may reasonably hope that there are some believers, and however this be, the persons thus assembling, in so far avow themselves

to be voluntary subjects of the gospel dispensation; nor is it our place to determine, what in many cases we cannot, who of them are or are not Christians, or whether or not they may not be all so, seeing that in the point of view in which they present themselves to our considerations, as also in the course of the service, they manifest themselves to partake with us in the acts of religious worship. There can be no doubt, then, in such a case, but we are to consider and address them as the professed worshipers of the true God through Jesus Christ. . . .[11]

These were the thoughts of Thomas Campbell on the subject of religious fellowship in March, 1812, just three months before accepting immersion for himself and his family. Thomas always sounded as if he excluded many people from fellowship, in principle, but in practice he was much more inclusive.

Next Steps

The adoption of immersion by the "reformers," as they were soon called, erected a barrier between them and the other churches, as most of their religious neighbors were Presbyterian. The clergy, especially, were alarmed at the rejection of pedobaptism and ecclesiastical authority. The bitter prejudice against and opposition to the Brush Run Church showed itself in many ways: in private conversation, in the pulpit, and in some instances in the economic boycott of members. On one or two occasions Thomas Campbell was molested as he was baptizing various individuals who wished to unite with the church, but his dignity and calm always secured the respect of most people. In the meanwhile, throughout the winter of 1812-1813, the members of the Brush Run Church met regularly in their meetinghouse near Buffalo Creek, even though the interior was still unfinished and the building without fire for lack of funds. They often visited at each other's homes and spent long hours in prayer and in examining the Scriptures.

It was natural that the adoption of immersion would bring the little group of Brush Run Church into more friendly relations with the Baptists. Although at this time there were few Baptists in the vicinity of Washington, they were quite numerous in the area just east of Washington, along the Monongahela River, and in the foothills of the Allegheny Mountains and had formed the Redstone Baptist Association for the purpose of fellowship.[12] In their preaching and visiting across the countryside, Thomas and Alexander Campbell became acquainted with ministers of various Baptist congregations who often urged them to join the Redstone Association. The Campbells, however, had several objections to such a union. The Brush Run Church did, of course, have the practice of immersion, but the churches of the Redstone Association had adopted the strongly Calvinistic confession of faith drawn up by the Philadelphia Baptist Association in 1742, and this was very similar to the Westminster Confession. Indeed, the only respect in which Brush Run Church could qualify as a Baptist church was in the form of baptism. It did not, however, accept the usual creed; it had another church organization; it differed on the matter of the nature of faith; the place of the New Testament in relation to the Bible; the qualifications necessary for baptism; the purpose of baptism; and the frequency of communion. They knew the Baptists did not share their views on the necessity of returning to the faith and practice of the primitive church and the simple confession of faith which they had adopted at their immersion.

The frequent invitations to join with the Redstone association were discussed at length by Thomas and his son. Alexander in later years confessed that he had formed a very unfavorable opinion of the Baptist preachers he knew and considered them "narrow, contracted, illiberal and uneducated men," but he was better pleased with the Baptists as a group than with those of any other denomination. He liked the way they read their Bibles, and seemed to care for little else in religion than "conversion" and "Bible doctrine." Some of the Baptist congregations began to send for Thomas and his son to preach for them and in the fall of 1812 Alexander attended a meeting of the association at Uniontown, Pennsylvania, where he was disgusted by what he saw and heard. On his return home he found that the Baptists themselves did not like the preaching of their leaders and continued to ask the Campbells to visit their churches and preach for them, though the father and son were not members of the Baptist church or any of its associations. The members of these churches, however, continued to press Thomas and his son to join the association.

In the fall of 1814 or early in 1815 the question of applying for admission to membership in the Redstone Baptist Association was discussed thoroughly by the members of the Brush Run Church. Their decision was to make application for membership in the association, and at the same time to write out a full statement of their beliefs. On eight or ten large pages the Brush Run Church restated their protest against creeds and expressed a willingness to join the association only "provided always that we should be allowed to teach and preach whatever we learned from the Holy Scriptures, regardless of any creed or formula in Christendom." Unfortunately, a copy of the document submitted to the association was not kept and when, at a later date, one was requested, the request was refused. When this document was presented to the Redstone Association, there was much debate, but it was finally decided to admit the Brush Run Church into fellowship, despite a small minority, consisting mainly of preachers, who objected and later caused much dissension, particularly as Alexander's views on doctrinal matters became more mature. It is important to note that the Brush Run Church was received as a whole, not as individuals. It was an exceptional case for which there was no known precedent in Baptist rules of procedure.

With their admission into fellowship with the Redstone Baptist Association, the reformers were again integrated with a larger fellowship, and their hope was renewed that they might carry on their work, not as a sect, but within one of the major denominations. The formation of a separate church organization was once again postponed, and Thomas Campbell, particularly, was glad to be affiliated with a recognized group again. The relationship thus established was to continue for seventeen years, though with mounting tension. From the beginning it was evident that Thomas and Alexander Campbell and their followers did not regard themselves as merged indistinguishably into the Baptist denomination and their sense of special mission did not diminish.

The adoption of immersion brought Alexander Campbell into a position of leadership in the Brush Run Church and in the religious community as a whole. His leadership in forming the relationship with the Baptists strengthened this position. In deciding to follow the example of his son in the question of baptism, Thomas Campbell in effect conceded to him the leadership of the movement begun by the father. Alexander became definitely the leader, and his father the follower, in the adoption of immersion. It now became evident to all, and to no one more than to Thomas Campbell, that the leadership of the movement and the defense of its principles must devolve upon the younger man. From this time forward, then, the son continued to develop the pattern of reforming the church to which he felt directed by his study of the New Testament. The concern of Thomas Campbell for the union of Christians on the basis of the Bible alone had led him into paths he had little suspected when he had begun to preach on the American frontier five years previously. As was said by Charles Louis Loos, who knew both the Campbells intimately:

> This was the father's task—to project the great reform. But to bring it to full development of purpose and constitution of life and then execute it with success, demanded qualities Thomas Campbell did not possess in the fulness of their required strength. This office fell providentially on his son.[13]

Thomas Campbell was now a man fifty years of age, with a rather large family to support. The movement which he had initiated called for one of younger years. The zeal and enthusiasm of his youth were past and he was quite content to let his capable eldest son take the initiative in developing their movement. It must not be assumed, however, that Thomas Campbell had no further contribution to make to the movement. Father and son worked together for the next forty or more years and Alexander continued to consult his father in all matters of interest to the movement. Until the end of Thomas' life he continued to be an adviser and helper to his son. Thomas Campbell was vitally interested in all that concerned the young movement and his son's leadership of it, but he was from this time forward the movement's counselor rather than its leader.

CHAPTER FIVE

ALEXANDER GAINS AN ABLE ASSISTANT

Migrations of 1813-1819

AS EARLY as 1811 Thomas Campbell had been preaching to interested groups on the frontier adjacent to Washington in the counties of eastern Ohio and western Virginia. In that period, it will be remembered, meetinghouses were few in number and preaching services were held either in the open or in public buildings such as schools or courthouses. Such services were usually well attended since many people were anxious to worship and the opportunity of hearing a preacher came only infrequently. Even before the Brush Run Church had been accepted into fellowship with the Redstone Baptist Association, various Baptist congregations had requested Thomas Campbell to preach for them, and after the admittance of the Brush Run Church into fellowship it was only natural that he was invited more frequently to visit Baptist churches.

Not long after the Brush Run Church united with the Redstone Association, Thomas became convinced that his ministry would have wider influence in another section of the country, and being best acquainted with the potentialities of the neighboring counties of Ohio, decided to sell his small farm near Mt. Pleasant in Washington County, and move ninety miles farther west to another farm about two miles from Cambridge, in Guernsey County, Ohio. Campbell at this time was nearly fifty-one years old and was more corpulent than in his youth. He was kindly and courteous in manner, serious in conversation, and deeply pious. He spoke with a slight Irish accent in a full voice resonant with animation and frequently took a pinch of snuff from the old gold box which at this time he invariably carried.[1] His family was maturing rapidly, for his oldest daughter, Dorothea, had married Joseph Bryant on January 13, 1813, and in November, 1813, just before the family moved to Ohio, eighteen-year-old Nancy married Andrew Chapman, a young Washingtonian. Besides his wife, Jane, two girls and two boys still remained at home: young Jane, aged thirteen; Alicia, seven; Thomas, eleven; and Archibald, nine. When the decision was made to move to Ohio, it was arranged that the married daughters and their husbands go along to assist in the management of the farm, and early in 1814 after the farewells were said, Brush Run Church was left in the care of Alexander Campbell and James Foster, who had been ordained elder.

Prior to the move to Ohio, Thomas Campbell had decided to follow Alexander's lead, as he had in the case of immersion, and preach without compensation. It was necessary, therefore, for him to provide an income from some other source for his still fairly large family. To add to his income Campbell opened and conducted a school in Cambridge, the county seat, where he held classes in a log building near the center of town. Here he enrolled his own sons and daughters. He used the remainder of his time to preach to the people of the community in a log-hewn meetinghouse on Pultney Ridge and in the Harmony Baptist Church near Cambridge, but with little success.

In the meantime, other members of the Brush Run Church decided to join the westward migration and move as a body to a site near Zanesville, Ohio, where they could establish a religious colony. Plans for the move were formulated under the direction of Alexander Campbell, who was especially enthusiastic about the project; but Alexander's father-in-law was against the proposed move because he objected to having his daughter and son-in-law so far away from him. In order to induce them to remain in Virginia, he deeded his farm to Alexander and moved his own family to Charlestown (now Wellsburg). Alexander agreed to this and, without his leadership, the others decided not to make the move. It is significant that the gift of the farm to Alexander established his financial security and was, therefore, highly important to the future development of the whole new movement.

Thomas Campbell kept himself busily engaged in teaching school at Cambridge, Ohio, and in preaching to the nearby churches during the remainder of 1814 and the greater part of 1815. Early in the fall of 1815, however, he received a letter from his old friend Thomas Acheson asking him to come to Washington to visit Acheson's brother David who was seriously ill and whose recovery, it was felt, could be speeded by the presence of his old and valued friend. Answering the summons, Campbell left his school in charge of other members of the family and paid a visit of several weeks to Washington. While there he heard of the favorable opportunities for a school in Pittsburgh and, what was to him of far more importance, of the possibility of establishing a church in the same place. He had become discouraged because the response to his preaching in Ohio had been meager and he was seriously in doubt as to whether he had found the right location for a successful ministry, even though his school had prospered. Therefore, he visited Pittsburgh and soon made the necessary arrangements to move his family there.

Campbell and his family, including the married daughters and their husbands, were then established in Pittsburgh by the late fall of 1815. There proved to be a definite need for a good school in Pittsburgh, and with the influence of two of the town's prominent citizens, James Irwin and Nathaniel Richardson who helped to gather the pupils, and with the help of personal friends, a large and successful school was soon under way. Campbell's reputation had preceded him, and the town parents were happy to have as teacher for their children a man who used the strict discipline of the British schools and who was, at the same time, deeply religious. His method of instruction not only gave a thorough scholastic foundation but also was concerned with his students' use of their time and opportunity.

When Campbell had been in Pittsburgh only a short time, Alexander visited him briefly on his way to Philadelphia. Alexander was starting on a tour of three or four months for the purpose of raising funds for a meetinghouse in Wellsburg and spent one Thursday evening with his father at the home of Richardson, who contributed the first twenty dollars toward the new building. The next morning Alexander set out by stagecoach for Philadelphia, where he arrived on December 28, 1815. He immediately wrote a letter to his Uncle Archibald at Newry, Ireland, in which he related his experiences in America and gave an interesting insight into his relations with his father at this time. He said:

> My father still resembles one of our planets in emigrating from place to place. He has lived in Washington and in the country; in Cambridge, ninety miles west, and now in Pittsburg. He is teaching a school in Pittsburg, worth, say, seven hundred dollars, and will be worth much more in a short time. As to our religious state, news, progress and attainments, I expect my father has written or will immediately write you. . . . What I am in religion I am from examination, reflection, conviction, not from *"ipse dixit,"* tradition or human authority. . . . Though my father and I accord in sentiment, neither of us are dictators or imitators. Neither of us lead; neither of us follow.[2]

Nathaniel Richardson at this time knew or cared little about the religious reformation which had sprung from Thomas Campbell's *Declaration and Address,* published only six years before. He valued the elder Campbell as a teacher, as a beloved guest and a devoted family friend. Richardson had enrolled his oldest son, Robert, in the academy conducted by the wise and kindly Thomas Campbell, and this son was later to assume an intimate association with the Campbell movement. Sitting under the tutelage of the elder Campbell and meeting the younger on the occasion of his brief visits, Robert was in a position to observe both men and record his impressions of their differing personalities:

> The father, full of affectionate sympathy and oversensitive in regard to the feelings of others, could not bear to inflict the slightest pain, and would rather withhold than to confer a benefit which could be imparted only by wounding the recipient. The son, with more mastery of his emotional nature, could calmly contemplate the entire case, and, for the accomplishment of higher good, could resolutely inflict a temporary suffering. The former was cautious, forbearing, apologetic; the latter, decided, prompt and critical.[3]

Since the major purpose of Thomas Campbell's move to Pittsburgh had been to have the opportunity to preach the restoration of the primitive purity of the church, he was not long in gathering other interested individuals about him and establishing a small independent congregation. The group met in the school building, practiced immersion, and each week observed the Lord's Supper which was followed by a sermon and a message of instruction. Campbell always spoke the truth as he saw it, without sparing the views of other religious groups, but always respecting their leaders, and welcoming to fellowship anyone who could give evidence of a sincere faith. Campbell presented an application for the admission of this congregation to fellowship at the annual meeting of the Redstone Baptist Association which was held in August, 1816, at Cross Creek Baptist Church, located three miles north of Wellsburg. It was here that the ministers and "messengers," appointed to represent the various congregations, gathered and among those who attended the meeting were Alexander Campbell and his wife; Thomas Campbell; Matthias Luce, who had immersed them; John Brown, and James Foster. Thomas Campbell well knew that he could expect opposition at the meeting and was undoubtedly prepared for the action of the association which was recorded in the minutes of the meeting for Saturday, August 31, 1816, and which stated:

7. A letter was presented by brother T. Campbell, from a number of baptized professors in the city of Pittsburg, requesting union as a church to this Association.

8. Voted, that as this letter is not presented according to the constitution of this Association, the request cannot be granted.

9. Voted, that brother T. Campbell be invited to take a seat in this Association.

10. Voted, that a committee be appointed to wait on the persons mentioned in the seventh article, to investigate the subject of their letter. Brethren D. Phillips, Luce and Pritchard are the committee to attend in Pittsburg, on the Saturday preceding the first Lord's day in November.[4]

The congregation organized by Thomas Campbell was denied admission as a church because its letter was "not presented according to the constitution of the Association," which required an acceptance of the Philadelphia Confession or an equivalent doctrinal statement. The association apparently had been taught to be more careful by their experience in admitting the Brush Run Church and were on guard against any more accessions at the recommendation of the Campbells. It is clear, however, that the association respected Thomas Campbell personally, for though they refused to recognize his congregation, they offered him a seat at the meeting. Further, the association was willing to go so far as to appoint a committee to investigate the Pittsburgh congregation to ascertain its orthodoxy.

At this same meeting Thomas Campbell presented a paper, called a "circular letter," which he had been asked to prepare at the 1815 annual meeting. He had been assigned the subject of the Trinity since the Baptist preachers were very anxious to hear what the Campbells had to say on this subject. This paper begins with a survey of the Scriptures for references to the three persons of the Trinity and continues:

... By his word, then, we learn that the divine name comprehends in it a plurality. . . . Father, Son and Spirit of God. . . . To us, then, who hold the Christian faith, there is but one God; the Father, of whom are all things, and we by him; and one Spirit who worketh all things, who inspires, animates and replenishes the whole body of Christ; divining to every man severally as he will. And these three are one. . . .

It appears to be a query with some who profess to hold this doctrine, whether it be correct to use the term *person* when speaking of the above distinct characters in the divine essence. As to this, let every man be fully persuaded in his own mind.

Campbell insisted that four things are palpable from the scriptural evidence: (1) that there are three distinct intelligent agents, subsistencies, or personal characters, in one Jehovah, (2) that in the exercise of one and the same divine energy or efficient will, these three are inseparable operators in every work, and (3) that the divine characters, the Father, the Son and Holy Spirit co-exist under relations which not only suppose and declare their essential unity, but also, with equal evidence, demonstrate a relative subordination according to the manner and order of their subsistence and operation and (4) furthermore, it is evident that each of the divine characters has a power peculiar to himself, by which they are distinguishable both among themselves and to mankind. Campbell concluded the paper with an exploration of some of the heretical teachings which he found in his day such as a denial of the essential Sonship of Christ.[5]

The minutes of the association reveal as the eleventh item of business for August 31, the approval of this paper, stating:

11. The circular letter prepared by brother T. Campbell was read and accepted without amendment.[6]

The paper was apparently satisfactory, even to the more orthodox members present since it was accepted without objection or amendment. The elder Campbell had presented the doctrine of the Trinity in language as close as possible to the language of the New Testament. It is interesting, indeed, that Campbell did not use the word "Trinity" once in the document, probably because he was convinced that only scriptural terms should be used and he had not found any use of the term in the New Testament.

This circular letter, in its general style and careful language, furnishes a marked contrast with the spirit of the "Sermon on the Law" delivered by Alexander Campbell at the same meeting—a contrast indicative of that which existed in the personalities of the two men. Alexander's sermon, based on Romans 8:3, with its emphasis on the distinction between the Old and the New Testament law and ordinances, in opposition to common Baptist acceptance, created considerable dissension. During the time the Campbells had been in the Redstone Baptist Association, there had been some opposition to them but, in general, there had been cooperation with them. After the delivery of this sermon, the opposition became and remained more pronounced. Thomas Campbell had revealed in this meeting, in consistency with his deepest principles, the focus of attention on uniting and reconciling Christians on the simple authority of the Bible, while Alexander had displayed just as clearly his characteristically iconoclastic tendencies.

After this meeting of the Redstone Association the bickering and controversy which ensued over the issues raised by Alexander in the "Sermon on the Law" were a source of deep discouragement to Thomas Campbell. He was greatly concerned over the direction the movement for scriptural union was obviously taking. In the seven years since the publication of the *Declaration and Address* he had, indeed, won few advocates to his cause. There were still not more than one hundred and fifty individuals, scattered among the Baptist churches of eastern Ohio, western Pennsylvania, and Virginia, who believed as Thomas Campbell did on matters of scriptural union and the restoration of the primitive Christian church. Thomas and Alexander Campbell alone were preaching in behalf of the movement among the various churches, for James Foster was caring only for the Brush Run Church. The response to Thomas' message in Pittsburgh had been decidedly disappointing even though the school still prospered.

In the spring of 1817 Mrs. Joseph Bryant's (Dorothea Campbell) health failed, and Thomas' daughter Nancy and her husband had returned to Washington County to farm. As a result of these circumstances Thomas Campbell was left with the entire responsibility for the large school which had developed in Pittsburgh. This was too great a burden on a man past the prime of life and, along with his discouragement over the lack of progress of his ministry in Pittsburgh, had much to do with Campbell's decision to move to Kentucky where he hoped that he would be able to minister to the religious needs of the newer frontier. Therefore, in the fall of 1817, Campbell took his family to Newport in Boone County, Kentucky, just opposite Cincinnati, and left them there for several months while he visited the numerous Baptist churches bordering the Ohio River. He found the Baptists here most cordial and hospitable and relatively liberal in their religious views, but he did not like the emphasis which they placed on the emotional experience in religion and on their lack of insistence on Bible study and family worship.

In the course of his travels he visited Burlington, a county seat of three hundred inhabitants, in the same county with Newport. The citizens were in process of erecting a schoolroom, and since they were in need of a teacher for the new school, they urged Campbell to move his family there and take over the teaching when the building had been completed. After a time Campbell and his family became an integral part of the community and his school was ever more popular, which made it also very remunerative. Pupils came from great distances to attend the school and Campbell's eighteen-year-old daughter Jane assisted in the school, soon becoming recognized for her ability as a teacher.

Campbell's chief interest was still in religion and he became the religious leader of the community. Most of the people in the community were Baptists, but there was no church or church building to house them. Shortly after moving to Burlington, Campbell began to give a course of lectures on the Bible to which the public was invited and, though only a few people accepted his teachings, the lectures were well attended. He continually encouraged family worship and the daily study of the Scriptures, and in his preaching Campbell emphasized the great need for a proper understanding of religion as well as the importance of an emotional experience. He set forth his views on the need for the reformation of the church, in the light of his findings on the importance of baptism, and sought to reveal what he considered to be the errors taught by other sects. During these years of 1817-1819 Campbell made several visits and preaching tours into Indiana where he found various religious groups at work. Here the theme of his message was little changed, for he sought primarily to show that the church of his day was far from being what the gospel contemplated. Campbell's approach was, however, always conciliatory and respectful, and he took care to avoid as much as possible a polemic or belligerent style.

The Campbell family was extremely happy in the congenial atmosphere they found in northern Kentucky. Just when it seemed as if they had at last found a permanent home, however, an incident occurred which suddenly changed everything. One Sunday afternoon in the summer of 1819 Campbell noticed a large number of Negro slaves amusing themselves in a grove near the school building, where he had frequently seen them before. He watched them for a time and ended by inviting them to come into the schoolroom, where he read the Bible to them, explained its meaning in a simple fashion, and taught them some hymns. The slaves enjoyed the meeting so much that Campbell arranged to have a similar service at a later date. He had no thought but that he was rendering a Christian service to the servants of some of the families in the community. Next day, however, one of his friends called on him and told him of a state law which forbade any address to Negroes except in the presence of one or more white witnesses. He had broken the law but was assured that no steps would be taken against him unless he repeated his Sunday meeting. It is clear that Campbell did not realize the reasons for the law, nor does it seem that he was aware of the early abolition movement under way in Kentucky at that time. He was shocked that a state should seek to prohibit religious teaching to anyone, even to slaves, and protested: "Can the Word of God be thus fettered in a Christian land?" His decision was made immediately: whatever it might cost, he would leave this community and go where he was free to preach unhampered. Moreover, he insisted that the remaining children of his family be allowed to grow to maturity and settle in a community of freedom. This decision to move both surprised and grieved the rest of the family who were quite attached to their new home. The community was similarly disturbed and both the residents of Burlington and Campbell's own family urged him to remain. But he refused to listen, for he felt that to remain would be incompatible with his own sense of Christian duty. Therefore, he immediately wrote to Alexander informing him of his decision to move and began to settle his business in the community.

While Thomas Campbell was living in Kentucky, Alexander continued to preach, ministering especially to the Brush Run Church, which met alternately between crossroads and Brush Run, and to improve his farm located near the village of Bethany. At the beginning of 1818, Alexander decided to open a school in his home for the purpose of training young men for the ministry. This academy, known as "Buffalo Seminary," soon attracted not only a large number of ministerial students but also young men who wished to study language and young people of both sexes who wanted simply to receive a good basic education and who attended as day students. Therefore, when Thomas Campbell wrote in the fall of 1819 that he was anxious to leave Kentucky, Alexander proposed to his father that he come and assist in the duties of Buffalo Seminary.

Thomas Campbell Returns "Home"

As soon as arrangements for the move could be completed, Campbell settled his family in Washington County, Pennsylvania, near the village of West Middletown, in the upper part of Brush Run valley. In this location he had the satisfaction of knowing that his family was away from the institution of slavery. He spent most of the time at Alexander's about seven miles away, assisted his son in the conduct of Buffalo Seminary, and resumed the pastoral care of the Brush Run Church. Both father and son were happy to be once again associated in their work. Thomas was glad to be back in the area and among the people he knew so well, to be back to the scene of his earlier efforts, and back to join his son in the work which was to see them cooperating happily until age and death claimed the father.

Campbell, on his return to western Pennsylvania and the northern panhandle of Virginia, found that during his absence of nearly ten years little effort had been made to advance the cause of primitive Christianity which he had sponsored in 1809 by the publication of the *Declaration and Address* of the Christian Association. These principles, along with the important modification brought about by the acceptance of immersion, had been accepted by only five small congregations, numbering in all not more than two hundred members. There was the Brush Run Church; two congregations in Brooke County, Virginia (Wellsburg and a church meeting in Alexander's home); one in Harrison County, Ohio; and one in Guernsey County, Ohio. The two congregations in Brooke County were chiefly the results of Alexander's efforts and the two in Ohio were the fruits of Thomas' labors during the year he had spent in that area. These five congregations had united by 1815 with the Redstone Baptist Association and were regarded by the Baptists of the time as members of their denomination. It is true that the terms of the union left the little group free to believe as it felt, but even with this stipulation they found their position uncomfortable, particularly after Alexander's "Sermon on the Law." Many of the Baptist preachers felt increasingly that the Campbells, father and son, were not orthodox and that they were leading the Baptist churches away from Baptist principles. On the other hand, the Campbells were cordially welcomed in many Baptist churches and among their members gained a large following, especially among the laymen.

Alexander had long been confined because of his duties in connection with Buffalo Seminary, but with the assistance of his father, he was freed to visit Pittsburgh and the churches near by. On one such visit early in 1820, he met for the first time a young Scottish Presbyterian, named Walter Scott, and found in him a congenial spirit. Scott agreed with the Campbells on the main features of their program and was prepared by education, natural ability, and religious devotion to become a fellow worker in the movement. Scott had arrived in Pittsburgh some time in 1818 from New York and Scotland, and had at that time come under the influence of a fellow Scotsman, named Forrester, in whose school he became an assistant. Forrester talked with Scott frequently on religious subjects and directed his study of the Bible, with the result that Scott soon gave up infant baptism and was immersed. At this time Scott took over Forrester's school and became acquainted with Nathaniel Richardson, at whose home he was a frequent visitor. Richardson's oldest son, Robert, formerly a pupil of Thomas Campbell's, was now a youth of thirteen and was enrolled in Scott's school. It was not long until Walter Scott met the elder Campbell and found in him a man of very similar temperament—a man whom he cherished from first sight as the most saintly man of his acquaintance. In these circumstances a relationship which was to bear much fruit later was thus begun between Walter Scott and the Campbells.

In the constant hope that unpleasant argument might be avoided, the elder Campbell had stated in the *Declaration and Address* that controversy formed no part of the intended plan and that, although written objections would be received, verbal controversy would not be allowed. Principally because of his father's objections, Alexander at first refused to engage in an oral debate with John Walker, a Seceder Presbyterian minister, of Mt. Pleasant, Ohio. The occasion for the debate was a challenge from Walker to a Baptist minister, a John Birch, or any other Baptist preacher of good standing whom Birch might choose to debate with him the question of baptism. Birch readily accepted the challenge and immediately wrote to Alexander Campbell urging him to meet Walker. Twice Alexander refused the invitation, but at the insistence of his friends and many of the Baptist preachers, he finally accepted only after having succeeded in convincing his father that while debates on human theories and opinions were to be avoided, there could be no valid objection to a public defense of revealed truth.

The debate was held June 19 and 20, 1820, at Mt. Pleasant, Ohio, about twenty-three miles from Alexander's home. He was accompanied to Mt. Pleasant only by his father and a few interested friends. The issue under discussion was the proper subject and means of baptism. Walker argued that baptism was the symbol of membership in the Christian church just as the practice of circumcision was a badge of membership in the Jewish church. Young Campbell's reply was that circumcision required only racial descent from Abraham, whereas baptism demanded faith in Christ. As he said: "Baptism is connected with the promise of the remission of sins and the gift of the Holy Spirit." Walker was inclined to repeat himself, so Alexander used his time during the debate to speak of the principles of the reformers; namely, the supreme authority of Scripture and the necessity of a positive scriptural command behind every religious institution. As to the correct form of baptism, Campbell tried to show that immersion was the teaching of the Bible. Most of those present agreed that Alexander was the victor. Thomas Campbell was called on to close the debate with prayer, and on their return to Bethany assisted in editing and publishing the debate as taken from the notes of the younger Campbell. The results of the debate were pleasing to both father and son because of the larger audience it gave for their views and for the fact that the debate had been conducted in an orderly manner.

From this time forward it was felt by the two that orderly discussion on clearly stated propositions was one of the ways by which biblical truth might be advanced. The significance of this first debate is that it made Alexander a recognized ally of the Baptists on the frontier and encouraged him to conceive of the possibility of religious reformation beyond the confines of a local congregation. Thomas Campbell himself never engaged in oral debate, but he was always interested in the debates of his son.

Alexander, in publishing the debate with Walker, soon realized the power of the frontier press and the eagerness of the people for religious literature, for the first edition of 1,000 copies was quickly followed by a second of 3,000. Immediately after the debate he began to receive large numbers of inquiries from interested individuals and within the next two years began to think seriously of issuing a monthly magazine especially devoted to the interests of the proposed reformation of the churches. This project and experiment in printing the debate mark an important point in the Campbell movement, for it is the first indication either father or son had that their views could be carried to a larger constituency than they could reach personally. Coincidently with the decision to publish a religious journal early in 1823, Alexander's health began to suffer from overwork. He therefore decided to close Buffalo Seminary which, though well attended, was not serving his purpose of training ministers for the cause of the reformation.

After conferring with his father and with Walter Scott, Alexander issued in the spring of 1823, the prospectus of a magazine which he had named the *Christian Baptist,* a title adopted with some misgivings since the term "Baptist" was thought sectarian. The first issue came from the press August 3, 1823, and was published monthly thereafter, until the close of 1830. The tone of the magazine was critical in the extreme of the clergy of the period and reflected Alexander's antagonism, especially to the Baptist clergy. The articles and essays were frequently sarcastic and ironical, and much in the earlier volumes of the *Christian Baptist* made fun of the ecclesiastical authorities of the day. The elder Campbell was aroused thoroughly by his son's boldness and sought to no avail to induce Alexander to adopt a milder policy. He then tried to tone down the periodical by contributing to the magazine essays which were of a less beligerent nature, and to which he signed himself "T.W."

Alexander's opponents in the Redstone Baptist Association had become increasingly active and were furious over the publication of the *Christian Baptist*. He learned that the opposition had determined to make a strong effort at the September, 1823, meeting of the association to have him removed from the fellowship. He conceived of a plan whereby he could defeat them by leaving the Redstone Association and uniting with the Mahoning Association of Ohio, as he had previously been urged to do. The Mahoning Baptist Association had been formed on August 20, 1820, just two months before the Campbell-Walker debate, under the leadership of Adamson Bentley, of Warren, Ohio, and Sydney Rigdon, Bentley's brother-in-law. Bentley and Rigdon had visited Alexander at Bethany and had every confidence in the Campbells and the correctness of their views.

A number of the members of the Brush Run Church lived in Wellsburg and it was therefore decided that Alexander should take membership with the little congregation there, and later to unite this congregation with the Mahoning Association. This matter was discussed in the Brush Run Church at one of its meetings and a church letter was granted to Alexander and to thirty-one of the other members. The letter, drawn up and issued in the handwriting of Thomas Campbell, attested:

Be it known to all whom it may concern, that we have dismissed the following brethren in good standing with us, to constitute a church of Christ at Wellsburg, namely:

Alexander Campbell, Margaret Campbell, John Brown, Ann Brown, Mary Sayres, Mary Marshall, Mary Little, Richard McConnel, Stephen Priest, Mr. Jones, John Chambers, Mary Chambers, Jacob Osborne, Susan Osborne, Mrs. Bakewell, Selina Bakewell, Mrs. Dicks, William Gilchrist, Jane Gilchrist, Mr. Brockaw, Nancy Brockaw, Alexander Holliday, Joseph Freeman, Margaret Parkinson, Jane Parkinson, Mrs. Talbot, George Young, Daniel Babbitt, Catherine Harvey, Mrs. Braley, Solomon Salah, Delilah Salah.

Done at our meeting, August 31st, A.D. 1823, and signed by order of the church.

Thomas Campbell.[7]

The Brush Run Church appointed its minister, Thomas Campbell, and two others as messengers to the Redstone Association, and Alexander planned to attend as a spectator. In September when the meeting of the association was called to order, Alexander was questioned by the association as to why he had not been appointed a messenger, as had been expected, and he explained to them that the church of which he was now a member was not connected with the Redstone Association. Alexander in this way checkmated his opponents and thus was enabled to remain free to preach among the Baptist churches the principles of reformation which he was coming to feel were God's revealed truth.

At the close of the Walker debate, Alexander had issued a challenge to any reputable pedobaptist minister to continue the debate on baptism and finally in May, 1823, he received a letter from a Mr. Maccalla, a Presbyterian minister of Augusta, Kentucky, accepting the challenge. It was then decided to have the debate at Washington, Kentucky, beginning on October 15. Often during the period between the Walker and the Maccalla debates, 1820-1823, the purpose of baptism had been discussed by Thomas and his son, as well as by Walter

Scott, with the result that the three of them had agreed on what they believed were the true and obvious teachings of the New Testament. These views were presented by Alexander in October, 1823, in the Maccalla debate but actually had been stated by Thomas Campbell in the second issue of the *Christian Baptist*, September 2, of the same year, in an article intended for the first number but delayed for lack of room. Thomas' first contribution to the new magazine was introduced by a letter to the editor offering an essay on "the power and primary intention of the gospel," the purpose of which was to further the object of the magazine. In this letter he said:

... please accept it as a token of sincere desire for the utility and success of your undertaking, and as a pledge on the part of the writer of his hearty determination to contribute any assistance in his power, to the accomplishment of so worthy an object.[8]

The essay itself is a study of the various passages of the Bible which deal with the purpose of baptism, which purpose Thomas considered to be the reconciliation of man with God in Christ, and a complete reconciliation of the sinner through the atonement of Christ, the effect of which was the full and free pardon of all men's sins. Thomas accepted the Scriptures as revealed truth, in the Lockean sense, and as the unquestioned evidence on which a Christian should base his beliefs. Granting this assumption, Campbell's was basically a rational approach to religion, and it is not surprising to find the phrase "it is evident" used many times in the article.

During the years after 1823, Thomas Campbell gave himself to his ministry with the Brush Run Church, which was still in fellowship with the Redstone Baptist Association, and to traveling among the various Baptist churches in the vicinity of West Middletown and Bethany. It is apparent on examination of the *Christian Baptist* that Thomas edited it on Alexander's frequent tours and absences from Bethany during these years. The assistance of his father enabled Alexander to make important contacts in Kentucky, Ohio, and as far away as eastern Virginia.

Thomas Campbell's second contribution to the *Christian Baptist* came as the result of an article, which had appeared in the March issue, written by Alexander on "Experimental religion" wherein he had given the impression of denying experimental religion, or religion of the heart, and insisted on "head" religion. It was written in answer to a charge of impiety made by some of the Baptists because Alexander had criticized the popular revival methods of the time. This article was destined to be an even greater source of offense to the Baptists than the "Sermon on the Law" had been. It was published in the absence of Thomas Campbell, who on his return rebuked Alexander for publishing such views before his readers were ready for them. In the June issue Thomas replied to Alexander's articles on experimental religion by addressing a letter to the editor, signed "T. W.," in which he said:

I was persuaded that it would likely given offense and that instead of obviating the charge it would rather increase it. I, therefore, could have wished, that you had treated that very delicate, and, at the same time, very important subject, in a different manner. I am not to be understood as objecting to the detection and exposure of a false and unscriptural exexperience.

. . . .

Upon the whole, it is evident that all the salvation that is known or experienced in this world, is in consequence, and by virtue of the knowledge and belief of the truth, which works effectually in them that believe.

To talk, therefore, of christian experience by any supposed operations of the Holy Spirit without the word, or previous to, and independent of, the knowledge and belief of the truth, is not only contrary to most express declarations of holy scripture and universally established fact, but to reason also. . . .

Let us have done then, with this unscriptural, indefinite, unmeaning phrase, which at best, is only calculated to perplex, mislead, and deceive. When we speak of our holy religion, let us speak of it, and distinguish it by proper epithets, such as the scriptures afford, instead of those vain delusive epithets, which the wisdom, or rather the folly, of men has invented.[9]

Thomas Campbell was thus trying to call Alexander back to the original conception of opposing such practices as they found about them on scriptural grounds only. Alexander was indulgent with his father but proceeded to follow the policy which suited his purposes more fully. Thomas, however, was not the only one to take exception to the controversial article, for Robert B. Semple, an influential Baptist minister of eastern Virginia and good friend of the Campbell's, wrote objecting in particular to the article and in general to the spirit in which the *Christian Baptist* was conducted.

Four months later, in October, 1824, "T.W." again contributed a letter to the editor, followed by an essay on "The Religion of Christianity." This letter to the editor indicated indirectly Thomas' criticism of Alexander's negative attitude evidenced thus far in the *Christian Baptist*:

> Sirs: In the numbers of this work already published, we meet with several essays upon the Christian religion, all justly tending to enhance its value by pointing out its consumate excellence. ... I could wish, however, to see those things more distinctly developed, not only by pointing out as above, the high and distinguishing peculiarities of the Christian religion; and by an upright endeavor, to extricate and defend it from the innumerable perversions and abuses with which it is ... corrupted and perverted ... but also by pointing out, and defending as clearly as possible, the religion of Christianity. ...[10]

In the essay on "The Religion of Christianity" which followed, Thomas Campbell sought to present the subject as he thought it should be presented:

The author and ultimate object of our holy religion, is the God and Father of our Lord Jesus Christ, by his Spirit, speaking in Christ and his holy apostles. The principle of this holy religion within us, is faith, a correspondent faith. . . . Thus we worship the Father, through the Son, by the Spirit, relying upon his teachings in and by the word, to lead us into all the truth which he has testified for our edification and salvation.[11]

He listed "three primary, comprehensive and all-important ordinances of the christian religion; the particular and individual observance of which, constitute the religion of every real christian." They are: (1) baptism, (2) prayer, and (3) the study of the Scriptures. He then asked the reader to compare these essential acts of Christian worship with some of the current views and practices such as infant baptism, set forms of prayer and the cold and formal reading of the Scripture found in some churches. He concluded:

From this brief scriptural view of the private and personal religion of every intelligent bible-taught christian, both internally and externally considered; and this briefly contrasted with the popular religion of the day, we may clearly perceive an essential difference, and be hereby enabled both to examine ourselves, and admonish others.[12]

It is a tribute to the independence of mind possessed by both Thomas and Alexander Campbell that father and son, although not always agreeing on certain of the conclusions reached or in the advisability of published writings, did agree on the great fundamental elements of faith, and in opposing opinions each allowed the other latitude. Alexander Campbell could not have done his work unless his father had formulated the principles, but certainly if it had not been for the determined spirit and incisive logic of the son, the movement would probably not have progressed as it did. Due mainly to the *Christian Baptist* and Alexander's preaching tours, from about 1825 there was growing tension between the Campbells and certain leaders and ministers of the Baptist churches. Alexander created further tension in the spring of 1826 when he published a modern language version of the New Testament translated by British scholars, George Campbell, James Macknight, and Philip Doddridge.

Thomas Campbell gave hearty approval to his son's efforts to secure the New Testament for the modern reader in a language simple and understandable to him. Thomas had been greatly disturbed at the use to which some ministers had put the Scriptures and had insisted that every Christian should read and interpret for himself. For this reason he had favored giving them the New Testament in readable language, and as he said on one occasion,

> What is the great difference between withholding the Scriptures from the laity, as the Romanists do, and rendering them unintelligible by arbitrary interpretations, forced criticisms and fanciful explanations, as many Protestants do, or making the people believe that they are nearly unintelligible by urging the necessity of what is called a learned clergy to explain them? If a translation can only be understood through the originals, might it not as well have been withheld? If the labors of a learned clergy be still necessary to render a translation intelligible, upon whose skill and fidelity as translators and upon whose judgment as expositors the people must still rely, and to whom they must still look up as their religious guides and dictators, of what use is a translation?[13]

The new translation, published by Alexander, was widely read and discussed, for the first edition was soon exhausted and a second edition was called for and evidently published, although there is no record of it. In the midst of these publishing and preaching activities the Campbells made ready to attend the annual meeting of the Mahoning Association. Walter Scott had moved to Steubenville, Ohio, from Pittsburgh some time earlier in the year, so Thomas and his son stopped at the Scott home to invite Walter to attend the meeting which was to be held at Canfield, Ohio, Friday through Sunday,

August 25-27, 1826. Alexander and two others were to represent the Wellsburg church; and Thomas, along with Sydney Rigdon and others, was invited to a seat. The following week the Redstone Baptist Association held its annual meeting. Thomas Campbell and two others represented the Brush Run Church and Alexander was there as "corresponding messenger" from the Mahoning Association. At this meeting the champions of orthodoxy, using a ruling of the previous year, rejected all church letters that did not refer to the Philadelphia Confession, ousting thirteen of the twenty-three churches in the association, among them, the Brush Run Church and its minister, Thomas Campbell. A minority of ten churches thus accused the majority of being guilty of Arianism, Socinianism, Arminianism, and Antinomianism. The representatives of the expelled churches met in a nearby house and heard a sermon from Alexander Campbell, after which it was agreed to meet in Washington, Pennsylvania, in November to form a new association. Accordingly, messengers were sent in November, 1826, to a convention which drew up a short constitution but made no mention of the Philadelphia Confession and declared as the second article: "We receive the Scriptures as the only rule of faith and practice to all the churches of Christ." This division of the Redstone Association in 1826 was but one of a series of separations which took place for the next five or more years among the regular Baptists and the reformers. It was indeed tragic that those who had gone forth so enthusiastically in 1809, preaching scriptural union, were now producing, not union, but division. Had the Synod of Pittsburgh been correct after all when, in 1810, it had said such a movement would divide rather than unite?

The first meeting of this new association was held on Friday, September 7, 1827, at which time the constitution drawn up the previous November was adopted. Four messengers were allotted to each church, and Brush Run

Church was represented by Thomas Campbell, Joseph Bryant, John Hawkins, and Joseph Matthews. Matthias Luce was chosen the moderator. The Brush Run Church, however, did not exist for many months after this as a distinct congregation, for it had been weakened in membership to such a degree that it seemed unwise for it to continue to meet. Consequently the remaining members, among whom were Thomas Campbell and his family, merged with the church which had been organized several years previously in Alexander's home at Bethany. Later in the fall of 1827 Thomas Campbell spent two months visiting and preaching among the leading churches of the Western Reserve, that section of northeastern Ohio originally reserved by the federal government to be granted to veterans of the American Revolution. He took with him, for companionship, his youngest son, the twenty-three-year-old Archibald, who preached his first sermons on this trip and later became a physician.

Typical of the religious climate produced by the Campbells at this time were the tensions which arose in the Stillwater Baptist Association of Ohio over the practice of weekly communion. This custom had been instigated through a young man, Cyrus McNeely, who had been impressed by the articles in the *Christian Baptist* on "Experimental religion" and who, joining the Wellsburg church in 1827, had later transferred to the Cadiz, Ohio, Baptist church, which belonged to the Stillwater Association. In due time this "heresy" of weekly communion was brought to the attention of the association, and when the vote was taken McNeely's position was upheld. A little later, McNeely again evoked the cry of "heresy" by baptizing a woman without himself being ordained— a violation of the association's rules. For this act McNeely had to stand trial before his brethren. He was ably defended by Thomas and Alexander Campbell, and when a vote was taken on the issue, the majority again upheld McNeely. Not satisfied with the way things were going, the minority group withdrew fellowship and formed a new association, thus leaving the remainder of the Stillwater Association in the hands of the reformers.

Activity on the Western Reserve

The Mahoning Association had met at New Lisbon, Ohio, in August, 1827, and, as the result of a request from one of its churches, had decided to appoint an itinerant evangelist. Walter Scott was present at the meeting, and when urged, he accepted the task, and entered the field almost immediately. Earlier there had arisen among many of the churches of the area an evangelistic awakening, which had spread to Ohio from Kentucky under the leadership of Barton W. Stone and others. From the first there were friendly relations between the Stone and the Campbell movements, and preachers of both groups took an active interest in the proceedings of the Mahoning Association.

From the first the movement of the reformers on the Western Reserve began to receive new growth from Scott's energetic and novel preaching, with its five-finger exercise of faith, repentance, baptism, remission of sins, and gift of the Holy Spirit. Scott was not a Baptist, except in his practice of immersion, but was a great student of the Bible, and a man with revolutionary methods. He used the school children to advertise his meetings, adopted the plan of calling for immediate acceptance of Christ, and of urging men in the phrases of the New Testament to be baptized for the remission of sins. Soon hundreds were being added to the churches of the Reserve and it was only natural that some of the members of the Baptist churches were disturbed by the addition of so many new members who did not fully appreciate Baptist traditions. This tended further to increase the tensions developing between the reformers and the Baptists.

By March, 1828, Alexander Campbell had heard reports of the growing success of Walter Scott on the Western Reserve and had become worried. He wondered whether Scott had allowed his well-known impulsiveness to run away with him, or whether his evangelistic fervor had broken loose from its proper moorings in knowledge and Scripture. The Reserve was at this time the chief stronghold of the Campbellian influence, and Alexander had no wish to lose it. His concern was shared by his father and it was decided that Thomas should visit the Reserve and examine for himself the results of Scott's endeavors. So Thomas Campbell saddled his favorite horse and visited the churches where Scott had been preaching. This took him to such places as New Lisbon, Fairfield, Warren, Braceville, Windham, Mantua, Mentor, Chardon, Hampden and Huntsburg. The elder Campbell heard for himself some of the sermons of Walter Scott and witnessed his methods with both surprise and pleasure. He saw clearly that Scott had added to the movement for reform a new element which had been lacking in his own work and that of his brilliant son. There is indeed a note of pathos in the letter he wrote from New Lisbon on April 9, 1828:

> I perceive that theory and practice in religion, as well as in other things, are matters of distinct consideration. . . . We have spoken and published many things *correctly* concerning the ancient gospel, its simplicity and perfect adaptation to the present state of mankind . . . but I must confess, that, in respect of the direct exhibition and application of it . . . I am at present, for the first time, upon the ground where the thing has appeared to be practically exhibited to the proper purpose.[14]

The simple truth is that the movement to restore a church based on the New Testament did not take hold firmly until Walter Scott began preaching on the Reserve and Barton W. Stone's "Christian" movement spread to Ohio. Without the impetus given by those movements,

Thomas Campbell's great dream of Christian union on a biblical basis would have quickly been passed over on the rapidly growing frontier.

This visit of Thomas Campbell on the Western frontier lasted from April until the annual meeting of the Mahoning Association, during which time he traveled and preached extensively throughout this section of Ohio. On June 9, 1828, Thomas wrote from Bazetta, Ohio, to his wife that:

> Nothing could reconcile me to this long and indefinite absence from you and our beloved children and grandchildren, but the work in which I am engaged. . . . I can truly say it is the work of the Lord; from the matter of it, the manner of it, the success of it, and from the outrageous opposition everywhere manifested against it. . . .

After reviewing his recent evangelistic successes, he continued:

> . . . I feel much stronger to speak, and to bear any kind of fatigue, than when I left home; and if there were ten more to aid the four or five of us who are at present engaged in this good work, with all the zeal and ability they could possess, they would not be sufficient to meet the demands of the public, or to occupy the ground that lies open before us.
>
> . . . .
>
> There are of this Church a good number of the old members, who, with thirty who have been baptized by us reformers, wish me to constitute them into a new Church, upon Gospel principles, before I leave this place; which I shall probably do. . . .
>
> Now, beloved, what shall we say to these things? I long to be with you for our mutual comfort; but can I, from any private consideration, withdraw from a work for which the Lord has been preparing me for more than twenty years; and for which, I presume, I was brought to this country. . . .[15]

Thus the sixty-five-year-old Thomas revealed his enthusiasm and zeal for the work which was developing under Walter Scott and the others. With him there was no sense of failure. He was content that the Lord's work should succeed and so gave himself untiringly to the cause for which he felt providence had long prepared him. Whatever the cost might be, he wanted to do all that was humanly possible to further this work of evangelism. The report in the June issue of the *Christian Baptist* was probably sent from Thomas and mentions the evangelistic endeavors of "Bishops" Scott, Rigdon and Bentley ("Bishop" being considered a New Testament term for the leader of a congregation) and the immersion within six months of about eight hundred persons, but modestly omits his own name. The fact remains, however, that in the months spent on the Reserve the elder Campbell conducted more than an investigation, for wherever he went he preached and counseled, strengthened and reinforced, the churches.

His influence was great among both the older and the younger preachers with whom he came in touch. One of the younger men he influenced was Symonds Rider from Hiram, Ohio, who heard Thomas Campbell preach at Mantua in June, 1828, and was baptized. Another of his new-found ministerial friends was a young Universalist preacher, named Aylett Raines, whom Campbell led into the reformers movement, and the two traveled and evangelized together for several months. People from all sects and religious groups were now being gathered into the reformers movement and the ability of the reformers to assimilate these individuals who came from diverse backgrounds proved to be a severe test of Thomas' principles concerning matters of faith and opinion.

Considering the members added, the new churches formed, and the large number of persons attracted from the ministry of other communions, the meeting of the Mahoning Association in Warren in August, 1828, took on more than ordinary interest. Alexander Campbell delivered the opening sermon on the Christian religion and divided his subject into three divisions: matters of knowledge, matters of faith, and matters of opinion.

Strangely enough, this position met its first test at the Warren meeting. Aylett Raines, who had been traveling with Thomas Campbell, was regarded by some with suspicion because of his Universalist views, but Thomas stood by him and held that as long as Raines believed, accepted, and obeyed Christ, he could hold what private opinions he wished, provided he did not preach them. Campbell said:

> Brother Raines and I have been much together for the last several months, and we have mutually unbosomed ourselves to each other. I am a Calvinist, and he a Restorationist; and although I am a Calvinist, I would put my right arm into the fire and have it burned off before I would raise my hand against him. And if I were Paul, I would have Brother Raines in preference to any other young man of my acquaintance to be my Timothy.[16]

In July, 1828, Thomas Campbell addressed a letter to the editors of the *Gospel Advocate,* edited at Georgetown, Kentucky, by J. T. Johnson and B. F. Hall, members of the Stone movement. This was in reply to an article which had come to his attention in the October, 1826, issue of the magazine. The elder Campbell in this letter, written for publication, outlined the main principles on which he felt all Christians could unite:

> Let all that bear the name of Christians, who are disgusted and aggrieved with the present corruptions and divisions existing among us, return to the original standard of Christianity, which is the New Testament, believe and obey the Gospel, as it is there recorded by the pens and from the lips of the holy apostles, and obey the law of Christ, by them enjoined upon the believers; receiving the Old Testament as of equal authority with the New, and making the divinely prescribed use of it; and let this suffice; that is, let all that professedly and practically do so, esteem and treat each other as brethren.

He then lists six propositions which he thought illustrated the principle:

> 1. That there was a time when all Christians composed but one sect.

2. That every one who believed the Gospel which the apostles preached, and was baptized upon a confession of this belief, was esteemed a Christian, and none else.

3. That all who believed and were baptized had the promise of the remission of their sins, and of the gift of the Holy Spirit. . . .

4. That specimens of the Gospel preached by the apostles are recorded in the Acts of the Apostles . . . so that we can be at no loss about the ancient apostolic Gospel. . . .

5. That the apostles, when commissioned to evangelize the nations, and to baptize the believers, were also instructed to teach them to observe all things that Christ had commanded for that purpose. . . .

6. That, therefore, believing the Gospel that the apostles preached, and obeying the injunctions which they delivered, completed the Christian character. Let, therefore, this faith and obedience be deemed sufficient, as it was at the beginning, and there is an end of all sectarian controversy.[17]

How deeply Thomas Campbell was affected and influenced by Scott's views would be difficult to evaluate. At least there is every indication that there was an exchange of thought and ideas. It is obvious that Thomas sincerely believed that he had recovered the "divinely appointed" and "effectual means" necessary to restore the purity of the church and ultimately the union of all Christians, if only they would listen and obey the simple commands of the Scriptures. At about this time the elder Campbell told an Ohio friend that:

If you attend the ministry of a Presbyterian, you will hear many good things; if you hear a Methodist, many glorious truths will be uttered; should the preacher be an Episcopalian, he may edify you; a Baptist preacher will say many things that are said in the Bible; the Universalist is not entirely ignorant of the gospel; the Unitarian's sermon is true in part; and the like may be said of every sect in Christendom; but among all these sects, without exception, nearly one-half you hear is false, or, to say the least, doubtful; that is to say, it is not to be found in the scriptures.[18]

Campbell was now riding with Walter Scott everywhere over the Reserve. The two men had become fast friends and proved to be an effective team. In his report to the association for 1828 Walter Scott recognized the help he had received from his fellow ministers. He reported:

> The signal success which has attended the labors of brothers Bentley, Rigdon and Gaston, is known to you all. Father Thomas Campbell has been about five months on the field, both increasing the number of Disciples, and building them up in all the wisdom of the Just One.[19]

During these months Campbell was frequently called on to arbitrate disputes in the various churches. On one occasion he was called to Sharon, just across the Ohio line in Pennsylvania, to end a quarrel which had begun when several recently immersed believers applied for admission to the Sharon church. Campbell pleaded, expostulated, reasoned, and prayed with them to receive the new converts on the Word of God alone and not on the articles of faith, but this was refused.

No sooner had Thomas Campbell returned home from the arduous preaching tour of the Western Reserve than he left, with Archibald again as his companion, on a tour of several counties in Pennsylvania, which extended as far as Somerset where they remained for three weeks. In Somerset they found a small church made up largely of pious women; but during their stay in the town, Campbell was able to add some thirty members to the congregation and gain for it some of the town's ablest masculine leadership. The winter of 1828-1829 was presumably spent by Thomas in preaching to the churches in the vicinity of Bethany and West Middletown.

In the spring of 1829 arrangements were completed for Alexander's famous debate with Robert Owen of England and of New Harmony, Indiana, the famous social experimenter and philanthropist. Owen had visited Bethany earlier and Thomas had witnessed the agreement drawn up between Owen and Alexander as to the conditions of their debate and had at that time met Owen who commented on the exceeding kindness and courtesy of the elder Campbell. The debate was held in Cincinnati, Ohio, from Monday, April 13 to Tuesday, April 21 on the question of Owen's "Social System" and on the part of Alexander was a defense of the Christian religion. Thomas accompanied his son from Bethany, was present for the debate, and remained in Cincinnati for some time preaching and baptizing converts who had been won from skepticism during the debate.

A little known pamphlet entitled "To the Religious Public" was published by the elder Campbell in May while still in Cincinnati following the Owen debate. He began:

> The following queries, for the purpose of promoting a genuine Scriptural reformation amongst the sincere professors of Christianity, are respectfully submitted to their consideration:

There were in all twelve questions asked by Thomas in the circular, designed to illustrate and promote the restoration of the New Testament church. The following questions were typical:

> 1. Is not the christian community in a sectarian condition, existing in separate communities alienated from each other?
> 2. Is not such a condition the native and necessary result of corruption; that is, of the introduction of human opinions into the constitution, faith, or worship, of christian societies?
> 3. Is not such a state of corruption and division anti-natural, anti-rational, anti-christian?
> 4. Is it not the common duty and interest of all concerned, especially of the teachers to put an end to this destructive and anti-scriptural condition?

And so the questions were propounded, with the author coming to the final conclusion:

> Upon the whole, these things being so, it necessarily follows, that christianity, being entirely a divine institution, there can be nothing human in it; consequently it has nothing to do with the doctrines and commandments of men; but simply and solely

with the belief and obedience of the expressly recorded testimony and will of God, contained in the Holy Scriptures, and enjoined by the authority of the Saviour and his holy apostles upon the Christian community.[20]

So it was that near the twentieth anniversary of the writing of the *Declaration and Address,* Thomas Campbell was still concerned to emphasize the cardinal doctrine of his lifetime ministry: the importance and centrality of the Holy Scriptures for the life of the Christian.

Such was the progress of evangelism in Ohio that, when the Mahoning Association met at Sharon, Pennsylvania, in the latter part of August, 1829, the messengers learned that another thousand converts had been added to the churches.

Editor Pro-Tem

Shortly before the Campbell-Owen debate Alexander had decided to discontinue the *Christian Baptist,* for he did not want the name Christian Baptist given to the movement which he and his father were leading. Another reason for its discontinuance was his desire to begin a new periodical of larger size and of somewhat different character. Walter Scott had proposed a periodical to be known as the *Millennial Herald* and in 1827 had issued a prospectus for such a magazine to be devoted to the exposition of his views of the primitive gospel. The project, however, had been abandoned when he became the evangelist for the Mahoning Association. As the subject of the Millennial period was at that time of great interest, Alexander decided to call the new periodical the *Millennial Harbinger.* Furthermore, it was his plan to make the new magazine milder in tone than the *Christian Baptist* and to include a wider range of subjects. Once Alexander made the decision to change magazines, he had the problem of finishing the program outlined for the *Christian Baptist* and beginning the *Millennial Har-*

binger, which he was anxious to have begin with the new year 1830. He solved this problem by having the last six months of the *Christian Baptist* run concurrently with the first six months of the new magazine. An unexpected problem presented itself on Alexander's election in the fall of 1829 as a delegate from his district to the convention called to revise the constitution for the state of Virginia—a convention which met at Richmond on October 5 and which remained in session several months.

As always, Thomas Campbell, the father, was there to take over. From time to time the father's name had appeared in the pages of the *Christian Baptist* and in January, 1827, he had written a short reply to a "Mr. D, a Skeptic." This was, however, his last major contribution until just before the meeting of the Mahoning Association in August, 1829, when he wrote an open letter "To the Religious Public" and for the first time signed his name, Thomas Campbell, instead of the initials, "T. W." This was a reprint of the pamphlet published in May in Cincinnati and appealed to all Christians and non-Christians to accept the New Testament as a basis for common belief. With Alexander away at the constitutional convention from September 22, 1829, until February 1, 1830, Thomas Campbell was kept busy editing and publishing the next five issues of the *Christian Baptist,* in which by a coincidence, the father had five contributions. The first of these was an unsigned feature called "Queries" which contained two questions and answers; one a biblical question of little interest and the other a question as to whether a single man or youth is eligible to be a preacher. The answer was that if Paul is accepted as a witness, he is not.[21]

Thomas Campbell's next contribution was published in the November issue of the *Christian Baptist.* In this issue "A Constant Reader" from King and Queen, Virginia, had written a letter to the editor concerning some questions and answers, which had appeared in the March and April issues of 1829, about modern preachers who preach a "mock" gospel in order to be popular. In his reply Thomas Campbell indicated that he felt the writer of the letter was deliberately trying to be captious and insisted that there were modern popular preachers who spoke of a supernatural power not mentioned in the Scriptures which intervened in the salvation of sinners. It was this that was called a mock gospel in the *Christian Baptist*. The elder Campbell concluded his reply by the statement that the "successive publication of this pure apostolic gospel is what we plead for, without any additions, or intermixture of human opinions." In this same issue "T. W." answered a query, "Did Christ die in our law room and stead, according to the popular preaching?" To which he replied: "This is one of the many ignorant, unprofitable, vain questions so strongly reprobated by the Apostle..."[22]

There are two major contributions of Thomas Campbell in the December, 1829, issue. The first is a letter to the editor which suggested that the purity of the church has been corrupted by the introduction of human opinions and observed that, therefore,

... the grand object of your periodical ... is the restoration of the ancient gospel and discipline, or order of things (as you term it) as the same was published and inculcated by the apostles ... I take the liberty of suggesting to you ... the imperious, and indispensable necessity of a strict and undeviating practical use of the holy scriptures in the inculcation of every item of faith and obedience.

. . . .

To conclude, respected sir ... I would beg leave to assure you, that all your labors, and those of your most zealous co-operants, will be measurably lost, nay, must eventually fail, unless those who professedly labor in the good cause, confine themselves to the inculcation of scripture doctrine in scripture terms; abstaining from all sectarian controversies, ancient or modern, and from inculcating anything as a matter of christian faith or duty, not expressly contained on the sacred page....[23]

The second letter to the editor in this issue, signed "T. W.," took Alexander to task for publishing the essays of Walter Scott on election in which Thomas suggested that if election was to be discussed, why not reprobation, eternal justification, original sin, imputed righteousness, consubstantiation, and other topics. He was obviously concerned that the proposed reformation be kept simple so that it would unite Christians as well as to purify the church. He feared that the movement was taking another direction and was getting away from a simple emphasis on biblical truth. He said:

> We, then, an advocate for the genuine radical reform, even for the restoration of the ancient gospel, and order of things established by the apostles, insist upon it, that we have nothing to do with sectarian controversies; with the theological contentions of the present or former ages; with any thing of the kind that happened since the apostle's day.

Thomas Campbell indicated that if he had simply wanted to rewrite the creeds, he would have stayed with the Westminster Confession of Faith. On this subject he said:

> The writer of this most seriously declares ... that were not the all-sufficiency of the holy scriptures, without comment or paraphrase, clearly demonstrable ... he would have either continued with his quondam brethren of the Westminster school, or joined with some of the modern creed-reforming parties: for, by no means would he have committed himself to the capricious and whimsical extemporaneous effusions of every one, who might have confidence enough to open his mouth in public.

He closed with an apology for having exceeded his bounds but excused himself on the basis that the sectarian evil he exposed was so prevalent:

> ... and especially as effecting the desired reformation in the hands of many, who, while they profess to advocate the all-sufficiency of the holy scriptures, to the rejection of everything of human invention or authority, are but making a new start,

to run the old race over again, by preaching every man his own opinions, reviving the old controveries, or producing new ones....[24]

A letter to "T. W." appeared in the issue published February 1, 1830—a letter which elicited the final response of Thomas Campbell in the *Christian Baptist*, for shortly thereafter Alexander returned and resumed the editorial desk. The letter asked "T. W." if he had assurance from the Old and New Testaments that he was a preacher. In his answer the elder Campbell urged all men to read the Scriptures and to believe the witness given there, and sought further to point out the weakness of much of the emotional preaching of the frontier.

Separation from the Baptists

It is difficult to give an exact date for the separation of the reformers from the Baptists. It is certain that the movement for separation was greatest during 1829 and 1830. An individualistic attitude in general dominated this period of American life, and emotionalism prevailed everywhere, especially on the frontier. It is not surprising, then, to find this spirit reflected in the life of Thomas Campbell and the Campbell movement. The tension between the reformers and the Baptists, which had first appeared after the preaching of the "Sermon on the Law" in 1816 and which had been increased with the publication of the first issue of the *Christian Baptist* in 1823, had been mounting for several years, and in August, 1829, the Beaver Baptist Association in western Pennsylvania, had published an anathema of the Mahoning Association of eastern Ohio, which charged them with "disbelieving and denying the doctrines of the Holy Scriptures." Apparently the conclusions which Thomas Campbell conceived to be so evident from a reading of the Scriptures were not so obvious to others. Specifically, they listed eight errors:

1. That there is no promise of salvation without baptism.

2. That baptism should be administered on belief that Jesus Christ is the Son of God, without examination on any other point.

3. That there is no direct operation of the Holy Spirit on the mind before baptism.

4. That baptism procures the remission of sins and the gift of the Holy Spirit.

5. That the Scriptures are the only evidence of interest in Christ.

6. That man's obedience places it in God's power to elect to salvation.

7. That no creed is necessary for the church but the Scriptures.

8. That all baptized persons have a right to administer the ordinance of baptism.[25]

The "Beaver Anathema" was widely circulated, and provoked both ratifications and additional denunciations from every quarter. The Appomattox Association of Virginia, the Baptist Association of Anderson County, the Elkhorn Association, and the Baptist Association of Sulphur Fork, Kentucky, all joined in the chorus. There was a general movement to purge the Baptist churches of the Campbells and their followers, and provoked by the successful evangelistic endeavors of Walter Scott, the reaction had set in which was to produce a clear separation of Baptists from the reformers.

An extended visit was paid to Kentucky and southern Ohio by Thomas Campbell in the spring and summer of 1830, doubtless because of the agitation within the Baptist churches against the Campbells. In April, Campbell wrote a letter from Maysville, Kentucky, to his wife in which he outlined his itinerary for the coming weeks and spoke of the kind reception he had received in that part of Kentucky. Some of the churches of the Bracken Association of Kentucky, anticipating the action of the association in excluding the reformers, had published a notice that a three-day's meeting would be held at Mayslick on Friday before the fifth Sunday in May, and that all who were favorable to the reformers were urged to attend. A large number of people responded to the call, among them Thomas and Alexander Campbell.

In June, 1830, a fraction of the Tate's Creek Association of Kentucky met and excluded those who had joined with the Campbells. They drew up a protest embodying the "Beaver Anathema" and added four more errors by stating that the reformers taught:

9. That there is no special call to the ministry.
10. That the law given by God to Moses is abolished.
11. That experimental religion is enthusiasm.
12. That there is no mystery in the Scriptures.

They closed their protest by saying: "We intend to have no controversy, but to remain as we are, the Tate's Creek Association of the United Baptists." This action was taken by ten of the twenty-six churches composing the association.[26]

Thomas Campbell himself was present at some of the association meetings that were decisive in making permanent the separation of the reformers and the Baptists. On the fourth Saturday in July, 1830, he attended the meeting of the reforming portion of the divided North District Association when it met at Spencer's Creek in Kentucky. Campbell sat on the platform along with John Smith, David S. Burnet, and Aylett Raines. The elder Campbell was also present the second Saturday in August, 1830, when the Elkhorn Association of Kentucky met at Silas Church in Bourbon County. He heard Jacob Creath, Sr., deliver a speech to the association in defense of the rights of the churches which Thomas said was the best he had ever heard. There was one especially stormy session with questions raised over the seating of certain messengers. Thomas Campbell must have viewed the turbulent scenes of the day with pain, for he sat with his head bowed in sorrow and later advised those contending for the reformers to withdraw. The session ironically closed with the entire association singing the Psalm: "Behold how good and pleasant a thing it is for brethren to dwell together in unity!"

Shortly after the meeting of the Elkhorn Association in 1830 Thomas Campbell wrote a letter to his wife which revealed something of his thoughts and outlook during this period. He had been absent from home for nearly six months and noted that in the forty-three years of their marriage he had been separated from home and family more than one-seventh of the time, and asked his wife to forgive him that wrong. After testifying to his good health he described something of the agitation in which he found himself. The letter, written August 20, said:

> I can give you no adequate idea of the weight and heat of the work in Kentucky. The outrageous and malevolent opposition is ripening the harvest for the reformers. A. Campbell, Campbellism, Campbellites, and heretics, are the chorus, the overword. . . . You cannot conceive what a terrible dust our humble name has kicked up. If it were not coupled with the pure cause of God . . . I should tremble for the consequences![27]

From the publication of the "Beaver Anathema" in August, 1829, until the withdrawal of the Kentucky associations in August, 1830, the final break with the Baptists was to all intents and purposes accomplished, although many separations and divisions of churches took place before these dates and many others after it. It may be said, therefore, that by the fall of 1830 the Campbells again found themselves forced to carry on their reformation outside the framework of a regular church system. In the seventeen years since the Brush Run Church had been taken into fellowship with the Redstone Baptist Association, several characteristic tenets had emerged from the Campbell's preaching and writing which clearly distinguished the reformers from the Baptists. By the year 1830 these distinguishing doctrines and practices could be summarized as: (1) the distinctions between the Old and New Testaments, with reliance on the New Testament as the source of authority for the church, (2) the purpose of baptism for the remission of sins, (3) the belief in faith as a rational act, (4) the operation of the Holy Spirit in conversion by means of the Word alone, (5) rejection of the Calvinistic idea that Christ died only for the "elect," (6) rejection of creeds and church covenants, (7) acceptance of members on confession of faith in Christ, repentance, and baptism without relation of an experience, (8) weekly observance of the Lord's Supper, (9) no special "call" to the ministry and no sharp distinction between clergy and laity, (10) ordinances administered by any believer, and (11) the denial of authority to associations to exercise power over the local congregation or to lay down conditions of fellowship or communion, as the Baptist associations had done when they excluded those churches not adhering to the Philadelphia confession.

The Campbells may have found themselves outside an established Christian denomination with some regret, but they did not for a moment despair. The situation on the American frontier was quite different from that which it had been when the father and son found themselves separated from the Presbyterians in 1809, for different forces were at work in America in the thirties. A new democracy had arisen, revealing its power in the election of Andrew Jackson to the presidency of the United States. Opportunity and optimism were the dominant themes of the new era. Never before had the frontier seemed more a land of boundless opportunity and never before had those who peopled it had a greater confidence in their ability to take full advantage of it. Thomas Campbell's vision of a church united on a scriptural basis was about to become manifest in a uniquely American religious movement.

Sydney Rigdon and Mormonism

One further incident brings this period of Thomas Campbell's life to a close. Mormonism appeared in northern Ohio in 1830 and chief among its promoters was Sydney Rigdon, a former Baptist preacher of ability and who has been previously mentioned as Adamson Bentley's brother-in-law. Rigdon had joined the reformers after 1823 and was known personally to Thomas and Alexander Campbell. The early conversion of Rigdon to Mormonism was of considerable importance to the Mormon movement, and it has been conjectured by non-Mormon scholars that he furnished a good share of the doctrinal content of the new religion. About this time Mormon headquarters were moved to Kirtland, Ohio, inasmuch as Rigdon was the minister of a church there. Rigdon made his home in Mentor, a town adjoining Kirtland, but was successful in attracting only a few followers to the new faith.

Alexander Campbell published an analysis of the *Book of Mormon* in the *Millennial Harbinger* as soon as Mormonism appeared, and later in the year 1830 Thomas Campbell went to Mentor to see what was happening. The logical excuse for such a trip was a visit to his youngest daughter, Alicia, who had recently married Matthew Clapp, the son of Judge Orris Clapp, a leader in the reformer's church in Mentor. During the winter of 1830-1831 Thomas was a guest in the judge's home and he, together with the Clapps and others, furnished effective opposition to any possible encroachment of the Mormons among the reformers of that area. The elder Campbell's wise counsels and great influence kept many from joining the Mormon movement. Thomas Campbell tried to draw Rigdon into a public discussion of the issue, but was not successful. From Mentor, Ohio, in February, 1831, he addressed a letter to Rigdon in which he said:

Nevertheless, I should now have visited you, as formerly, could I conceive that my so doing would answer the important purpose, both to ourselves and to the public, to which we both stand pledged, from the conspicuous and important stations we occupy—you as the professed disciple and public teacher of the infernal Book of Mormon, and I as the professed disciple and public teacher of the supernal books of the Old and New Testaments of our Lord and Saviour Jesus Christ, which you now say is superceded by the Book of Mormon, is become a dead letter, so dead that the belief and obedience of it, without the reception of the latter, is no longer available to salvation. To the disproof of this assertion, I understand you to defy the world. . . . I, therefore, as in duty bound, accept the challenge and shall hold myself in readiness, if the Lord permit, to meet you publicly, in any place, either in Mentor or Kirtland, or in any of the adjoining towns that may appear most eligible for the accomodation of the public. The sooner the investigation takes place the better for all concerned.

The proposition that I have assumed, and which I mean to assume and defend against Mormonism and every other *ism* that has been assumed since the Christian era, is the all-sufficiency of the Holy Scriptures, of the Old and New Testaments, vulgarly called the Bible, to make every intelligent believer wise to salvation, thoroughly furnished for any good work.[28]

In the rest of the letter Thomas enumerated propositions to which he would give attention in such a meeting, six of them having to do with the claims of Mormonism. Rigdon did not reply to this, Thomas Campbell's only known challenge to oral debate, but is reported to have thrown it into the fire. In the spring, Thomas Campbell said farewell to his friends and daughter, Alicia, and returned to his home near West Middletown.

CHAPTER SIX

VENERABLE FATHER CAMPBELL

Efforts on Behalf of the Disciples

IN THE summer of 1831 Thomas Campbell went to New Lisbon, Ohio, along with Alexander, to attend the first big "yearly meeting" of Ohio Disciples. Six hundred persons were served communion in a grove south of town at this meeting where the subject of the churches' cooperation in supporting itinerant evangelists was discussed. Doubtless Thomas Campbell had something to say on this since it had been a principal interest of his since his days in Ireland. In late November, 1831, the elder Campbell set out on horseback to visit the churches of eastern Virginia. The separation of the Baptists from the reformers, or Disciples of Christ as they began to be called about this time, was still in progress and Campbell took advantage of the opportunity of making contact with many new adherents of the reformation movement which had sprung up in nearly all of the Baptist churches.

Thomas Campbell arrived in Fredericksburg on a Friday near the end of December and was invited by the pastor of the Baptist church to preach the following Sunday. On the next day Robert B. Semple, one of the well-known Baptist preachers, was introduced to Thomas. They became immediate friends, went to church together on Sunday, assisted each other in the communion service and continued conversing throughout the rest of the day. Interestingly enough, the elder Campbell's was the last sermon Semple heard before his sudden death on Christmas Day, 1831. One cannot assume that Semple agreed with what Thomas Campbell said, but their meeting was significant in that it proved that fraternal relationships were still possible on an individual level despite the bitter feelings existing between the Baptists and the reformers, or Disciples of Christ. Ironically this meeting which had been so satisfactory to Thomas was immediately used by the Baptists to create difficulties for him in his visit to the Virginia churches. Articles in the *Religious Herald,* a Baptist publication printed at Richmond, denied that Campbell had had the friendly visit with Semple before his death, and accused him of fabricating the story in order to induce Baptist churches to leave their association and become reformers. Thomas after learning of this wrote a letter to Alexander for publication in the *Millennial Harbinger,* in which he said, "... You will perceive by the documents before me, that every nerve has been strained to invalidate my relation of the friendly interview that took place between myself and brother Semple." Thomas had sent documents verifying the facts of the case, and the whole tone of his letter shows how deeply he felt the injury.[1]

Such misconceptions and misunderstandings, created by the opponents of the Campbells among the Baptists, served to accelerate the division among the churches. Soon after the elder Campbell's arrival at Richmond in December, 1831, the Baptist pastor there and others opposed to the reformers requested all those favorable to the Campbells' views to withdraw and become a separate church. Sixty-seven of the church members, many of them persons of influence, withdrew, and immediately began plans for a place of worship. Thomas was delayed in Richmond until March by a serious illness. In a letter home he spoke of a fall from his horse, the effects of which had been giving him difficulty, which is not surprising considering his sixty-eight years. By March

4, 1832, however, he had sufficiently recovered to preach to the new congregation which had come out of the Baptist church, and which has become known as the "first full-fledged Church of Christ in Virginia."

While on this extended visit to Virginia, Thomas was assisting Alexander in the revision of the translation of the New Testament which had been issued in 1826. Alexander was in process of bringing out a new edition, stereotyped and pocket-sized, for economy and convenience. In a letter dated December 24, 1831, written from Loys, Virginia, Thomas commented on his experiences and travels. He then proceeded to advise Alexander in no uncertain terms of his expectations for the new edition:

> I feel infinitely more concerned for your intended publication of the New Testament than for anything you have ever attempted to publish. I beg and beseech you to look to the Lord continually for the guidance and superintending aid of his Holy Spirit; also to guard most rigidly against all philosophical, theoretical, and theological leanings. Let the translation be purely classical upon the established principles of philological, idiomatical, and grammatic criticism. Further, that you will not only duly attend to the corrections that I have already put into your hand in the small manuscript that I left with you, as well as what yet remains to be presented as soon as I have finished my review of your last edition, but also that you will grant me the indulgence of revising with you all the improvements you may have made out and collected, before you put them down in the improved and corrected copy to be stereotyped, before it is delivered for that purpose to the engraver.[2]

Apparently the elder Campbell spent all of the spring and summer of 1832 preaching and visiting the churches of Virginia, for he wrote from Spottsylvania the first day of August outlining his appointments for the next few weeks and indicating his intention of arriving home by September 1. He proposed to visit Fredericksburg, Warrenton, and Winchester, preaching on the way but, because of the heat of the summer and weight of his baggage, he did not expect to travel very fast. In reference to the difficulties with the Baptists, he counseled good will and Christian love, saying:

> The opposition here are doing all they can, but the cause of the reformation is daily gathering strength—is in the ascendant. If the public advocates from the pulpit and the press would only keep their temper, use soft words and hard arguments, it would progress still more. . . . May we not expose evils without exposing the persons that practice them, further than to endeavor affectionately to convince them that they are wrong? . . . I most cordially wish never to see or hear one ironic hint, one retalitive retort, by any friend or advocate of the reformation. . . . Speaking the truth in love is the Christian motto. . . .

The revision of the New Testament was still in progress and Campbell continued in his letter:

> I think long, my dear son, to be home, not only for the sake of my family enjoyments, but, in a peculiar measure, for the sake of a final revision of your intended impression of the New Testament. Were this satisfactorily accomplished I should be comparatively at ease about other achievements. It was with great reluctance I left home on that account.[3]

When at length the third edition, and later, the fourth or stereotyped edition appeared, the third paragraph of the Preface contained the following tribute to the scholarship and assistance of the father:

> The sheets of the third edition, after having been repeatedly read by myself and others, were submitted to the examination of Thomas Campbell, sen., and of Francis W. Emmons, to whom we are much indebted for the care which they have bestowed on them, and the numerous suggestions with which they have favored us. Their classical and biblical attainments have been of much service to us, and to the public, in the completion of this work.[4]

Thomas Campbell arrived home in September, 1832, after an absence of over nine months, in time to attend a meeting of the Wellsburg congregation. On September 6, 1832, this congregation passed a resolution appointing Robert Richardson clerk (Richardson had moved to Wellsburg some years previously) and named Richardson, John Brown, F. W. Emmons, H. N. Bakewell, and Thomas Campbell members of a committee on "godly edification." This committee was asked

> ... to consult together and make such arrangements for the proper ordering of the public exercise of the church, the times of meeting, etc., as may tend to promote the edification of the disciples, by calling forth the gifts of each member for the benefit of all.[5]

The meeting also voted to ask "Father Campbell" to take up his residence in Wellsburg for the purpose of "assisting us in acquiring a knowledge of the scriptures and getting things into better order among us." The elder Campbell agreed to this and subsequently moved for a time to Wellsburg. The committee on "godly edification" was later reappointed and charged with the additional responsibility of disciplining offenders against the regulations of the church.

In the December, 1832, issue of the *Millennial Harbinger*, Thomas Campbell contributed an article bearing the lengthy title "A Word to the Disciples of the Ancient Gospel in Behalf of the Reformation and for the Consideration of Opponents." Thomas, so recently returned from his Virginia tour, was quite concerned over the bitter feelings which he had encountered between the Baptists and Disciples of Christ. In this article "Father Campbell" sought to persuade his readers to consider the truth as he saw it. He took up the various objections to the proposition that theological differences are formed by as just reasoning as are scriptural differences. The last and most important of the objections considered was the point raised by some that

> We want personal reformation, practical and experimental religion enforced, instead of so much declamation against sectarianism.

Answer: Who can enumerate the evils of sectarianism? But is there no personal reformation in a strict conformity to the faith and practice expressly inculcated upon the disciples of Christ in the New Testament? Is there no practical and experimental religion in the belief and obedience of the gospel and law of Christ, as preached and taught by the Apostles? ... This puts us in mind of the clamorous outcry of the sectarian religionists in our Lord's time, who had made void the word of God by their traditions; they stigmatized him a Sabbath-breaker, a winebibber, a friend of the publicans and sinners, etc. But he was a reformer.[6]

Things were indeed not always peaceful in the churches of the young movement of Disciples of Christ. Thomas Campbell, however, long experienced in matters of dissension, was well qualified to restore order and Christian fellowship when the occasion demanded. Such an incident occurred during the winter of 1832 or the spring of 1833 while Campbell was resident in Wellsburg and attending services there. A young preacher was speaking on the subject of "The Holy Spirit and How He Operates," and was trying to convince his hearers that "the Spirit was the Word and the Word was the Spirit," which was contrary to the general belief of most of the congregation. He was mentally keen, but theologically dogmatic and there was an opinionated self-confidence in his words. At the close of the young man's sermon, before the congregation could be dismissed:

Father Campbell arose, with the dignity and solemnity of a patriarch, as he was, and spoke for some ten or fifteen minutes in reply. Ah, with what force and plainness for the truth! and yet, with tenderness and kindness for the young man. He completely used him up. He did it as no one present could have done.[7]

Discussion with Stone on the Atonement

There is little information on the relations of Thomas Campbell and Barton W. Stone, and it is in fact not even known if they ever met personally. It is known, however, that the elder Campbell questioned some of the doctrinal positions which Stone held, and after the union of the Campbell and Stone movements beginning in 1832, Thomas Campbell and Barton Stone entered into what may be called a written debate through the pages of the *Christian Messenger,* Stone's magazine, and the *Millennial Harbinger.* This arose from a letter Thomas Campbell published in the June, 1833, issue of the *Millennial Harbinger* addressed to a Kentuckian, William Z. Thompson, who had sent the elder Campbell a review copy of a book on the atonement written by a Noah Worcester. Thomas' letter in reply, which served as a review, precipitated an extensive correspondence between the elder Campbell and Stone which continued through four issues of the *Millennial Harbinger.* Campbell's criticism of Worcester's views of the atonement was that he said that the sacrifice of Christ by God was a display of love not of wrath. Campbell answered with "scriptural testimony" that he believed Christ's death on the cross was for love *and* wrath. In this letter Thomas Campbell revealed his doctrine of the atonement:

1. Christ died for both love of God and his wrath at man's sins.
2. God laid on Christ the iniquity, that is the punishment due to the iniquity of us all.
3. Without the shedding of his blood there is no remission of sins.
4. Christ suffered for our sins that he might redeem us from this present evil world, according to the will of God our Father.

To conclude, if we could be saved in a way honorable to God, without the sacrifice of his Son as a sin offering, we certainly could have been saved without his peculiar doctrines or example, and consequently without his birth, life or death. . . . Believing as I do, that it was not possible that any one of our race could be saved without the sacrifice of the Lamb of God, I must hold every attempt to explain it away into a mere moral example, or a display of love, without regard to justice, as tending to subvert the basis of the divine government. . . .[8]

Stone in his reply took Campbell to task for saying that he believed it impossible for any of the human race to be saved except by the sacrifice of Christ. In the August *Millennial Harbinger* the elder Campbell answered: "Respected Brother: I AM sorry to find that you disapprove of my remarks upon N. W. . . . .'s 'view of the atonement,' " and proceeded to defend himself by saying that he only quoted Scripture. After a lengthy and sometimes heated discussion of his views, Campbell closed with words of good will:

. . . let us leave behind us the weapons of that unprofitable and pernicious warfare—imbibe the spirit, and adopt the phrase, of our divine instructors; that, practicing and speaking the truth in love, we may be conformed to them in all things, and thus adorn our holy profession.[9]

In the October and November issues of the *Millennial Harbinger* the same controversy over the atonement and Worcester's book is continued. Stone answered Thomas in the *Christian Messenger* and both are in process of ironing out differences between them on shades of meaning, especially on those which were involved in Stone's scruples against the vicarious sufferings of Christ. The fifth and final article appeared in the December issue of the *Millennial Harbinger* and Thomas Campbell proposed to close the discussion. He said:

And now, dear brother, I have done with my reply to your remarks on my letter; and can truly say with you, "it was not my purpose to attempt a reply to all *you* have written." A few prominent points only of your strictures have I noticed. There are a few gospel facts, which I consider as axioms; I have, therefore, doubted the truth of every doctrine, that stands in opposition to these.

. . . .

And now, respected brother, farewell. . . . I little thought when I wrote to gratify friend Thompson, that it should prove an occasion for what has taken place between us; but I humbly hope that it is all for good; and do, therefore, cordially submit it to the divine disposal, and to the serious consideration of an inquiring public.[10]

Barton W. Stone closed his side of the discussion with the observation:

> Some of our weak brethren are afraid that the passing remarks of Brother Thomas Campbell and myself will ultimate in controversy, and injury to the cause in which we profess to be engaged. We have been solicited by them to desist and by others of stronger minds, lest that which is lame be turned out of the way. As a Bishop must not be self-willed, I have yielded to their wishes.[11]

But not all of those concerned viewed the debate in this light. John B. Howard of Paris, Tennessee, editor of the *Christian Reformer*, read these controversies and suggested:

> ... If brother Campbell has been mainly instrumental in stripping the gospel of the human appendances, additions and glosses by which it was clogged and obscured, it must be acknowledged that father Stone was greatly instrumental in preparing the people for its reception. The pious, venerable and able fathers, Stone and Thomas Campbell, would suit well for co-editors.[12]

The truth of the matter was that many of the Campbell's followers doubted that Stone was sound and completely scriptural in his views. In many ways Barton W. Stone was too tolerant and exhibited the open mind too much to suit the Scripture-centered Thomas. In the five contributions published in the *Millennial Harbinger*, the elder Campbell tried to point out what he considered were the defective views of Stone. Thomas Campbell saw Stone as satisfied with a moral theory of the atonement, and sought to show that, while this moral theory was not wrong, it did not satisfy all the teachings of the Scriptures on the subject. The elder Campbell did not denounce Stone, but expressed an earnest desire that each might attain the full truth, and that full truth could be discovered only in the Scriptures.

Last Active Decade: 1833-1843

In early October, 1833, Thomas Campbell left his home at Wellsburg, and in company with Alexander, B. F. Hall from Kentucky, and two of Thomas' granddaughters, Maria and Eliza, traveled across Virginia, arriving in Richmond, on October 24. The congregation at Richmond was worshiping in its new building which was called "Sycamore Meetinghouse" because of the large tree which shaded its door. At Richmond the party divided, with Alexander and Hall going on to New York, and Thomas Campbell to North Carolina, where he planned to visit and preach as he might have opportunity. At this time North Carolina had a population of 750,000 persons, of which one half million were white. Only eight per cent belonged to any church; consequently the field of evangelism was an open one. But the aging Thomas Campbell was not able to take full advantage of the opportunities for religious growth which were present. At this time he was well into his seventieth year and lacked the physical vigor and energy with which to capture the minds of strangers even though his heart was aglow with the cause to which he was committed.

The elder Campbell's tour of North Carolina lasted for over six months, through the winter of 1833 and into the spring of 1834. He addressed his final reply to Barton W. Stone on the atonement from Edenton, North Carolina, on November 5, 1833, where he stayed until the middle of February as the guest of a Thomas Whaff. From Edenton he moved to Greenville where he stayed in the home of a General William Clark, who was a fellow minister and a friend of the movement of Disciples of Christ. Clark had been the first subscriber to the *Millennial Harbinger* in North Carolina. Thomas Campbell's message was not enthusiastically received, and he wrote a letter to his daughter Dorothea (Mrs. Joseph Bryant) from Greenville on February 17, 1834, in which he confessed that he had had frequent feelings of loneliness and discouragement. On such occasions he took consolation in prayer, and afterward he stated:

> ... I feel consoled, refreshed, and delighted, and only at a loss for the presence of some kindred mind to whom I could communicate and with whom I could reciprocate my feelings; and being deprived of this privilege, I return again to my chamber or the fireside whence I set out.
>
> Thus you have, in brief, the history of my course since my arrival in this State; except that I have occasionally been reading and writing in defense of the reformation as opportunity offered.[13]

On March 7, 1834, Campbell wrote his wife of his discouragement over the slowness with which results were achieved. He nostalgically recalled their sharing together the joys and hardships of a minister's calling, and described the religious conditions of the community:

> Religion here appears to be at a very low ebb, both with regard to its exhibition and effects. We anticipate a meeting of the few friends of reform—I mean the preachers—on the last Lord's day of this month, and the two preceding days, not far from this place, for the purpose of concert concerning our future proceedings; after which, if spared, I shall shortly write you our conclusions.[14]

Sufficient progress had apparently been made by the newly organized congregation at Greenville to permit them to plan a union meeting of Disciples of Christ in this area for March 28-30, 1834, the first in the state. At that time an observer noted certain facts about the impression the venerable Father Campbell gave, reporting that Campbell preached sitting down with a large Bible from which he frequently read. He described Campbell as wearing his white hair long, with a patriarchal effect.

From Pantego, North Carolina, Campbell wrote his wife, April 9, 1834, that he hoped to be in Richmond,

Virginia, by May 1 and would stay there indefinitely before returning home. He summed up his entire experience of nearly six months by saying:

> I never had my mind so much disciplined, in any given period of my life, as since I came to this place. It has been to me a kind of exile, as was Patmos, to the beloved apostle. It seems to me as though I have been among a kind of people different from any with whom I have been formerly acquainted. . . . I am now about to leave the State without having found a strong attachment but to a very few.[15]

He became despondent, and dwelt on thoughts of death and eternity as he wrote:

> I wish you, my dear, to inculcate on all our children, as you have opportunity, that the great business of time is to prepare for eternity, by abounding in the work of faith, the labor of love, and the patience or perseverance of hope in our Lord Jesus Christ; that they may be enabled to teach their children . . . for alas! this important duty is greatly neglected in our day, by the great majority of professed Christians, of all denominations, in our highly favored country. . . . I remain, most sincerely and affectionately, your husband till death. . . .[16]

It is evident that not a little of Thomas Campbell's discouragement was due to his failure in North Carolina—a failure which he believed stemmed from the opposition of the Baptists. There can be no question but that there was opposition. The decrees of the Dover Association in the fall of 1832, calling on Baptist churches everywhere to exclude Disciples of Christ, had crossed from Virginia into North Carolina and were being read and circulated among the Baptist churches. While he was at Edenton, from November to February, he witnessed the exclusion of the group of Disciples of Christ from the church there, and the Yeopim Union Meeting of this area appointed a committee called "The Committee on the Case of the Campbellite Reformers." This committee made its report in three resolutions, the third of which stipulated that it was

... due to the cause of truth and Christian concord to guard our brethren against the ministrations of the one, Thomas Campbell, a teacher of Campbellism, who has been for some time visiting among our brethren, carrying with him letters of recommendation from persons residing in Edenton, and laboring, it is believed, to disseminate his peculiar sentiments among our people.[17]

Thomas Campbell answered these attacks in a small pamphlet of sixteen pages, entitled *On Religious Reformation*. There was very little new in the document for it contained only the preface and selected excerpts from the printed *Declaration and Address*, the pamphlet published in Cincinnati, in May, 1829, and short quotations from the *Millennial Harbinger* (for 1831, No. 12, pp. 567-568), Calvin's *Institutes* (Book 4, chap. 10), and an essay by a Dr. Worcester entitled "False Standards Occasion False Estimates." The purpose of the pamphlet was stated in a short introduction as follows:

Having happened in eastern Virginia, as in many other places distant from our commencement, that various mistakes and discordant misrepresentations, injurious to the proposed reformation, have been unhappily indulged and officiously propagated, charging the reformers with a fickle unprincipled versatility, and the reformation with almost every thing deemed erroneous, it appears a duty we owe to ourselves, and to the public, in behalf of the all-important cause in which we are engaged, to give a public exhibit of the following well authenticated documents.... Impressed with these sentiments (the result of the rigorous investigation of upwards of twenty years, during which time the following specifications and assumptions ... have been subjected to the strictest scrutiny of objecting opposers of every description, without even the alleged detection of a single error; which, however, is not the alone ground of our confidence, which is more especially founded upon the materials of which these specifications and assumptions are composed, namely; express scripture testimony, undeniable facts, and universally acknowledged principles, which, we are persuaded, no rational professor of any sect *ever did*, or *can pretend, to call in question*,) we submit as follows:

It is clearly seen in the above introduction that the elder Campbell was trying to show that the reformation of the churches which he proposed was no new thing and that there were printed documents available as evidence that this was no ephemeral movement led by a "here today, gone tomorrow" leadership. Thomas insisted that in spite of all the opposition no opponent had ever shown a scriptural reason as to why he should give up the reformation principles. He closed with this same view:

> ... all the sects are offended. And why? We shall leave it to them to say; for they have not yet, no not one of them, presented any relevant reason, why we should desist from urging the indispensable duty, absolute necessity, and vast importance of the reformation for which we plead. ... We shall take leave of this subject, and of the public for the present, by respectfully assuring all concerned, that if they; or any of them, will convince us of inculating any error, either of faith or practice, that we shall candidly relinquish it, and thank God and man for the discovery. Also, that if they will shew us how we may, without giving offence, plead the cause of a reformation, which involves the glory of God and happiness to mankind, we shall thankfully adopt it. Farewell.[18]

From May, 1834, to April, 1835, little is known of Thomas Campbell's activity. It may be assumed, however, that he returned safely to his home at West Middletown, Pennsylvania, not far from Bethany and undoubtedly preached among the churches of the area. About the middle of April, 1835, Alexander left on a trip of two-and-one-half-months duration and, as usual, the elder Campbell assisted his son by taking over the editorship of the *Millennial Harbinger*. Alexander had left a number of articles for insertion, but the editor *pro tem* himself did considerable writing. In the preparation of the May issue the elder Campbell answered letters of February 18 and 20 from John R. Howard of Paris, Tennessee, addressed to his son and

> ... containing some matters for publication, which I have arranged in the following order, upon which I shall, in my son's

absence, offer a few responsive remarks; not intended, however, to supersede anything that he may think proper to add, at his return, after their publication.[19]

In an extremely verbose section Thomas proceeded to answer such questions as: are the sufferings of Christ vicarious? If so, how or in what sense, are they vicarious? Were they to appease the wrath of the Father against sinners? How are his sufferings and death to affect sinners? To all these questions Thomas Campbell's final appeal was to the Scriptures, and wherever possible he avoided a personal reply, letting the Bible speak for itself. In this same May issue "M. Winans" of Jamestown, Ohio, wrote showing himself concerned with certain individuals who refused to partake of the Lord's Supper because of a supposed grievance against other members of the congregation. Thomas replied that the Scriptures were perfectly plain concerning "our relative duties with respect to our offending brethren." Further on in this issue there was a letter signed "M. T.," dated February 14, 1835, from Pittsburgh, which made an inquiry concerning the term "evangelist," suggesting that the office expired with the apostolic age. The elder Campbell replied by tracing the derivation of the word "evangelist" from the Greek and from references to the word in the New Testament and in the early church. He concluded that "the intention of the aforesaid gifts, have an equal reference to the whole christian community, to the end of time."

At this time Thomas Campbell and his wife made their home with their third daughter, Jane, who had married Matthew McKeaver some years previously, and who lived near West Middletown, Pennsylvania, about seven miles from Bethany. Alexander had not been gone from home for long when his mother, then nearly seventy-two years old, was taken with what proved to be a fatal illness. Her husband was constantly at her bedside, and they spent many hours talking of their life together.

She passed away quietly on April 28, 1835, with her companion of nearly fifty years and their youngest son, Archibald, at her side. She was buried in the family cemetery at Bethany, and several days later Thomas wrote an account of the mother's death for their daughter Alicia Clapp at Mentor, Ohio. This letter, later published in the *Millennial Harbinger*, revealed the tenderness of affection in which Campbell held his wife and paid tribute to her faithfulness in training the children and managing her large household. He noted that within the last eight years he had been gone from home three fourths of the time, and that she had borne the extra burdens gladly, feeling herself a part of his ministry. He concluded:

... and now, dear daughter, what remains for me, thus bereft of my endearing attached companion, from whose loving faithful heart, I am persuaded, I was not absent a single day of our fifty years connexion ... yes, what now remains for me, without any worldly care, or particular object of worldly attachment,—but, with renewed energy—with redoubled diligence, as the Lord may be graciously pleased to enable, to sound abroad *the word of life*....[20]

Therefore, in May, 1835, in spite of his recent loss, Thomas Campbell continued to edit and read proof for the June issue of the *Millennial Harbinger*. In it the elder Campbell continued the answers to his son's voluminous correspondence which had raised many questions of church government and theological interpretation. At last, his patience exhausted, Campbell used these many letters as the excuse for a two-page discourse on the movement which he had fathered:

In the absence of the Editor, we feel induced, by the above communications, to express a feeling of deep regret, that a reformation, which we humbly suggested, and respectfully submitted to the consideration of the friends and lovers of truth and peace throughout all the churches, more than twenty-five years ago, for the express purpose of putting an end to religious controversy among christians, should appear to take the unhappy turn, to which with painful anxiety, we have seen it verging for the last ten years. . . .

It is clear that Thomas Campbell was vitally concerned with the direction in which the movement seemed to be going and expressed himself as he had done on other occasions, as being opposed. He was vainly and somewhat futilely trying to call a halt to tendencies which already were out of hand. The spirit of many who were writing and preaching was a grief to the mind of Thomas Campbell and, after quoting a section from the *Declaration and Address*, continued:

. . . And had the advocates of the proposed reformation continued to sustain and enforce it, as in the document referred to, we are constrained to believe, that the sectarian popular objections which have been brought against it, and with which its progress has been unhappily embarrassed, could never have been advanced by any, who acknowledged the all-sufficiency, and alone-sufficiency, of the belief and obedience of the Holy Scriptures, in their obvious grammatic sense, for the salvation of sinners; for the perfect edification of the christian church, independent of all human opinions and inventions of men.

Father Campbell concluded his attempt to restore the original motivation of the movement by trying still another time to emphasize the authority of the Bible as alone sufficient for the Christian:

. . . For instead of detecting and exposing the supposed errors of any of the *existing isms* of sectarian christendom, our controversies should have been confined to *verbal criticism* about the literal, contextual, and analogical meaning of the sacred text . . . all of which would have a direct and proper tendency to make us better acquainted with the true, literal and figurative meaning of the language of the sacred volume.[21]

This article is important, for it indicates that Thomas Campbell realized that the movement had taken a direction which he had never intended when he first set forth the principles of the *Declaration and Address*. It would not be correct, however, to deduce from such an article that Thomas and Alexander Campbell were fundamentally opposed to each other or that they quarreled over the matter. Thomas was blindly and stubbornly staying by his original purpose of proposing Christian union on the basis of biblical authority, and failed utterly to see the end toward which such scriptural interpretation was taking them. In a very real sense this article summarizes the frustration and incipient tragedy of Thomas Campbell's life.

There is little record of Thomas Campbell's activities from the summer of 1835 until the fall of 1838. Only a fleeting glimpse is caught of his movements during this period. Although Alexander was gone from home even more than before, Thomas did not often edit the *Millennial Harbinger,* for his son had secured the services of Robert Richardson as co-editor. The elder Campbell spent the summer of 1836 in northern Ohio, probably with his daughter Alicia at Mentor, for Alexander wrote his wife on June 11, 1836, from Lake Erie: "My father left me in good health yesterday morning and will spend the summer in the Lake country." About this time Thomas Campbell's second son, Thomas, Jr., must have died, for there is no record of him after this period. It is generally understood that he was a physician and surgeon and lived in or about Bethany. His wife was supposedly an invalid and preceded her husband in death. There were no known children. The circumstances surrounding his death are unusual, for there was no mention of the event in the *Millennial Harbinger* or other family records.

In the fall of 1838 Alexander set out on a trip of several months' duration, and as Richardson was also absent from Bethany, his father was once more left with the responsibility for preparing copy for the *Millennial Harbinger.* The November issue contained a query from

"M. Winans" of Jamestown, Ohio, as to whether the word Satan should be translated "punishing" in the New Testament. The elder Campbell gave his usual answer that scriptural authority alone could have any weight in such a matter and quoted many passages that would oppose such a rendering. A letter from Thomas M. Henley of Hillsborough, Virginia, dated December 28, 1838, addressed him as "Beloved old brother T. Campbell, learning from brother Alexander, when he was at my house, you would attend to the Harbinger, I address you as Editor...."[22]

Toward the end of 1838 and the beginning of 1839 the attention of Thomas Campbell was challenged by the report he read of a Christian union convention which had been held August 21, 1838, at Syracuse, New York. This report, taken from the *Union Herald* of August 31, 1838, was published by him in the January and February *Millennial Harbinger* so that all might be informed of this new proposal for the union of Christians. There was a report from a committee on resolutions which presented what it considered fundamental propositions for Christian union. They simply required that a candidate should profess a belief in the Lord Jesus Christ. In an address which followed, the evils of sectarianism were brought to the attention of the Christian world, and the duty of immediate union was emphasized. The plan of union proposed was to search out the Scriptures and find the example of Christ, which was considered the supreme law of the church. This convention rejected all human creeds and the authority of ecclesiastical bodies. The second meeting of the Christian union convention was held at Cazenovia, New York, on January 30 and 31, 1839, and was duly reported in the *Millennial Harbinger* by its editor *pro tem*. The sessions at Cazenovia revealed that the convention felt that theological agreement was the way to Christian union. Thomas followed the printed report of the Cazenovia meeting by recording his reactions to it:

> And first, upon the whole, we greatly rejoice, that this all important subject of Christian union is beginning to awake the public attention, not only in the State of New York; but, in some measure, throughout Protestant Christendom.

The elder Campbell then reviewed the efforts he had made thirty years previously to promote the same cause and quoted at length from the propositions of the *Declaration and Address*. He then proceeded with his reactions to the proposal:

> Second, as to the propositions adopted by the Convention, they appear too indefinite; and, of course, have a tendency to produce difficulties, both to the candidates for Christian fellowship, and also to those who are to admit and receive them.

The difficulties to which he referred were contained in the first and second propositions of the committee on resolutions which provided that the candidate for church fellowship be accepted merely on his statement of belief in Jesus as Lord and Savior. Thomas Campbell called the attention of his readers to the position which he and Disciples of Christ had taken:

> Whereas, if, in stead of these perplexing and almost insoluble difficulties, teachers and churches would proceed upon the divinely prescribed practice of the Apostles; namely, to preach the gospel . . . and upon his being confessedly convinced and disposed to obey it, then to baptize him into the name of the Father, and of the Son, and of the Holy Spirit . . . and afterwards carefully teach the baptized to observe all things taught by the Apostles as expressly recorded in the New Testament. . . . And it is only by thus assuming and acting upon original ground, as we have proposed, that ever the modern churches can be reduced to New Testament order, so as to exhibit the divine costume of the apostolic churches.

The reports of the Christian Union Convention and Thomas Campbell's reaction to it give opportunity to evaluate his mature thinking on the subject of Christian union. In doing this one finds that in the thirty years since the publication of the *Declaration and Address* he had steadily moved toward a position of strict interpretation of the New Testament as the only basis for the union of Christians and apparently had not fully realized the difficulty of a uniform interpretation of scriptural truth. To him it was all plainly written and, if the Scriptures were accepted as divinely inspired, only needed to be read to be understood. This position is further defined in a succeeding issue of the *Millennial Harbinger* in an article on "Christian Union" which lists in sixteen steps the platform upon which a united church of the New Testament pattern could be built. This served to crystallize Campbell's thinking of a few years earlier and indicates a position which he was to hold from this time on.[23]

In early 1839 Thomas Campbell wrote an article entitled "The Divine Order for Evangelizing the World, and for Teaching the Evangelized How to Conduct Themselves." He was increasingly concerned about the hundreds of new congregations of Disciples of Christ that were developing in almost every state of the union and wished to instruct them in the proposed church order and organization. This was the purpose of this article and a subsequent series on "The Direct and Immediate Intention of the Christian Institution." In the first article Thomas Campbell urged the churches to study the Bible assiduously:

> Let the church then take up its Book, and read and study it. . . . Thus will the church resume its proper character; that is, the school of Christ, disciples, Christians; and will not henceforth shame its Master, through its stupid, wilful, shameful ignorance of his only Book.

In a series of essays on the "Christian Institution" Thomas suggested that the members of the church meet together each Sunday at ten o'clock and remain together four hours with a half-hour recess between each two hours. The worship should commence with singing, prayer, and reading of the Bible, followed by a period of teaching, the Lord's Supper, and with more preaching and teaching, close with assignment of Scriptures to be studied in the coming week and the taking of an offering. He suggested the items to be kept in a church record book: (1) a statement of the basic belief of the congregation, (2) the names of the members, (3) a record of additions, by baptism, by letter, or otherwise, (4) a record of deaths and of those dismissed for cause, and (5) an account of contributions and expenditures. The elder Campbell even offered a suggested statement of purpose for a congregation, emphasizing the acceptance of the Holy Scriptures alone, "as the only perfect and all-sufficient expression of the divine will" and stating that the proposed congregation will make a "rule *of* them and be ruled *by* them."[24]

These essays only carried into application Thomas Campbell's basic concern that the Bible be read and studied to gain a knowledge of God, of man, of sin, of Christ, of his salvation, of the means of enjoying it and of its consequences. He said:

> Therefore, as often as we open the blessed Book, it should be with the precise and real intention of acquiring a more perfect knowledge of these all-important topics, that so we might still be adding to our faith....[25]

Alexander returned home shortly after the first of April, 1839, and relieved his father of the duties of editor. In August and September of the same year Thomas Campbell was on a preaching tour of Pennsylvania, but Alexander published in the *Millennial Harbinger* an essay of the elder Campbell on "Personal and Family Devotion," and explained that his father had not seen Alexander's article on a similar subject in the August issue.

After Thomas pointed up the importance of Bible-reading, he proposed that each family have a period of Bible reading at each meal:

> ... when they meet for breakfast, let them first take their spiritual meal, thus socially beginning the day with God—by reading a certain select portion of his word, with suitable questions, remarks, and exhortations for this purpose.... This may be conveniently done by asking the following pertinent questions according to the respective capacities of the guests, viz.—1. Who is the writer or speaker of the portion read, or of any particular part of it? 2. To whom is it written or spoken? 3. What historic facts are contained in it? 4. What commands are contained in it? 5. What doctrinal declarations? 6. What invitations? 7. What promises? 8. What threatenings? Lastly, the why, when, and where those things were spoken or written, still remain to be considered, and are circumstances sometimes worthy of particular attention, in order to a correct understanding of particular passages.[26]

Aside from the relative merit of the suggestions concerning daily devotions in the family, this article is noteworthy in that it points to certain basic principles of biblical interpretation and criticism which are taken for granted today, but which were startling when they were first written down over one hundred years ago. It is interesting that Thomas Campbell would suggest that facts of historical criticism such as when and where the book had been written, and to whom, were important to the understanding of a biblical passage. On the other hand, embedded as they were, in the midst of so much other material, these suggestions were passed over for many years as of little significance.

In 1839 and early 1840 a long-smoldering fire broke forth over the "name" for the movement: whether it should be "Christian" or "Disciples of Christ." The question actually went back to a period as early as September, 1824, when Thomas Campbell had shown a distinct preference for the single designation "Christian" in an article for the *Christian Baptist* entitled

"Essay on the Religion of Christianity," in which he had much to say about the Christian's being baptized "into" the name of the Father, Son, and Holy Spirit rather than "in" the name, in the sense of imparting authority.[27] Alexander had not concurred with his father, but was willing to admit that the name Christian was proper and appropriate and only wished that all were worthy of it. Alexander preferred the name "disciple" as being more humble and of earlier and more frequent use in the New Testament. Another reason for his lack of enthusiasm for "Christian" was that the Christian connection group had appropriated the name and that group's anti-Trinitarian speculations had subjected them to the charge of Arianism. This was the period of increased contact with the Stone movement of Kentucky, and Alexander did not want to leave himself open to such a charge. These discussions anticipated the real problem which became increasingly evident about 1830 in the separation of the "reformers" from the Baptists over what the new congregations thus established were to be called. Another indication of the gathering storm was the publication in 1835 of a hymnbook for the use of the churches. It was edited by Walter Scott, Alexander Campbell, Barton W. Stone and John T. Johnson, and called *The Disciples' Hymn Book*. Scott, along with Stone and Thomas Campbell, objected to the name chosen, preferring the name "Christian." Alexander held out for "Disciples" against them but later changed the name to *Christian Hymn Book*. When the controversy broke out anew in 1840, Walter Scott expressed himself very decidedly in favor of "Christian." Alexander raised the problem with a lead article in the August, 1839, issue of the *Millennial Harbinger,* in which he asked: "What shall we be called?" and suggested four alternatives: Disciples of Christ, Christians, Reformers and Campbellites, and showed that only two, "Disciples of Christ" and "Christians" were scriptural. In a second article, appearing in the September number, the son reiterated his objections to "Christians" on the basis of the use of the name by New England groups who were Unitarian. Alexander gave as his reasons for the choice of "Disciples" that it was more ancient, descriptive, scriptural and unused. Thomas Campbell came out, along with Barton W. Stone, Walter Scott and others, for "Christian." Thomas' contribution to the discussion is titled simply "Communication":

> Notwithstanding all that has been said . . . in relation to the name by which the advocates and subjects of the proposed reformation should be known, it would appear that there is none so eligible or suitable as the name Christian: and that for the following reasons:—1st. Because of the radical and comprehensive import of its appellative signification. 2d. Because of its scriptural consistency with the intention of the proposed reformation.[28]

The father and son did not quarrel over the question of the name, but each used what he pleased, and on different occasions both men used both names. Nevertheless, despite the counsel of his father and the desires of Barton W. Stone and Walter Scott, Alexander Campbell exerted his powerful influence for the name "Disciples of Christ" and ultimately gained the victory, as this is the name by which the movement is known today.

In December, 1839, Thomas Campbell was editor of the *Millennial Harbinger* for a short time while Alexander was away for a few weeks, and he wrote concerning ordination (men are to be set aside and ordained); nonresistance (not taught in either the Old or New Testaments); and on self-education (it is necessary to attain the good life). In this same volume the elder Campbell had an essay on "Church Edification," which appeared in two parts and in which he considered the purpose of the church and the "progressive edification and ultimate perfection of every individual member."[29]

As early as October, 1839, Alexander Campbell had advanced the "Plan of a Literary, Moral, and Religious School" in the pages of the *Millennial Harbinger*. During the winter of 1839-1840, these ideas matured to the point that Alexander decided to proceed to the organization of a college for the training of young men—a college which would emphasize in its curriculum physical sciences and humanities, and include the teaching of the Bible as a textbook. Early in 1840, therefore, Alexander Campbell called together eighteen men who were to serve as incorporators of the college, and Thomas Campbell was one of them. Looking around him at the first meeting he saw such leaders as his son Alexander and his son-in-law, Matthew McKeaver, three sons-in-law of Alexander: John C. Campbell, Albert O. Ewing, and Robert Y. Henley. In addition to those having connections with the Campbell family, there were the influential Adamson Bentley of Warren, Ohio, and Samuel Church of Pittsburgh; still others who lived in the vicinity: Robert Richardson, Campbell Tarr, and William Stewart. The purpose of the meeting was to draw up articles of incorporation and to prepare the petition to the legislators of Virginia for a charter. To that end Alexander Campbell and his son-in-law, John C. Campbell, formerly a Virginia legislator, and then a prominent Wellsburg attorney and banker, set off for Richmond in February, 1840. They returned the next month with a charter (issued March 2, 1840) which stipulated:

> That there be, and is hereby erected and established, at or near Bethany, in the county of Brooke, in this Commonwealth, a seminary of learning for the instruction of youth in the various branches of science and literature, the useful arts, agriculture, and the learned and foreign languages . . . and be it further enacted, That the said Seminary shall be known and called by the name of Bethany College.[30]

The first meeting of the trustees of the new institution was held on Monday, May 11, 1840. Those present were:

Thomas and Alexander Campbell, Robert Richardson, Robert Y. Henley, Matthew McKeaver, John C. Campbell, Samuel Grafton, William Stewart, and Robert Nicholls. John Campbell moved that Thomas Campbell be elected chairman, and it was unanimously approved. Alexander was named treasurer, and a building committee was appointed. The meeting was then adjourned to reassemble Friday, September 18, at Bethany. The second meeting was held as scheduled, and again Thomas Campbell presided. A report from the secretary indicating a bond had been posted by the treasurer was accepted and the treasurer made a report of monies received. The building committee was authorized to erect such buildings as they thought necessary. William Stewart moved that they proceed to the election of a president of the college to which office Alexander Campbell was elected. He was requested to submit a plan of study and to make inquiry regarding professors and other officers necessary to open the college as soon as possible. These minutes were signed by Thomas Campbell as president *pro tem*.

Plans for such an institution must have warmed the heart of the seventy-seven-year-old Thomas, for of all the leaders of the movement of Disciples of Christ, he had had the most extensive formal training. Barton W. Stone had attended a frontier academy for a short time, Walter Scott had finished the University of Edinburgh; and Thomas' son, Alexander, had attended the University of Glasgow for a period of some months, but only Thomas Campbell had completed both the university course and several years of training at a theological seminary. Moreover, he had conducted several schools, had helped educate young ministers and sensed the need of both an educated ministry and constituency. It is probable that only advancing age hindered him from taking part side by side with Alexander in soliciting funds for the infant institution.

Thomas Campbell continued to write for the *Millennial Harbinger* and in the February, 1840, issue there was a long article on "Church Edification" which followed the two-part article that had appeared the previous year. In the new article the elder Campbell suggested that the Scriptures revealed the proper activity for Christians and suggested that the occupation of the Lord's Day was to spend much time in the study of the Bible. He further suggested:

> . . . surely four or five hours per week, spent together for this blissful purpose, should seem but a short space; and so it must and will, if we be not carnally-minded; and even if we be, it can only be cured by persevering in spiritual exercises.[31]

From June through August, 1840, Thomas was again serving briefly as editor while "my son, Alexander," was absent from home on one of his many trips across the countryside.

In a private letter to A. S. Hayden, a young minister of Ohio, Thomas Campbell revealed his philosophy of how to establish a new congregation. Apparently Hayden had written to Bethany seeking advice on opening a church in Cleveland, Ohio, in cooperation with interested citizens of that community. Thomas suggested that Hayden visit the people concerned, preach and pray with them for a few weeks and tell them his intention, which Campbell would conceive to be that of preaching the doctrine of Disciples of Christ and teaching religion from house to house. The elder Campbell further suggested that if they seemed agreed after such a visit, Hayden should locate with them for one year in order to make a trial of what could be done. Having located his family, Hayden was urged to devote his time to reading, meditation, prayer and to the public and private preaching of the word and to an insistence on family worship.[32]

The religious education of the young always concerned Thomas Campbell. He had worked hard to bring up his own family in "the nurture and admonition of the Lord" and was active in the lives of his many grandchildren and in their training. It was not as a mere theorist, therefore, that he wrote in the August issue of the *Millennial Harbinger* a choice essay entitled: "Family Education: The Nursery." In this article Thomas revealed a knowledge of child psychology and educational concepts far in advance of his day. He wrote:

> Though the pages of the Harbinger have furnished its readers with many useful suggestions upon the all-important subject of family education . . . yet the particular duties of the primary department—that of the nursery, do not appear to have been distinctly considered. Now it is in the plastic subjects of this department, that the formative impressions of human character are inlaid. The infant sees, feels, and retains the impressions made upon its perception, long before it can think for itself; yes, indeed, these constitute the very elements of its thoughts and desires; or its aversions.[33]

He suggested that the child be trained by relating the love of the earthly parents for the child to the care and love of the heavenly Father. The elder Campbell felt that the child's food and clothing should be "plain, simple and suitable" and should answer the purpose of health and convenience rather than to pamper the appetite and to build pride. He concluded: "Upon the whole;—these things being evidently so, there must be pious spiritually-minded Christian parents, before there can be pious obedient children. . . ."

August also saw the publication of the first in a series of seven essays by Thomas Campbell on "A Scriptural View of Christian Character and Privilege." The succeeding articles in the series appeared in the September, 1840, issue and in the March, April, May, and December issues of 1841. The seventh and last contribution on this subject was in the January, 1842, issue of the *Millennial Harbinger*. The purpose of the series was exactly what was indicated by the title, for it was a survey of the scriptural references which pertain to Christian character. The elder Campbell was concerned with the indications of a growing materialism which by the 1840's was increasingly evident on what had been the frontier when Campbell first came to western Pennsylvania thirty years before, for he concluded:

> The all-important intention of the above collection of scripture testimony for the development of Christian character, has been occasioned by a deep and painful conviction of the sad and almost universal deficiency, in this respect, every where manifestly evident, though apparently little noticed. When we consider the peculiar distinguishing attributes of Christian character . . . we are ready to exclaim,—what is become of Christianity!!! Where is the Christian to be found![34]

The articles which followed developed the "scripture testimony" and divided the analysis of Christian character into eight sections. In the March, 1841, article Thomas explained that through the winter months, from September, 1840, until February, 1841, he had been away preaching, and expressed his regret that all the Scripture was quoted in the 1840 volume. He closed the series with the injunction: "We must, therefore, make our holy religion our main business, our chief concern, if we would realize and enjoy it."

Aside from the series on Christian character, Thomas Campbell made two other contributions to the 1841 volume of the *Harbinger*. In the April issue someone signed "T. H." asked about the advisability of traveling preachers and evangelists securing recommendations from recognized congregations and the elder Campbell's answer stated that they should do so in order to protect themselves and the congregations. In the November number Thomas had an article entitled: "A Scriptural View of the Agency of the Holy Spirit in the Conversion and Salvation of Sinners—According to the Gospel."

This was another survey of the Scriptures in order to secure the evidence for a Christian belief in the work of the Holy Spirit in conversion. He referred almost entirely to the New Testament, and the main argument was simply that one cannot separate the power of the Holy Spirit from the effect of the importance of the Word of God in conversion. In such articles Thomas Campbell always showed himself thoroughly versed in the Bible and in this essay he anticipated by more than two years the treatment of the subject by Alexander in his debate with Nathan L. Rice at Lexington, Kentucky, in November, 1843.

Retirement and Reflection

From 1843, about the time of his eightieth birthday, until his death, Thomas Campbell, with few exceptions, stayed in retirement at Bethany. He made his home with Alexander and his few wants were cared for by the family. Thin and drawn in middle age, the elder Campbell grew more portly in his later years, and his eyes grew dim from much reading. He continued to wear his flowing white hair so long that it fell down over his shoulders. In his retirement Thomas took an active interest in all that concerned the movement of Disciples of Christ, kept up an extensive correspondence, wrote occasionally for publication and once or twice ventured forth to preach and teach as in former days. In 1840 Alexander had built an octagonal study for himself adjacent to his home and had left his older study, across the road from the house, available for his father. In these days of retirement and reflection the elder Campbell would spend many hours in the neat little brick study in meditation and prayer. He joined the family morning and evening for devotions and at these times he and Alexander alternated in reading the Scriptures and in reciting the portions memorized during the day.

In April, 1843, grandfather Campbell addressed a long letter to Alexander's daughter, Margaret, on the occasion of her fifteenth birthday. She was attending a "female seminary" conducted by P. S. Fall, an early leader of Disciples of Christ of Frankfort, Kentucky. In this letter to his granddaughter, Thomas tried to expound the invaluable meaning of the Christian faith and in the tenderest terms he described the joys of the Christian life.

About this time J. R. Frame, an evangelist, paid a visit to Bethany and proposed to Thomas Campbell a period of joint service with him to the churches of Ohio. Thomas agreed to consider the request and replied to Frame in a letter, dated May 16, 1843:

> I should be very glad to cooperate with you in this good work, for all the purposes you mentioned when you were here: but my son, Alexander, is quite opposed to my proceeding farther in itinerant labors at my advanced age of eighty years. He rather urges the application of my time to writing, and to local labors in the vicinity of Bethany. However, what I shall do I have not finally determined. But if I conclude to cooperate with you a part of this summer, I shall endeavor to be with you at the time and place mentioned.[35]

In this same letter the elder Campbell presented Frame with three "hints" on the purpose of evangelism: (1) the purpose of the gospel is to remake a person and should be fully taught before baptism, (2) the baptized person should be taught to follow all the commands of the New Testament, and (3) family worship is next in importance with its emphasis on the reading of Scripture and prayer.

Thomas Campbell's love for people and preaching must have led him to disregard his son's advice, for he met Frame in May at the Harmony meetinghouse not far from Cambridge, Ohio, where he had preached in 1814-1815. He must, indeed, have enjoyed visiting the friends and acquaintances of that period, and especially seeing the pupils of his school at Cambridge, who were now grown and had families of their own. All that summer he preached in Guernsey, Muskingum, and Washington counties in Ohio, and surprisingly enough, not only to congregations of Disciples of Christ, but in Baptist and Cumberland Presbyterian churches as well. He still preached sermons of two hours' duration. At Beverly, about twenty miles above Marietta, Ohio, he became ill with fatigue and overwork, but he soon recovered and proceeded on the tour. The congregations were strengthened by his preaching and many people were won to Christianity. About this time the elder Campbell gave up drinking either tea or coffee, and later on this trip he received the gift of "second sight" and was able to read without spectacles for several years. By the end of the summer he returned home to Bethany by way of the Ohio River, greatly exhausted and affected by the heat. He was never to go forth on such a tour again.

On May 25, 1843, Alexander addressed a letter to his father in Ohio, asking him to reply to an inquiry on "figurative allusions to baptism." Thomas' answer was printed in the June, 1843, issue of the *Millennial Harbinger,* in which he stated that on the basis of scriptural interpretation all institutions of a religious nature were figurative, and "baptism being of this class, must, of course, be so too." On November 15, 1843, the venerable Father Campbell addressed a letter to his companion of the summer months on the value of time. He said to Frame:

> O What a waste of our precious time in this carnal, ungodly age! If the time that is spent in mere trifling—in talking, and thinking about things of no value, or to no real purpose, was spent in reading, memorizing, studying, meditating upon, and conversing about the contents of the Holy Scriptures, and in praying to and praising God about them, O what hundreds—yes, thousands—of pages of the Good Book would be read, understood, possessed and enjoyed, for one there is at present![36]

Another letter was sent to Frame on January 8, 1844, in which Thomas apologized for having so long delayed in answering Frame's letter of September 27, 1843. He said: "I have been so situated for some months past, that I could pay but little attention to letter-writing." The purpose of the letter was to discuss further the idea of baptism as it relates to Christian training:

> Baptism but brings us into the church—the school of Christ. We have then to be taught to observe all the THINGS which he commanded . . . amongst which, the training up of the children in the nurture and admonition of the Lord, is a most important item. Children cannot have one religious idea but what they learn from their parents and teachers. They obtain the ideas of sensible objects by the natural use of their senses, but not so of spiritual things, for faith comes by hearing the word of God. . . .
>
> You see, then, dear brother, that laboring to make disciples, and duly training them afterwards, are two very different things; and that the latter is by far the more important, for what use in persuading a person to go to school, unless he be duly taught afterwards?[37]

On January 17, 1844, Thomas Campbell wrote a lengthy letter to "S.R.J." in which he reviewed the reasons for the movement of Disciples of Christ and made it clear that he felt some individuals were emphasizing the wrong things. The letter is typical of Thomas' thoughts of the period which were characterized by this evaluation of his life's work. He said:

> The reformation which we propose as defined in the fourth page of our Declaration and Address . . . expressly excludes the teaching of anything as a matter of the Christian faith or duty for which there can not be express terms or by approved precedent. Upon these propositions the Baptists at first cordially received us and some years afterwards were excited to reject us . . . nevertheless, we have always considered and treated them as brethren as far as they would permit us; and as far as I am concerned, always intend to do so. And in the meantime we would humbly advise you so to treat them. . . .

Dear Brother: Christian union upon Christian principles is our motto, our object. Now to perfect this union in faith and holiness ought to be our grand concern. For what is profession without possession?[38]

This letter was published in the March, 1844, issue of the *Millennial Harbinger*. In the same issue a letter from "T.C." to "D" written in February is published. Typical of many of Thomas Campbell's letters at this time, it replied to a question concerning the order of the church and what should be done to discipline elders who were neglectful of duty. Campbell urged "prayer and fasting."

From the frequent references Thomas Campbell made during these years to the *Declaration and Address* it can be supposed that he spent many of his hours of retirement in reflection on that document. In May, 1844, he referred to the Address when he published an article called "An Address to all our Christian Brethren—Upon the Necessity and Importance of the Actual Enjoyment of Our Holy Religion." This article, as was true of several mentioned before, endeavored to direct the attention of the growing movement of Disciples of Christ to the original purpose of the *Declaration and Address*, that of encouraging Christian union on the authority of the Bible alone. The elder Campbell was indirectly voicing his criticism of those individuals who were seeking to lead the movement into doctrinal and speculative emphases. In this regard he said:

Although the promotion and maintenance of Christian union upon Christian principle, is a most important and indispensable duty; yet as it consists in the detection and correction of erroneous opinions and practices, and thus employs the mind in abstract speculations; it is, therefore, unfavorable to those mental exercises, in which the enjoyment of our holy religion consists.

According to that highly important portion, if a man had all attainments, that grace or nature could confer, and yet had not

Christian love, he would be a mere cypher in Christianity; he would not have the first principle of it. . . . Theorizing, criticizing, and practicing, are very different exercises. We may be proficients in the two former, and very deficient in the latter. . . . Wherefore, my beloved brethren, if you would really enjoy our holy religion, you must preserve and abound in the exercises of evangelical faith, hope and love.[39]

In a long "P.S." Campbell enjoined the brethren to read and reread his advice in these matters and in addition to consult frequently the "gracious declarations, invitations and promises of the blessed gospel."

The lead article in the November, 1844, issue of the *Millennial Harbinger* was entitled "A Synopsis of Christianity" and was introduced by his son, Alexander, who said that the article was a summary of all his father's seventy years thinking on the Christian religion, sustained by many quotations from Scripture. Alexander apologized for the length and seeming redundancy of the writing, explaining that his father was "fond of the old style of expressing himself." Immediately following this introduction Thomas plunged into his "synopsis" of the Christian religion:

> Christianity is emphatically, supereminently—yea, transcendently, the religion of love: that is, of affectionate attachment, benevolence, and beneficence; for its Divine Author, subject matter, and effects, are all love in the highest possible degree. . . . So are all its grand fundamental facts, the effects of divine love. Namely, 1st. The divine assumption of our humanity in its present debased degraded condition. 2. The personal gift of the Holy Spirit to inhabit our nature, thus assumed. 3. The deep humiliation, cruel maltreatment, tremendous sufferings, and ignominious death of this glorious personage, our Divine Emanuel. 4. His glorious resurrection and infinite exaltation above all heavens. 5. The mission and descent of the Holy Spirit upon the disciples on the day of Pentecost, to dwell in them, and to be with them for ever; and likewise in and with all them that should believe through their word.

Now, if it be scripturally evident to demonstration, from the above mentioned facts and documents (and we humbly presume it is), that our holy religion, in its Divine Author, subject matter, and effects, is pure and perfect love; what remains, then, but that we so avail ourselves of it, as to get into the actual possession of this blissful attainment? . . .[40]

In the remaining pages of the article the venerable and aging Campbell called as witness and authority the multitude of scriptural passages which seemed to him to bear out his introduction and to prove the "gospel facts." In doing this he made a distinction between the Old and New Testaments, and always based conclusions on the New Testament.

Views on Slavery

For many years prior to 1845 both Thomas and Alexander Campbell had been urged by their friends to speak openly on the growing tension between the northern and southern states on the question of slavery. From the second decade of the nineteenth century this was the dominant political issue in the United States, and by 1830 the first period of antislavery agitation had come to an end, and a new and more aggressive movement began. This new phase of antislavery agitation was brought about chiefly by two factors: (1) the increased demand for cotton and (2) the rise in the North of a new and aggressive antislavery leadership. The new antislavery movement found ready support among church people, and it was not long until the question of slavery became a religious issue of prime importance. This radical support of the abolition movement among the churches of the North was met by proslavery defenders in the South.

The Campbells, placed geographically as they were, not far from the Mason-Dixon line, had their attitude on this vexing question solicited by many. In some matters the convictions and attitudes of the two Campbells, father and son, were so interwoven that it is difficult to separate them, and this was particularly true on the question of slavery. The father's views on preaching the gospel to the slaves have been shown in his hasty departure from Kentucky in 1819. Alexander at one time had owned a few young slaves, but these had been freed on reaching maturity. Neither the father nor the son had publicly declared their position at the beginning of the year 1845, the year that was to bring the issue to a head in several denominations. In May, 1845, the Baptist convention met at Augusta, Georgia, and voted to organize a "Southern Baptist Convention" and the crisis had been reached in the General Conference of the Methodist church in New York in May, 1844. This conference occupied itself in the closing days of the session with drawing up a Plan of Separation, which resulted in the founding of the Methodist Episcopal Church, South, in 1845. The Presbyterians, however, remained united until 1861 and did not divide until after the outbreak of the War between the States.

It was, therefore, with more than casual interest that the readers of the *Millennial Harbinger* opened their copy for January, 1845, to find a statement from Alexander Campbell in the "Preface," which he traditionally wrote for the first issue of each year, that

> Our position, as a religious community, in the pending controversy between the North and the South, on the subject of Slavery, seems also to call for some attention from us. Our duties should be clearly defined and our attitude in respect to those conflicting views fully ascertained. To these subjects we must pay such attention as the crisis demands. We commence the volume with a statement of the views of Elder Thomas Campbell on this complex subject, elicited from him some few years ago. . . .[41]

The father had written his views on the subject of slavery privately to Cyrus McNeely of Ohio in August, 1841, and it was this letter which was now carefully revised by the elder Campbell and published under his supervision. As was usual with Thomas Campbell, he began with a full listing of all biblical references on the subject of slavery and servitude beginning with Genesis and continuing through the New Testament. Upon this "evidence" he proceeded to draw the following deductions:

1st. That slavery, or servitude, of the most servile and degrading character, was divinely pronounced and inflicted upon a portion of the human family, on account of sin. . . .

2d. That to have and to hold servants, as purchases and permanent property, is divinely permitted. . . .

3d. That this state or condition of servitude, or slavery, was sometimes voluntary; but that in many cases it was involuntary. . . . These things being evidently so, it necessarily follows, that, according to the express tenor of the divine legislature above referred to, "all men are" not "born free and equal:" consequently, are not the subjects of equal rights. Nevertheless, it is equally evident . . . that all possess natural rights, of which they cannot be deprived upon any pretence. . . .

4th. That as fraudulent and violent means of reducing persons to slavery . . . are divinely prohibited . . . and especially as the Christian is divinely commanded to love his neighbor as himself, and to do to all as he would have them to do to him, therefore Christians should have nothing to do with encouraging involuntary servitude.

From these studies the elder Campbell concluded that

Upon the whole, with respect to American slavery, wherever distinguished by any inhuman and antichristian adjuncts, by any unnatural, immoral, and irreligious usages, we may justly and reasonably conclude that as Christianity and truly moralized humanity prevail, it must and will go down; and that, in these respects, no Christian can either approve or practise it. . . . Wherefore, it becomes the American people, both as citizens and Christians, to consider these things, and so to discharge their duties, both civil and religious, for the amelioration and ultimate abolition of slavery; especially those of them that have embraced the gospel.[42]

Neither the father nor the son approved the abuses of power connected with slavery but at the same time found themselves in opposition to the extremes of the anti-slavery forces.

By putting Thomas' letter in the January issue of the magazine, Alexander was preparing the way to declare himself on this question. From the series of articles by Alexander entitled "Our Position to American Slavery" which began in the February, 1845, issue, it was apparent that Alexander did not entirely agree with his father on the subject. Alexander found himself possessed by an understanding appreciation for the problems of his brethren of both the North and the South; he, therefore, took a mediating position. He objected to the institution of slavery, but objected more to the methods of the abolitionists. As he interpreted Scripture, he thought slavery was acceptable in God's sight, and from the political standpoint, he upheld the institution because it was sanctioned by law. Economically and socially, he was against slavery and thought the country would be better off without it. In short, he felt that the slavery question was "a matter of opinion" and should never be made a test of fellowship. Actually this viewpoint, while unpopular with both North and South at the time, enabled the adolescent movement of Disciples of Christ to remain united throughout the entire period of civil strife.

From March to May, 1845, Alexander was away from Bethany on an extended tour of the South and his father again served as editor of the *Millennial Harbinger*. Thus the elder Campbell took occasion in the May issue to state further his position on slavery:

> I am not, therefore, to be considered as advocating the cause of American slavery; nor, indeed of slavery of any kind, absolutely considered; but only in so far as the Bible authorises it; and when managed accordingly, to the real good of the parties. This far the church is concerned, and no farther. That is, to see that the parties do their duties to each other according to the law of Christ; and if not, to cast them out of his church. . . .[43]

It is apparent that the Campbells did not sidestep their responsibility in helping Disciples of Christ decide the church's attitude on the slavery question. It would be difficult, indeed, to measure the influence of Thomas Campbell, first, over his son, and secondly, over the entire movement, in keeping that movement from dividing over this question and following in the path of their religious neighbors.

"Faithful Unto Death"

In this same May issue of the *Millennial Harbinger* there was a "Brief Scriptural Exhibition of the Laws and Duties of Matrimony" from the pen of the eighty-two-year-old father. After the usual survey of all Scripture on the subject it was apparent that the elder Campbell was opposed to divorce for he felt that the family relation was the basis of society. The May issue also contained answers to questions submitted by one of the readers on the office of deacon and elder and in regard to discipline in the church. Still another communication from Thomas Campbell's hand is included in this issue, addressed to N. H. Finney, a converted atheist who was on his way to New England to evangelize. Thomas advised him on the scriptural basis of the movement of Disciples of Christ and on the need to preach the truth in love. He closed with what is possibly the last treatment by Thomas Campbell of the subject of baptism:

> What a pity that Christians should be divided by a difference about the one baptism, which is the very door of the church, by which we enter into the one family,—under the one Father! . . . For no person was considered a Christian in the apostolic churches, who had not confessed Christ as his Lord and Saviour in baptism. . . . And this difference not only about the action to be performed, but also about the proper subject of it! Alas! Alas! this radical evil! But we cannot help it. All that we can do is to show from the Good Book, that neither the action or the subject is left indefinite. . . .[44]

For the next several years, from 1845 to 1851, Thomas Campbell seemed to be content to settle down among his relatives, manuscripts, and books.[45] Some of his unpublished manuscripts were readied for the press and during Alexander's extended tour of Great Britain and the continent in 1847, while W. K. Pendleton and Robert Richardson edited the *Millennial Harbinger*, several of these manuscripts found their way into its pages. In the June, 1847, issue there was a letter on "Baptism" which reviewed Thomas' previous teachings on the subject and the Scriptures pertaining to it. A long article on "Christian Society" appeared in the July issue, prepared in June, which dealt with a Christian's conversation:

... his conversation must be divine, unless he acts out of character and disobeys his Creator and Redeemer. We do not mean, however, that a Christian must be always conversing about divine things, but that his conversation must be always governed by divine law. Christians must necessarily converse with the world, and with each other, about worldly things, as far as necessary; yet redeeming the time, as much as possible, for better purposes.[46]

Thomas Campbell passed his days quietly in study and meditation, but during the summer of 1847, his hearing and eyesight began to leave him once again and he found himself more confined than ever. He wrote to his daughter, Dorothea Bryant, who, with her husband and family had moved to Marion, Ohio, that:

... my hearing is a little dull, and my sight is much more so. I can scarcely see to walk along our common roads, or distinguish faces; it has been growing sensibly more dim every week since I saw you; so that I scarcely attempt to write ... in looking over my old religious manuscripts, I have selected a few of them for publication in the *Millennial Harbinger*, two of which are already published in the last two numbers. I have also selected one for the next. . .[47]

The article to which father Campbell referred was another essay on "The Means of Enjoying Our Holy

Religion," in which he attempted to answer the question "What are the divinely appointed means for the enjoyment of the proposed salvation?" His answer:

1. A reverential, sincere, persevering, studious attention to the holy scriptures, in order to a clear apprehension and distinct retention of their doctrinal contents. 2. A conscientious practical attention to the divine commands and promises, prohibitions and threatenings, contained in the sacred volume, so as consciously and gratefully to embrace and obey the former; and, with equal scrupulosity, to guard against and avoid the latter. This two-fold use of the divine volume, for the threefold purpose of acquiring that knowledge, faith and obedience, which constitute our present salvation, and prepare us for the enjoyment of that which is yet to be revealed in the last time, is the constant and immediate duty and high privilege of every disciple of Christ. . . .[48]

In the September and December issues another two of the elder Campbell's manuscripts are put to press. They are among the longest documents he had yet submitted but contain little that is new or of more than passing interest. The September article had been written April 16, 1832, and was addressed to "The Brethren who meet at Matthews . . . Thomas Campbell sendeth Christian salutation" in which he attempted to explain and defend the reformers from the attacks they were then receiving from the Baptists.[49] The article in the December issue bore the intriguing title: "The Disease, the Cure, and the Means of Enjoying It," which on examination turns out to be another scriptural view of man's depraved condition, the provisions of God to remedy that condition, and the means of continuing in God's grace, once it has been attained. This was by far the longest article Campbell ever submitted to the *Millennial Harbinger*.[50]

Shortly after 1848 the dimness noted during the summer of 1847 turned into total blindness which must, indeed, have been a privation to one who enjoyed reading so much. He bore his burden with resignation and patience, however, and retained a vigorous mind. It was his pleasure, during his blindness, to talk with the many visitors who came regularly to Bethany on business or to confer with Alexander. He enjoyed reciting the various hymns and hundreds of scriptural passages with which his memory was stored, but always with a comment or explanation as to the meaning of the hymn or passage in the Christian life. Sometimes he would courteously request a visitor or a member of the family to read a certain hymn or portion of the Scripture which he wanted to hear or to memorize. As the years passed, friends and relatives became more and more aware of his frailty, and he was asked to preach a "farewell" sermon at the Bethany church. He consented and it was arranged for him to speak on Sunday, June 1, 1851. He became quite interested in what he would say on the occasion and had Alexander's wife read many passages of Scripture to him, as he prepared himself, especially the story of the Good Samaritan.

Thomas Campbell was then eighty-eight years old, and when at last the day arrived, he was so enfeebled that he could not get into a carriage or buggy, fearing high places. Despite the spring rains, a large horse-drawn sled was used for transporting him to the old stone meetinghouse, where he was met by two deacons of the church and escorted down the center aisle to a special seat near the front. A large congregation had gathered to hear the widely known and venerated patriarch, among them a large number of girls from the McKeaver's female seminary at West Middletown and students from Bethany College. Thomas' daughter, Jane, and his son-in-law, Matthew McKeaver, were there; but Alexander did not get to hear his father, for he was away on a trip. W. K. Pendleton, Alexander's son-in-law and professor at Bethany College, took down the message in its entirety and described the aged preacher and man of God as impaired somewhat in memory but able to speak in a clear and distinct voice. It is significant that Thomas chose as his text Matthew 22:37-40: "Thou shalt love the Lord thy God with all thy heart, and with all thy soul, and with all thy mind . . . and thy neighbor as thyself." Campbell declared as his purpose in the sermon that "I am, by his strengthening grace here to commune with you, as best I can, upon the common duties, privileges and hopes of the people of God." He urged that Christians search the Scriptures night and day "that we may come rightly to apprehend and truly to realize the revealed character of our God, and thus fully to enjoy his salvation." He closed by saying:

. . . I can say no more to you, as the last words of a public ministry, protracted, under the merciful care of our heavenly father, for more than three-score years, in this my farewell exhortation to you on earth—I can say no more than what I have already so often urged upon you. . . .[51]

Early in 1853 James Challen, a great admirer of the "venerable Father Campbell" and the publisher of a Disciples magazine in Philadelphia entitled *Ladies' Christian Annual,* journeyed to Bethany to interview Thomas Campbell for his paper. His report indicated that

. . . In the absence of his son Alexander, he daily leads in family worship. . . . His memory, is, of course, very defective. . . . He sits in his comfortable armchair before the fire throughout the day, occasionally rising to change his position or for exercise. He still shaves himself, and attends to his toilet with scrupulous exactness. He retires to his chamber alone, in accordance with his own wishes, and rises without any aid from the family, as he is extremely reluctant to give the least possible trouble to any about him. His wants are all fully anticipated, and every possible attention paid him by every member of the family, not only from a sense of duty, but from pure affection. Indeed, no one can be near him without loving him. He is so kind and gentle, so courteous and bland, and so grateful even for the smallest favors. . . .

He still carries about him his old watch, and daily has it set to correspond with the family timepiece. . . . Time with him was always a sacred thing; he knew its value, and still prizes it. . . .[52]

This article was to appear in the *Ladies' Christian Annual* for January, 1854, together with a steel engraved lithograph from an oil painting produced when Campbell was about seventy years old. Challen had written, nearly a year earlier, "Soon, very soon will he pass away from among us," and hardly had the magazine been published in 1854 when word arrived that Thomas Campbell, "the venerable Father Campbell," had died on January 4, a month before his ninety-first birthday.

CHAPTER SEVEN

THE SUMMING UP

DESPITE his advanced age, Thomas Campbell remained in fair health until just a few weeks before his death. He retired and rose at regular hours, slept soundly and had a good appetite, but about the middle of December, 1853, he was stricken suddenly with an illness which affected his digestive system. He was patient and calm during the three weeks of his illness, and remained bedfast only four days. He told Alexander when he was first stricken, "I am going home and will soon pass over Jordan," and rejoiced in the prospect. His mind was clear and strong but because of an extremely sore mouth he could talk but little and his last days were spent almost in silence. The end came on Wednesday, January 4, 1854, about seven o'clock in the evening, at Bethany in the house which had been his home for many years. His children and his grandchildren were gathered around him when, without struggle, he gently breathed his last. He was laid to rest in the family cemetery at Bethany by the side of the wife who had been his helpmate for so many years. Even though they had realized his great age, his wide circle of friends and acquaintances were shocked and saddened when they received word of the death of "Father Campbell." Because he had not been aggressive like his son, he had made no enemies and had gained a host of lifelong friends. He had lived a long and useful life and in his lifetime had witnessed the growth of Disciples of Christ from a small group into a religious movement having followers in most of the United States.

The February, 1854, issue of the *Millennial Harbinger* carried the notice of the elder Campbell's death and the resolutions made by the students of Bethany College which testified to the esteem and affection in which he was held. In the same issue Robert Richardson wrote the obituary notice for the *Harbinger* with a heavy sense of personal loss:

I have to announce to the brethren and friends of the reformation, the death of the venerable Thomas Campbell, Sr. He died on the evening of Wednesday, January 4th, having attained to the advanced age of ninety-one years, lacking about a month.

Preceding a brief account of Campbell's life, Richardson eulogized him:

. . . Our beloved Father Campbell had been so long and so earnestly devoted to the cause of religious reformation, for which alone he seemed to live and labor, and had made, while thus engaged, so many journeyings through different parts of the United States, that he had formed a very widely extended circle of acquaintances and friends, to whom he was justly endeared, not only by these labors of love, but also by personal qualities so engaging as to command universal love and veneration.

Never was there an individual who manifested greater reverence for the Word of God, or a truer desire to see it faithfully obeyed. Yet this trust in the Divine word was not with him a mere verbal confidence, a faith or knowledge, like that of some professors, merely intellectual—lexical and grammatical; for never was there one who more fully recognized the spirituality of the gospel, or sought more diligently to impress all around him with the importance of the Holy Spirit in the salvation of the soul . . . and never was there one who more fully exemplified the doctrine which he taught, or whose life was more evidently guided by the teachings of the spirit, and controlled by the Divine principle of love to God and man.[1]

Alexander spoke of his father's death in a letter written January 24, 1854, to a Brother Dungan of Baltimore:

. . . I presume you may have already heard that Father Campbell has joined the Church above and entered into rest, where the wicked cease from troubling and the weary are at rest. . . . I never knew a man, in all my acquaintance with men, of whom it could have been said with more assurance that he "walked with God." Such was the even tenor of his path, not for a few years, but a period as far back as my memory reaches. . .[2]

Thomas Campbell was the second of the "big four" of the early leaders of Disciples of Christ to die. Barton W. Stone had died in 1844, and Walter Scott died a few years after Thomas, in 1861. Alexander was the only one of the original founders who remained, and his health began to decline the year of his father's death.

Those who had known Thomas Campbell, especially the friends of his last years, remembered a courteous and kindly old gentleman, who was most pious and devout. The sketch sent by Walter Scott from Mayslick, Kentucky, May 8, 1860, and written for publication in the *Millennial Harbinger* is typical of those incorporated by Alexander in the memoirs of his father which he published. Scott said, in part:

Touching his religion, he was the most devout man I ever knew. He loved God, and adored him for the gift of his Son in our great redemption. He was a man of prayer, a man of reading, a man of holy meditation, excogitation, and reformation. He was fond of the analogies between the two Divine systems, nature and religion, and read with delight, in the works of God, the spiritual relations of the universe. . . He had tasted of the sovereign and universal good, and his heart was in the heavens. He was the most exemplary man I ever saw. His memory is blessed.[3]

An early Disciple publication, the *Christian Age* for 1853, carried a tribute to Thomas Campbell which is valuable in showing something of the affection with which the elder Campbell was regarded and the impression of saintly benignity which he gave:

I felt a spirit of deep reverence upon me in the presence of this man of God, beyond that which I have ever felt in the presence of any other man. His age, his long experience in the ways of God, his sincere devotion to truth and righteousness, his untiring labors in the ministry for more than the ordinary limit of the life of man, the simplicity of his life, the patriarchical grandeur of his appearance, and his unaffected piety, left a deep impression on my mind which cannot easily be effaced.[4]

The estimate of Errett Gates, writing in 1904, illustrates the typical view of the elder Campbell fifty years after his death. Gates paints the picture of a man who "loved God and all men," and portrays him as one who longed for the fellowship of all God's people—a man of profound spirituality, Christlike gentleness and sweetness of spirit. In short, an echo of the judgment of Thomas Campbell's contemporaries. It was Gates's judgment that:

> Sectarianism and division wounded his heart and contradicted his nature. It was his discovery that the will of God as expressed in the New Testament was opposed to division that touched his gentle spirit into prophetic fervor.[5]

James Harvey Garrison, a second generation leader of Disciples of Christ, dedicated one of his volumes to Thomas Campbell and in doing so gave the evaluation current in his day:

> To the memory of Thomas Campbell, saintly pioneer, who, in an age of religious strife and bitterness, breathed the sweet spirit of peace and catholicity, and who, moved by the Spirit of Christ, lifted a banner of unity which is today an ensign of hope to millions of longing souls who are praying for a united church.[6]

In 1909 a great convention was held at Pittsburgh, Pennsylvania, celebrating the one hundredth anniversary of the publication of the *Declaration and Address*. Already the name of "Father Campbell" had become legendary, and he was described as "unselfish and self-sacrificing . . . willing to take the lowest place in the kingdom . . . a man of faith and prayer." One of the speakers at the centennial celebration said:

Thomas Campbell was a mild and kindly spirit, and while it may be granted that there was a period in which definition and argument were necessary . . . we shall have more and more use for that broad and conciliatory spirit that pervaded the "Declaration and Address." We shall do well in the opening of our second century to study the life and writings of this godly man.[7]

Archibald McLean, the beloved missionary leader of the brotherhood and fourth President of Bethany College, wrote on that occasion that Thomas Campbell was a Christian gentleman in the truest sense of the word. It was McLean's judgment that Campbell always avoided sarcasm and irony in speaking and writing, and that he was a man of catholic sympathies. McLean illustrated his point by recalling some of the expressions Campbell used to greet those who differed from him: "Dearly beloved brethren . . . you lovers of Jesus and beloved by him . . . our brethren in all denominations."[8] Clinton Lockhart, later President of Texas Christian University, in his address at the convention gave an inventory of those things inherited by the movement from Thomas Campbell:

1. His personal experience with the partisan spirit of his time.
2. The invaluable truth that sectarianism is sin.
3. The discovery that in opinions Christians are and ought to be free from ecclesiastical domination.
4. His insistence on a careful definition of the limits of the faith essential to salvation and to fellowship.
5. His rediscovery of the apostolic terms of fellowship and the ordinances of baptism and the Lord's Supper.
6. The proposed basis of Christian union, letting the Scriptures alone mark the common pathway of personal and congregational conduct.[9]

In the fifty years since the elder Campbell's death the idea of his imperturbable good will, his piety, and his emphasis on a scriptural basis for Christian union, had been uncritically accepted by most of those who had shown interest in his life and contribution. This does not imply that there was always agreement as to Thomas Campbell's major contribution to the movement of Disciples of Christ. Herbert L. Willett at the 1909 convention characterized that contribution as follows:

> When one turns to ask what was the essence of his message, the answer must be given in clear and emphatic form. Mr. Campbell did not concern himself with a variety of interests. . . . He held to one principle and to one alone—the union of God's people. To that one theme he devoted his life; he lived for nothing else . . . the one principle which absorbed him and claimed his life, was the truth that the church is ideally one, and ought to realize that unity in actual and visible experience. . . .[10]

W. T. Moore, who compiled the first comprehensive history of the movement, gave a still different emphasis:

> . . . All his contributions breathed the same spirit as that which was manifest in the "Declaration and Address." . . . In every sentence he ever wrote, and in every sermon he preached, love was the supreme characteristic.[11]

From these excerpts and evaluations of the first decade of the twentieth century it is obvious that the judgment of Thomas Campbell's contemporaries, especially those who knew him in retirement as the "venerable Father Campbell," had been accepted at face value and that no serious effort had been made to study either his life or contribution. Most of those who wrote and spoke in the early years of this century simply reflected the impressions of the earlier period.

The only recent study of Thomas Campbell's life, William Herbert Hanna's *Thomas Campbell, Seceder and Christian Union Advocate*, still emphasized the Christian union activities of Thomas' life and had as its main purpose the attempt to prove that Campbell was at first a sectarian-minded Seceder Presbyterian but that later when he made the great discovery of the "apostolic church" on the American frontier, he became an advocate of Christian union for the rest of his life. The following quotation summarizes Hanna's viewpoint:

> This present critical age must bear witness to the clarity of vision, both mental and spiritual, of our subject. Whether defending himself in the heresy trial, or advocating Christian union and apostolic Christianity, he was neither foggy nor muddy in ideas. ... He saw as a way to reunion and unbroken fellowship among believers a re-assessment of the place of Christ and the apostles in the church and a devaluation of creeds "of human composure" as tests and bonds of fellowship. He set Christ in and over the entire church without apology in true Pauline fashion, and registered his dependence absolutely upon the apostolic writings for knowledge of the life and revelation and will of Jesus Christ.[12]

In a final chapter, entitled "The Plea and Plan: Amend or Adopt?", Hanna asserted that Thomas Campbell had rediscovered the essential truth of Christian union so long hidden from Christian eyes:

> In the century and a quarter since 1809, there have sprung into existence several scores of new sects and parties, denominations and communions under the Christian banner. So what? The older Christianity becomes, the more plagued by partyism does it become? The more Christian union is advocated, the more it is disregarded and shown to be impossible of attainment? In a sense, there is a gain in the very multiplication of divisions, for it demonstrates that human creeds are unable to unite Christians. So was the contention of Thomas Campbell. ... The breaking up of denominations and the breaking down of denominational walls would seem to be incidental to the making of one fellowship, one church, not a huge ecclesiasticism, but in Christ.[13]

Two statements of more recent date must be mentioned. One of these was made by Winfred Ernest Garrison, son of James H. Garrison, and himself a student of the history of Disciples of Christ. In one of his books about Disciples of Christ he gives a cursory review of the life and contribution of Thomas Campbell and expresses his belief that

... After the "Declaration and Address," Thomas Campbell never wrote a line, delivered a speech, or made a decision which had any marked effect on the faith or fortunes of the movement which he had started.[14]

The second statement gives the judgment that

... The brotherhood, though it has honored Thomas Campbell and Barton W. Stone, as great men, nevertheless has followed in patterns set by Alexander Campbell, Walter Scott, David Staats Burnet, and Isaac Errett.[15]

It is the judgment of the present writer that Thomas Campbell was active not only in assisting Alexander but also in helping to make the basic decisions which confronted the young movement after 1809. It is evident from the facts that Campbell influenced the "brotherhood" known as Disciples of Christ much more fundamentally than has been commonly recognized. In organization patterns, in methods and publications, and in institutional development, the communion may have followed Alexander Campbell, Scott, and the others but in its inner spirit and its penetrating emphasis on the Scriptures the influence was primarily that of the elder Campbell.

Before proceeding further with the evidence for this judgment however, mention must be made of one or two theories that have been tentatively advanced as to the real contribution of Thomas Campbell to the movement. Nothing has been written to prove the idea, but from time to time the theory has been advanced among students of the movement of Disciples of Christ that there was a serious quarrel between Thomas Campbell and his son. This theory has been built around the possible jealousy of Thomas over the assumption of leadership by Alexander and over the disagreement expressed in the pages of the *Millennial Harbinger* on the name of the movement and the direction which it took. The facts, however, do not in any way substantiate such a conjecture. Another school of thought has tried to see in Thomas Campbell an irenic, tolerant, and truly liberal leader, if only his true nature were known and if he could have been freed of a dominating son. As proof of this theory its advocates point to the elder Campbell's attitude toward pedobaptism at the time of the writing of the *Declaration and Address* and his later acceptance of immersion, supposedly to keep peace with Alexander. Those who advance this theory have felt that Thomas came to immersion reluctantly and was really indifferent on the subject. Again, the facts do not warrant such a conclusion. After his acceptance of immersion for himself, Thomas Campbell sincerely and consistently preached and believed that this was the true teaching of the New Testament.

As the story of Thomas Campbell's life is pieced out from the scanty materials which have been preserved for us, simple candor compels us to confess that he was not a great man in the sense of much that the world calls greatness. Though gifted with excellent intellectual ability, he was not outstandingly brilliant. Though effective in public speech and writing, he had few of the attributes of a great preacher, and in his writing used a verbose style ill-suited to the American frontier. Yet, he was a humble and sincere, pious and devout, minister of the gospel of Christ. He clung steadfastly to whatever he believed was the expressed teaching of the Scriptures, and consistently preached and taught his honest convictions. Not possessing the full powers of dynamic leadership of his more gifted son, Thomas Campbell willingly stayed in the background of the movement which his document and principles brought into being. The elder Campbell's inadequacy as a vigorous leader first became apparent in the confusion and uncertainty which he evidenced when confronted by the opposition of the presbytery and later by the synod. He was not able to see clearly the direction in which he was going and was therefore hardly in a position to give leadership to others. Over and over again in the *Declaration and Address* and in the Christian Association, Thomas Campbell disclaimed any desire for leadership or for the formation of a movement, even when it was obvious that this was the only way in which the purposes of the group could hope to be accomplished. Even Alexander, young as he was, could see the mistake of the attempt at union with the Presbyterian Synod of Pittsburgh.

Thomas Campbell's desire, during all of these events, was to be left alone to minister to people as a simple clergyman, with the privilege of preaching and teaching his convictions without interference. When challenged he unhesitatingly defended his position, but it was not a task which he relished. Only when Alexander proved to be more outstanding than his father—in leadership, preaching, and organization—was the permanence of the movement brought into being by the father assured. The ineptness of the catechetical question at the time of the formation of the Brush Run Church and Thomas' awkwardness in performing the first immersion of this church are but symbols of his ineffective, though well-meaning, leadership. His personal acceptance of immersion as the express teaching of the New Testament, following the lead of Alexander, crystallized the establishment of a new sect. In later years his futile attempts to call the movement away from bitterness and controversy, and to get it to return to the fundamental principle of the *Declaration and Address,* that of Christian union on a return to New Testament teaching, were an anticlimax. In the sectarian spirit which had developed within the movement itself, to "restore the purity of the early church," there was little hope that those who followed the ambitious Alexander Campbell and the fiery Walter Scott would listen to the peace-loving old man, no matter how "venerable" or devout.

It is not in these areas that one must turn for a true conception of the contribution of Thomas Campbell. This can be revealed only after the known facts of his life have been carefully fitted together and reviewed. That he was pious is well attested to by the many references in his life story to the practice of daily devotions in the family, dating from the earliest days of his married life in Ireland. He was theologically a Calvinist and remained one, in every point except baptism, to the end of his days. There is no proof to the contrary and his writings in the *Millennial Harbinger* are evidence of this position. With all of his many admirable qualities, Thomas Campbell was undoubtedly tedious at times. It is recalled that as a young minister he received a severe caning for keeping his aged father too long on his knees at prayer. His sermons were more than two hours in length, and his contributions to the religious publications of his son were anything but brief. Walter Scott put it kindly when he said on one occasion that "... he often protracted his speech to a great length—the manners and the taste of the times demanding it...."

These, however, are only superficial attributes and qualities of the man. They are not the qualities for which he is, or deserves to be, remembered. It must never be forgotten that Thomas Campbell was chief teacher of his son Alexander. It was he who guided much of Alexander's elementary training in Ireland, and it was he who prepared him for the university. Since Alexander had had only a relatively few months at the university, it was the father who continued the son's training in this country. There is ample material available for a full study of the influence of Thomas Campbell on his son, Alexander, and it will doubtless one day be made. But more important than this is the contribution of the *Declaration and Address* to the shelf of the church's literature on Christian union. The *Declaration and Address* is a significant document, and the formulation and statement of its principles alone would entitle Thomas Campbell to an honored place in the history of the brotherhood of Disciples of Christ and of the ecumenical movement.

While it is true that Thomas Campbell's most progressive and creative years were those up to and including the writing of the *Declaration and Address* and the formation of the Christian Association of Washington, it is equally true that the last half of his life had its contribution to make also. It is not entirely fair to Campbell to say that he had no effect on the movement after 1809. The essential importance of those years after 1809 is the elder Campbell's steadying influence on the newly formed sect. While the father and son did not always agree on teachings and the advisability of published writings, they did agree on the great fundamentals, and more importantly still, Thomas Campbell provided stability to the young movement and served as a check against the son's excesses. Thomas was not the only stabilizing influence, to be sure, but as Alexander's father and chief counselor, he was in a better position to exercise that power than either Barton W. Stone or Walter Scott. Alexander Campbell had a commanding personality which enabled him to become the outstanding leader of the four men, but he lacked the temperament which made for the stability of the group. Walter Scott, Barton W. Stone, and especially Thomas Campbell, gave Alexander crucial assistance in keeping Disciples of Christ from utter confusion in those early days of the movement when ministers from diverse backgrounds were being assimilated into the movement and so many new members and churches were added. A friend of Alexander's in the movement observed:

> Brother Campbell's weakness was in his ambition: he could not brook the idea of having a rival; he would rather have been the first man in a village, than the second man in a city.[16]

Robert F. West, writing of this weakness of Alexander Campbell and of the several movements that made up the brotherhood of Disciples of Christ, expressed the idea of stability in the following manner:

> Alexander Campbell was willing to feed the young movements after they got into the world and he wanted the credit. But he needed the advice and help of Scott, Stone, and his father or he would have strangled the infants with excessive and irregular feedings. He knew better about the protection, defense, and inspiration of the children than about the more stabilizing elements of their inner growth.... The others had the humility, the sympathy, and the consistency which help to sustain the growth of churches in Christian history.[17]

It must be said, however, that while the idea of stability explains something of the contribution of the last years, one must search further for the key that will unlock the door to the truth about Thomas Campbell. He was devout and pious; he was considered irenic; and he did advocate Christian union on a scriptural basis, but there is something more. These factors in and of themselves are inadequate to describe the man and his total contribution.

When all the known facts are assembled and when his life is viewed as a whole, it becomes transparently clear that Thomas Campbell was simply a man of the Book. He was an educated but humble and believing Presbyterian minister, who, studying the Bible constantly, opened his mind and heart to receive God's truth as it was revealed to him through the pages of the Scriptures. He studied God's word diligently, and therein sought salvation for himself and his fellow man. Early in life he turned to a study of the Scriptures and spent much time even as a youth seeking God's will for his life. When he had established his family, it became an invariable rule with him to memorize some portion of the Bible every day and to seek to interpret its meaning for the day's tasks. This was a lifelong habit. As a young minister Campbell centered his personal study and spiritual development on the Bible. It is recalled that Alexander saw his father in middle age surrounded with religious literature but studying only the Scriptures. It was most significant when Thomas Campbell took the catechism away from the children of his parish for fear that they would confuse the language of the catechism with that of the Word of God. Campbell's opposition to secret societies in the midst of the political troubles in northern Ireland was based in large measure on the principle that they were anti-Scriptural. The experience with the Independent congregation at Rich Hill gave him an opportunity to know some of the outstanding religious leaders of his day, and influenced him in such matters as the observance of communion and evangelical preaching, but the Haldanean emphasis on the importance of the Bible must not be overlooked. It was here he learned to reverence the Scriptures as the only true guide in religion. When the time came for the elder Campbell to leave for America and thus to be separated from his family for some months, perhaps forever, his last words of advice were to study the Gospels.

Thomas Campbell had become aware of the divisions within the church even before he left Ireland for America, for he had labored without success to bring together the Burghers and Anti-burghers of his native country. It is important to note that his interest in uniting these factions was not a conscious effort at Christian union. His real concern was that the divisions within the church were a hindrance to many men and women in accepting the gospel, thus denying themselves the opportunity of salvation. When Campbell was again confronted with a divided church on the frontier of western Pennsylvania, his concern and compassion for the spiritually needy individuals he found there turned his attention once again to the evils of a sectarian church. But while his attention was momentarily diverted to the subject of

Christian union, when the libel presented by the presbytery stated that what he taught was not in keeping with "secession testimony," Campbell made his appeal to the Scriptures. When one considers the entire orientation of his life to this point, it can be seen how natural it was that he should turn to the Bible as the basis for all beliefs and practices. Here was the guiding principle for the Christian. The Christian should accept this, and all else will follow.

The meeting at the home of Abraham Altars at which the rule "Where the Scriptures speak, we speak; where the Scriptures are silent, we are silent," was adopted, revealed more of the truth about Thomas Campbell than has been commonly realized. The *Declaration and Address,* while it had much to say on Christian union, had as its central idea Thomas Campbell's determination to find a basis for Christian faith in the Bible alone and from this foundation eventually to see the union of all Christians. The emphasis, however, was on the importance and authority of the Scriptures. Campbell would have agreed to the idea that the Scriptures are all-sufficient and alone-sufficient as the subject matter of faith and the rule of conduct for the Christian. In the *Declaration and Address* the way to Christian union based on an exact conformity to the Bible is set forth. When the thirteen propositions of the Address are considered, it is discovered that more of them emphasize the place of scriptural truth than deal with the problem of Christian union. Campbell's program is fully summed up in the twelfth of these propositions when he suggests that all that is necessary to the union of the church is for members and ministers to keep close to scriptural authority and for all church activities to follow only the example of the primitive church exhibited in the New Testament, without any addition whatever of human opinions.

After the publication of the *Declaration and Address* in 1809, Thomas Campbell proceeded to act on the principles contained in that document, but in reality, no more so than he had done before. Before long he adopted immersion and gave up infant baptism, but only because he came to believe it was the express teaching of the New Testament and was therefore no longer a matter of "human opinion." It was precisely the same reason that had led him to reject the Confession of Faith when he first came to America. When Alexander decided on the ministry as a lifework, Thomas urged him to study the Bible for six months. In all future questions Thomas Campbell appealed to the evidence of the Scriptures in such a way that it is discernible as a formula in all his writings for the *Christian Baptist* and the *Millennial Harbinger*. Invariably the elder Campbell stated the problem or question under consideration, searched the Scriptures for what they had to say, and from this evidence made his judgment. This was true whether the question concerned Christian union, the religious education of the young, family worship, or slavery. Only the importance of the Scriptures in Thomas Campbell's life could have caused him to view Alexander's publication of the New Testament translation as the most important thing his son had ever done. In the discussion with Barton W. Stone on the atonement, Thomas stood on the Scriptures alone.

Thomas Campbell considered the quest of man's life a search for the salvation of his soul. It was his belief that God, in his infinite wisdom, had given the means and knowledge of that salvation in his revelation to man contained in the Holy Bible. With Campbell, a simple appeal to Scripture was regarded as decisive in relation to every matter of a spiritual nature. On the other hand, the innumerable religious questions which might be discussed, but which do not directly concern personal salvation, were to be deemed without authority over the conscience, and as of too little importance in themselves to be the subjects of debate or strife. The elder Campbell did not regard theological speculation as worthy of even a moment's consideration and always wanted to know how a religious inquiry would in any way affect an individual's salvation before he would attempt to answer it. If the question were considered important, he would turn to the evidence of God's revelation, the Bible, and seek the answer.

The elder Campbell had at first proposed Christian union on the basis of an essential core of Christianity to be discovered in the Scriptures and on which all Christians could agree. There was to be liberty for varieties of opinion on all matters on which they differed. Disciples of Christ, however, did not stand on this tolerant ground for long after they had discovered the "ancient order of things" for the churches and the "gospel restored" as the plan of salvation and the test of fellowship. Here were distinctive things that they held as essential to the unity, as well as the purity of the church. The movement, following Thomas Campbell's example, insisted that these things were not opinions but truths clearly and unmistakably revealed in the Word of God. The true emphasis on Christian union was actually the contribution of Barton W. Stone, evangelistic method was the contribution of Walter Scott, while formulation, publication, and popularization was the contribution of Alexander Campbell. But the emphasis of the movement of Disciples of Christ on the importance and authority of the Scriptures in faith and order is the contribution of Thomas Campbell, man of the Book.

NOTES

INTRODUCTION

1. Charles Louis Loos, "Introductory Period," *The Reformation of the Nineteenth Century*, p. 65.
2. Alexander Campbell, *Memoirs of Elder Thomas Campbell*, p. iv.
3. *Millennial Harbinger*, 1854, pp. 181 ff.

CHAPTER I

1. Benjamin Lyon Smith, *Alexander Campbell*, p. 44.
2. Robert Richardson, *Memoirs of Alexander Campbell*, I, 23.
3. For most of the material in this section the writer was dependent on Robert Richardson, *Memoirs*, I, pp. 21-25.
4. George Stewart, *The Story of Scottish Education*, p. 125.
5. For example, in an article for the *Millennial Harbinger*, Vol. IV, No. 6, June, 1833, he says: "Yet, were I to philosophize, I would say with Young, 'A God all mercy is a God unjust.'"
6. David Murray, *Memories of the Old College of Glasgow*, pp. 205 ff.
7. Alexander Campbell, *Memoirs of Elder Thomas Campbell*, p. 9.
8. *Ibid.*, pp. 194-204.
9. Alexander Campbell, *op. cit.*, pp. 208 f.
10. *Ibid.*, pp. 210 f.
11. *Ibid.*, pp. 213 f.
12. Robert Richardson, *op. cit.*, I, 81.

CHAPTER II

1. Henry Steele Commager, *The American Mind*, pp. 3 ff. See also W. E. Garrison's incisive analysis of the American frontiersman in *Religion Follows the Frontier*, pp. 55-58.
2. Alexander Campbell, *Memoirs of Elder Thomas Campbell*, pp. 20 f.
3. *Minutes of the Synod of the Associate Churches*, quoted in Hanna, p. 29.

4. Richardson, *Memoirs of Alexander Campbell*, I, 85 f.

5. *Minutes of the Chartiers Presbytery*, p. 122, quoted in Hanna, p. 31.

6. *Minutes of the Chartiers Presbytery*, p. 124, quoted in Hanna, p. 33 f.

7. Richardson, *op. cit.*, I, 88 ff.

8. Condensed from the *Minutes of the Chartiers Presbytery*, pp. 132-137, quoted in Hanna, pp. 39-43.

9. Thomas Campbell's answers to the seven charges are from the *Minutes of the Chartiers Presbytery*, pp. 139-141, quoted in Hanna, pp. 46-50.

10. *Minutes of the Synod of the Associate Churches*, quoted in Hanna, p. 68.

11. Alexander Campbell, *op. cit.*, pp. 12-15.

12. *Ibid.*, p. 16.

13. Richardson, *op. cit.*, I, 229.

14. Alexander Campbell, *op. cit.*, pp. 17 f. The italics are a part of the original document.

15. Acheson was sometimes called "General," but was really Lieutenant Colonel Commandant of the Twenty-second Regiment Pennsylvania Militia.

CHAPTER III

1. Letter of James Foster quoted in Alexander Campbell, *Memoirs of Elder Thomas Campbell*, pp. 19 f.

2. Thomas Campbell, *Declaration and Address of the Christian Association of Washington* (Washington, Pa.: Brown and Sample, 1909), p. 2.

3. The best interpretation of the *Declaration and Address* is that of Frederick D. Kershner, *The Christian Union Overture* (St. Louis: The Bethany Press, 1923).

4. Thomas Campbell, *op. cit.*, p. 3.

5. *Ibid.*, p. 6.

6. *Ibid.*

7. *Ibid.*, pp. 7 f.

8. *Ibid.*, p. 8.

9. *Ibid.*, p. 9.

10. *Ibid.*, p. 10.

11. *Ibid.*, pp. 10 f.

12. *Ibid.*

13. *Ibid.*

14. *Ibid.*, pp. 15 f.

15. The thirteen propositions are found in the *Declaration and Address*, original edition, pp. 16 ff.

16. Frederick D. Kershner, *The Christian Union Overture*, p. 26.

17. Thomas Campbell, *op. cit.*, pp. 18 f.

18. *Ibid.*, p. 23.

19. John Locke, "An Essay Concerning Human Understanding," *Great Books of the Western World*, Vol. 35, ed. Robert Maynard Hutchins (Chicago: Encyclopaedia Britannica, Inc.,

1952), Book IV, Chap. XVI, Sec. 14.

20. John Locke, "A Letter Concerning Toleration," *Great Books of the Western World*, Vol. 35, ed. Robert Maynard Hutchins (Chicago: Encyclopaedia Britannica, Inc., 1952), p. 4.

21. *Ibid.*, p. 5.

22. *Ibid.*

23. *Ibid.*, pp. 7 f.

24. *Ibid.*, p. 14.

25. *Ibid.*, p. 22.

26. Charles Louis Loos, "Introductory Period," *The Reformation of the Nineteenth Century*, ed. by J. H. Garrison (St. Louis: Christian Publishing Company, 1901), p. 41.

27. Thomas Campbell, *op. cit.*, p. 24.

28. *Ibid.*

29. *Ibid.*, p. 54.

30. *Ibid.*, pp. 55 f.

31. *Ibid.*, p. 55.

CHAPTER IV

1. Thomas Campbell, *Declaration and Address*, p. 52.

2. *Records of the Synod of Pittsburgh*, pp. 71 f.

3. *Ibid.*, p. 75.

4. Richardson, *Memoirs of Alexander Campbell*, I, 335.

5. Alexander Campbell, *Memoirs of Elder Thomas Campbell*, pp. 23 f.

6. Richardson, *op. cit.*, I, 251.

7. *Ibid.*, I, 390 f.

8. Thomas Campbell, *op. cit.*, p. 10.

9. These quotations are from a letter of Thomas Campbell to Alexander, quoted in Richardson, *op. cit.*, I, 414 f. Richardson says: ". . . (He) was an accomplished penman, and who wrote a hand so elegant that at a very short distance the eye could not distinguish it from copperplate engraving." Richardson, *op. cit.*, I, 443.

10. Letter from Thomas Campbell to Alexander, quoted in Richardson, *op. cit.*, I, 417 ff.

11. These quotations are from a letter of Thomas Campbell to Alexander, quoted in Richardson, *op. cit.*, I, 449-453.

12. *Ibid.*, I, 436. Richardson says that "Redstone" was the name of an old Indian fort on the Monongahela River, about sixty miles north and east of Pittsburgh, w h e r e the town of Brownsville is now located.

13. Charles Louis Loos, "Introductory Period," *The Reformation of the Nineteenth Century*, p. 65.

CHAPTER V

1. Chilton in *Centennial Convention Report*, p. 352. Thomas Campbell later gave up the habit of taking snuff. See Alexander Campbell, *op. cit.*, p. 277.

2. Letter of Alexander Campbell, quoted in Richardson, *Memoirs of Alexander Campbell*, I, 466 f.

3. Richardson, *op. cit.*, I, 482.

4. *Minutes of the Redstone Baptist Association*, quoted in Richardson, *op. cit.*, I, 480.

5. The circular letter on the Trinity is given as an Appendix in Richardson, *op. cit.* (Library edition, Philadelphia: J. P. Lippincott and Company, 1868), I, 539-555. This quotation from I, 540 f.

6. *Minutes of the Redstone Baptist Association*, quoted in Richardson, *op. cit.*, I, 480.

7. Richardson, *op. cit.*, II, 69, footnote.

8. *Christian Baptist*, September 2, 1823, pp. 11 f.

9. *Christian Baptist*, June 7, 1824, p. 65.

10. *Christian Baptist*, October 4, 1824, pp. 98 f.

11. *Ibid.*

12. *Ibid.*

13. Richardson, *op. cit.*, II, 144 f.

14. Letter from Thomas Campbell to Alexander, quoted in A. S. Hayden, *History of the Disciples in the Western Reserve, Ohio* (Cincinnati: Chase and Hall, 1876), p. 148.

15. Alexander Campbell, *Memoirs of Elder Thomas Campbell*, pp. 143 f.

16. Hayden, *op. cit.*, p. 168.

17. Alexander Campbell, *op. cit.*, pp. 185 f.

18. *Christian Baptist*, July 6, 1829, p. 565.

19. Stevenson, *Walter Scott, Voice of the Golden Oracle*, p. 101.

20. Thomas Campbell, *On Religious Reformation*, a pamphlet published in Virginia or North Carolina about 1831.

21. *Christian Baptist*, September 7, 1829, p. 581. This article is unsigned and was discovered and verified as an article of Thomas Campbell's by cross-checking Alexander Campbell's list of the contents of the seven volumes of the *Christian Baptist*.

22. *Christian Baptist*, November 2, 1829, p. 596.

23. *Christian Baptist*, December 7, 1829, p. 608.

24. *Christian Baptist*, December 7, 1829, p. 612 f.

25. Gates, *The Early Relation and Separation of Baptists and Disciples*, pp. 91 f.

26. Williams, *Life of Elder John Smith*, p. 308.

27. Alexander Campbell, *op. cit.*, pp. 151 f.

28. Hayden, *op. cit.*, pp. 217 f.

CHAPTER VI

1. *Millennial Harbinger*, 1832, p. 169.

2. Alexander Campbell, *Memoirs of Elder Thomas Campbell*, p. 174 f.

3. *Ibid.*, pp. 167-170.

4. *The Sacred Writings of the Apostles and the Evangelists of*

Jesus Christ, Commonly Called the New Testament (Third Edition—Revised and Enlarged, Bethany, Brooke County, Virginia: Alexander Campbell, 1832), ''Preface to the Fourth or Stereotype Edition,'' p. 57.

5. Goodnight and Stevenson, *Home to Bethphage*, pp. 62 f.

6. *Millennial Harbinger*, 1832, pp. 584 f.

7. Letter from W. F. Emmons, quoted in Alexander Campbell, *op. cit.*, pp. 281 f.

8. *Millennial Harbinger*, 1833, p. 253.

9. *Ibid.*, 1833, p. 423.

10. See *Millennial Harbinger*, 1833, p. 503, p. 548, and p. 594.

11. *Christian Messenger*, Vol. 7, p. 293.

12. *Christian Reformer*, 1836, p. 819, quoted in Ware, *Barton Warren Stone, Pathfinder of Christian Union*, pp. 309 f.

13. Alexander Campbell, *op. cit.*, pp. 152 ff.

14. *Ibid.*, p. 158.

15. *Ibid.*, p. 161. Alexander, visiting the same area in 1838 had the same feeling for he wrote in his journal: ''I am convinced that more than half the white population of the Carolinas and Georgia are an age behind the same class in the North and West of our national patrimony.'' See Richardson, *Memoirs of Alexander Campbell*, II, 450.

16. *Ibid.*, pp. 163 f.

17. Ware, *History of the Disciples in North Carolina*.

18. Thomas Campbell, *On Religious Reformation*, no date of publication.

19. *Millennial Harbinger*, 1835, pp. 206-211.

20. *Ibid.*, 1835, pp. 284-287.

21. *Ibid.*, 1835, pp. 272 f.

22. *Millennial Harbinger*, 1839, p. 66.

23. *Ibid.*, 1839, pp. 130-164 give the complete story of this Christian union convention and Thomas' reaction to it.

24. *Ibid.*, 1839, pp. 26-30.

25. *Ibid.*, 1839, p. 42. Another in this series appeared in the May, 1839, issue, pp. 216-220.

26. *Millennial Harbinger*, 1839, pp. 392-395.

27. *Christian Baptist*, September 6, 1824, p. 99.

28. *Millennial Harbinger*, 1840, pp. 19 ff.

29. *Ibid.*, 1839, pp. 569-575; pp. 576 f, and 596. Also, pp. 462-466 and pp. 591 ff.

30. *Charter of Bethany College*, quoted in Goodnight and Stevenson, *op. cit.*, p. 99.

31. *Millennial Harbinger*, 1840, pp. 56-60.

32. Alexander Campbell, *op. cit.*, pp. 164 ff.

33. *Millennial Harbinger*, 1860, pp. 340-345.

34. *Ibid.*, pp. 345-349.

35. *Ibid.*, 1851, pp. 450 f.

36. *Ibid.*, 1852, pp. 94-97.

37. *Ibid.*, 1853, p. 215. This letter was not published until nearly ten years after it was written and one suspects only then so that the name, Thomas Campbell, could be kept before the public.

38. *Ibid.*, 1844, pp. 102-105.

39. *Millennial Harbinger*, 1844, pp. 199-203.

40. *Ibid.*, 1844, pp. 481-491.

41. *Ibid.*, 1845, p. 2.

42. *Ibid.*, 1845, pp. 3-8.

43. *Ibid.*, 1845, pp. 196-200.

44. *Ibid.*, 1845, pp. 229-232.

45. Richardson, *op. cit.*, II, 605, spoke of a preaching tour to Ohio in the summer of 1846 in company with J. R. Frame. However, J. R. Frame, writing in July, 1860, gave the date as 1843, which date has been accepted by this writer as the actual time of the visit. See Alexander Campbell, *op. cit.*, p. 293.

46. *Millennial Harbinger*, 1847, pp. 394-401.

47. Alexander Campbell, *op. cit.*, pp. 166 f.

48. *Millennial Harbinger*, 1847, pp. 443-450.

49. *Ibid.*, 1847, pp. 491-503.

50. *Ibid.*, 1847, pp. 661-675.

51. The full address may be found in Alexander Campbell, *op. cit.*, pp. 215-234 and in the *Millennial Harbinger*, 1854, pp. 133-145.

52. Alexander Campbell, *op. cit.*, pp. 287-288.

CHAPTER VII

1. *Millennial Harbinger*, 1854, pp. 116-119.

2. Letter of Alexander Campbell, quoted in Richardson, *Memoirs of Alexander Campbell*, II, 605 f.

3. Letter of Walter Scott, quoted in Alexander Campbell, *Memoirs of Elder Thomas Campbell*, p. 279.

4. Article in *Christian Age*, 1853, quoted in Smith, *Alexander Campbell*, pp. 299 f.

5. Errett Gates in Alexander Young, *Historical Documents Advocating Christian Union*, pp. 34 f.

6. James Harvey Garrison, *Christian Union, A Historical Study*. Dedicatory page.

7. C. M. Chilton in *Centennial Convention Report*, p. 351.

8. *Program of the International Centennial Celebration*, pp. 38 f.

9. Clinton Lockhart in *Centennial Convention Report*, pp. 360 ff.

10. Herbert L. Willett in *Centennial Convention Report*, p. 359.

11. Moore, *A Comprehensive History of the Disciples of Christ*, pp. 465 f.
12. Hanna, *Thomas Campbell, Seceder and Christian Union Advocate*, pp. 208 f.
13. *Ibid.*, pp. 215 f.
14. W. E. Garrison, *Religion Follows the Frontier*, p. 88.
15. Shaw, *Buckeye Disciples*, p. 155.
16. W. D. Frazee, *Reminiscences and Sermons*, p. 115.
17. West, *Alexander Campbell and Natural Religion*, p. 229.

BIBLIOGRAPHY

A. Memoirs

Campbell, Alexander (ed.). *Memoirs of Elder Thomas Campbell.* Cincinnati: Bosworth, Chase and Hall, 1871.

Campbell, Mrs. Selina Huntington. *Home Life and Reminiscences of Alexander Campbell.* St. Louis: John Burns, 1882.

Richardson, Robert. *Memoirs of Alexander Campbell.* 2 vols. Cincinnati: The Standard Publishing Company, 1913.

—. *Memoirs of Alexander Campbell.* Vol. I. Library Edition. Philadelphia: J. P. Lippincott and Company, 1868.

B. Biographies

Goodnight, Claude, and Stevenson, Dwight E. *Home to Bethphage.* St. Louis: Christian Board of Publication, 1949.

Hanna, William Herbert. *Thomas Campbell, Seceder and Christian Union Advocate.* Cincinnati: The Standard Publishing Company, 1935.

Smith, Benjamin Lyon. *Alexander Campbell.* St. Louis: Bethany Press, 1930.

Stevenson, Dwight E. *Walter Scott: Voice of the Golden Oracle.* St. Louis: Christian Board of Publication, 1946.

Ware, Charles Crossfield. *Barton Warren Stone, Pathfinder of Christian Union.* St. Louis: Bethany Press, 1932.

Williams, John Augustus. *Life of Elder John Smith.* Cincinnati: The Standard Publishing Company, 1904.

C. Periodicals and Reports

Centennial Convention Report. Cincinnati: The Standard Publishing Company, 1909.

Christian Baptist. Edited by Alexander Campbell. Seven volumes in one, 1823-1830, ed. by D. S. Burnet. 13th edition, Cincinnati: H. S. Bosworth, 1861.

Millennial Harbinger. Edited by Alexander Campbell, et. al. Bethany, Virginia. Volumes for 1830-1854.

Program of the International Centennial Celebration and Conventions of the Disciples of Christ. Pittsburgh, Pennsylvania: n. p., 1909.

Records of the Synod of Pittsburgh. Pittsburgh: Luke Loomis, 1852.

D. Books

Athearn, Clarence R. *The Religious Education of Alexander Campbell.* St. Louis: Bethany Press, 1928.

Campbell, Thomas. *Declaration and Address of the Christian Association of Washington.* Washington, Pa.: Brown and Sample, 1809.

Campbell, Alexander, and Owen, Robert. *Debate on the Evidences of Christianity.* London: R. Groombridge, 1839.

Commager, Henry Steele. *The American Mind.* New Haven: Yale University Press, 1950.

England, Stephen J. *We Disciples, A Brief View of History and Doctrine.* St. Louis: Christian Board of Publication, 1946.

Fortune, Alonzo Willard. *The Disciples in Kentucky.* Published by the Convention of the Christian Churches in Kentucky, 1932.

—. *Origin and Development of the Disciples.* St. Louis: Bethany Press, 1924.

Garrison, James Harvey. *Christian Union, A Historical Study.* St. Louis: Christian Publishing Company, 1906.

—. (ed.) *The Reformation of the Nineteenth Century.* St. Louis: Christian Publishing Company, 1901.

—. *The Story of A Century.* St. Louis: Christian Publishing Company, 1909.

Garrison, Winfred Ernest. *Religion Follows the Frontier.* New York: Harper and Brothers, 1931.

—, and DeGroot, Alfred T. *The Disciples of Christ, A History.* St. Louis: Christian Board of Publication, 1948.

Gates, Errett. *The Early Relation and Separation of Baptists and Disciples.* Chicago: Donnelly and Sons Co., 1904.

Hayden, A. S. *Early History of the Disciples in the Western Reserve, Ohio.* Cincinnati: Chase and Hall, 1876.

Hicks, John D. *The Federal Union, A History of the United States to 1865.* Boston: Houghton Mifflin Company, 1937.

BIBLIOGRAPHY

Kellems, Jesse Randolph. *Alexander Campbell and the Disciples.* New York: R. R. Smith, Inc., 1930.

Kershner, Frederick D. *The Christian Union Overture, An Interpretation of the Declaration and Address of Thomas Campbell.* St. Louis: Bethany Press, 1923.

Locke, John. *An Essay Concerning Human Understanding.* Vol. 35 of the *Great Books of the Western World.* Edited by Robert Maynard Hutchins. Chicago: Encyclopaedia Britannica, 1952.

———. *A Letter Concerning Toleration.* Vol. 35 of the *Great Books of the Western World.* Edited by Robert Maynard Hutchins. Chicago: Encyclopaedia Britannica, 1952.

Moore, William Thomas. *A Comprehensive History of the Disciples of Christ.* New York: Fleming H. Revell and Company, 1909.

Murray, David. *Memories of the Old College of Glasgow.* Glasgow: Jackson, Wylie and Company, 1927.

The Sacred Writings of the Apostles and the Evangelists of Jesus Christ, Commonly Styled the New Testament. Third Edition—revised and enlarged. Bethany, Brooke Co., Va.: Alexander Campbell, 1832.

Shaw, Henry K. *Buckeye Disciples.* St. Louis: Christian Board of Publication, 1952.

Stewart, George. *The Story of Scottish Education.* London: Sir Isaac Putnam and Sons, Ltd., 1927.

Sweet, William Warren. *The Story of Religion in America.* New York: Harper Brothers, 1950.

Van Kirk, Hiram. *The Rise of the Current Reformation.* St. Louis: Christian Publishing Company, 1907.

Walker, Williston. *A History of the Christian Church.* New York: Charles Scribner's Sons, 1917.

West, Robert Frederick. *Alexander Campbell and Natural Religion.* New Haven: n. p., 1948.

Wish, Harvey. *Society and Thought in Early America.* New York: Longmans, Green and Company, 1950.

Young, Charles Alexander. *Historical Documents Advocating Christian Union.* Chicago: The Christian Century Company, 1904.

E. Encyclopaedias

Encyclopaedia Britannica, Eleventh Edition. Cambridge, England: University Press, 1910.

The New Schaff-Herzog Encyclopaedia of Religious Knowledge. New York: Funk and Wagnalls, 1911.

F. *Additional Sources*

Ainslie, Peter. *The Message of the Disciples for the Union of the Church.* New York: Fleming H. Revell Co., 1913.

DeGroot, Alfred T. *The Grounds for Divisions Among the Disciples of Christ.* Chicago: privately printed, 1940.

Garrison, Winfred Ernest. *An American Religious Movement.* St. Louis: Bethany Press, 1940.

—. *Alexander Campbell's Theology.* St. Louis: Christian Publishing Company, 1900.

Morrison, Charles Clayton. *What Is Christianity?* Chicago: Willett, Clark and Company, 1940.

Robinson, William. *Declaration and Address With an Introduction.* Birmingham, England: The Berean Press, 1951.

INDEX

A

Acheson, Hannah, 58, 68f., 70f.
Acheson, Thomas, 98, 125, 161, 174
Ahorey, 33, 35, 38, 47, 100
Altars, Abraham, 97f., 140, 154
American frontier, 60ff., 213f.
Anderson, Dr. John, 74, 76ff., 84, 87
"A Scriptural View of Christian Character and Privilege," 244f.
"A Scriptural View of the Holy Spirit," 245f.
Associate Synod of North America, 68f., 72, 84-91, 93ff.
"A Synopsis of Christianity," 251f.
Authority of the Scriptures, 117f., 123, 232f.
"A Word to the Disciples of the Ancient Gospel," 220f.

B

Ballymena, 31f.
Baptists, 168ff., 172, 180f., 184f., 193f, 195, 197, 209ff., 212f., 216f., 219, 227
Beaver Anathema, 209f., 212
Bethany College, 241ff., 259, 263, 266f.
"Brief Scriptural Exhibition of the Laws and Duties of Matrimony," 256
Brush Run Church, 150ff., 154, 160, 167ff., 174, 183, 189f., 195f.

Bryant, Mrs. Joseph. (Dorothea Campbell), 173, 180, 226, 257
Buffalo Seminary, 183f., 187
Burlington, Kentucky, 181ff.
Burnet, David S., 211

C

Calvinism, 65f., 82, 97, 121, 159, 168, 201
Cambridge, Ohio, 172ff., 247f.
Campbell, Alexander
  birth, 32
  education, 33f., 44
  arrival in America, 101, 103
  decision on lifework, 139
  assumption leadership, 145-148
  marriage, 150
  ordination, 156
  correspondence with father, 162ff.
  Campbell-Walker Debate, 185f.
  Campbell-Maccalla Debate, 189f.
  Campbell-Owen Debate, 203f.
Campbell, Archibald (son of Thomas), 196
Campbell, Mrs. Thomas (Jane), 31f., 102, 159, 212, 230f.
Campbell, Thomas
  conversion, 23
  at University of Glasgow, 26
  at Whitburn, 29
  marriage, 31
  ordination, 33
  as minister, 35
  diary of, 36
  prayer life, 37
  sermon style, 38f.

292 INDEX

and secret organizations, 41f.
and children, 43, 101
an Old-Light, Anti-Burgher, Seceder Presbyterian, 46
independence of mind, 46
and the Independents, 46
and sectarian spirit, 52
attempts at union in Ireland, 52-55
removal to America, 57f.
sails for America, 58
arrival in America, 68
immersion of, 157f.
on baptism, 190f.
editor and publisher, 206f.
on the atonement, 222
later years, 246ff.
on slavery, 252ff.
farewell sermon, 259ff.
Campbell, Thomas, Jr., 233
Cannamaugh, 73ff., 79
Chapman, Mrs. Andrew (Nancy Campbell), 173
Chartiers Presbytery, 69f., 73f., 78, 85ff., 92ff.
Christian Association of Washington, 100ff., 105, 108f., 115f., 135, 139f., 147ff., 150
Christian Baptist, the, 187f., 192f., 196, 200, 205f., 207, 209, 238f.
Christian Messenger, the, 222f.
Christian union, 160, 234ff., 236
"Church Edification," 240, 243
Civil Commotion in Ireland, 39-42
Clapp, Mrs. Matthew (Alicia Campbell), 214f., 231, 233

D

Declaration and Address, The, 100ff., 105-137, 180, 184, 205, 232f., 250, 265
propositions of, 116ff.
fundamental principles of, 123
Disciples of Christ, 132, 216, 221, 226, 235, 238f., 255

E

Essay Concerning Human Understanding, 34, 126ff.
Evangelical movement, 51f.
"Experimental Religion," reply to, 191f.

F

"Family Education: The Nursery," 244
Frontier, description of, 60ff.

G

Garrison, James Harvey, 265
Garrison, Winfred Ernest, 136, 268f.
Glas, John, 49
Glasgow, University of, 24ff., 125
Guernsey County, Ohio, 172f., 184

H

Haldane, James and Robert, 48, 50f.
Hanna, William Herbert, 267f.
Hill, Rowland, 47f.

I

Immersion, 152ff., 155, 159f., 167
Independents, the Scottish, 46-51, 126
Infant baptism, 98f., 152ff., 156, 159

J

Jardine, George, 28

L

Letter Concerning Toleration, 34, 126
Libel against Thomas Campbell, and his answers, 78ff.

INDEX   293

Locke, John, 34, 110
  life of, 126ff.
  philosophy of, 127-132
Loos, Charles Louis, 171

M

McKeever, Mrs. Matthew (Jane Campbell), 230f., 259f.
McLean, Archibald, 266
McNeely, Cyrus, 196f., 253ff.
Maccalla-Campbell Debate, 189f. There is some discrepancy as to the spelling of Maccalla's name. The spelling followed in this book is that used by Campbell in the publication of the debate. In a book written by Maccalla and published in 1828 the author's name in the title page is spelled "M'Calla"
Mahoning Baptist Association, 188, 194, 197, 200, 205f., 209
Mentor, Ohio, 214f.
Millennial Harbinger, 128, 205f., 217, 220f., 222ff., 225, 229, 231, 233f., 237, 243, 248, 253, 255, 258, 263
Mormonism, 214ff.
Movements for Christian Union, 66

N

Newry (Ireland), 21, 23, 33, 38
New Testament translation, 194, 218f.

O

On Religious Reformation, 228f.
Orangemen, Society of, 39
Owen-Campbell Debate, 203f.

P

"Peep-o'-Day Boys," 40
"Personal and Family Devotion," 237

Pittsburgh, Pennsylvania, 69f., 174ff., 180
Premillenarianism, 112f.
Presbyterians, regular, 65f., 67, 126, 141f., 167
Protest and Appeal, The, 85ff., 123

R

Raines, Aylett, 200f., 211
Redstone Baptist Association, 168ff., 176f., 179, 184, 188, 190, 195
Reformation movement, 160, 212, 216
Reformers, 197, 200, 209f., 214, 216
Reid, Thomas, 26, 125
Revolutionary War and effect on religion, 60, 62, 66, 112
Richardson, Robert, 176, 185, 220f., 233, 241, 257, 263
Rich Hill, 33, 43ff., 52
Richmond, Virginia, 217f., 225f.
Rigdon, Sydney, 200, 214ff.

S

Sandeman, Robert, 49f.
Scott, Walter, 185, 187, 190, 194, 197f., 199, 202f., 205, 208, 239, 264
Seceder Presbyterians, 22, 38, 45
  Anti-Burghers and Burghers, 29, 34, 45, 52f., 55, 68, 72f.
  "Old-Light" and "New Light," 45
Second Awakening, the 63f.
Sectarian spirit
  in Ireland, 51f.
  on American frontier, 64ff., 72f., 83, 103
Semple, Robert B., 192, 216f.
Sermon On the Law, 179f., 184, 209
Sharon, Pennsylvania, 203

Sheepbridge (Ireland), 22f., 32
Somerset, Pennsylvania, 203
Stone, Barton Warren, 66, 197f., 221ff., 239, 264
Synod of Pittsburgh, 141, 144, 154, 195

T

"The Direct and Immediate Intention of the Christian Institution," 236f.
"The Divine Order for Evangelizing of the World," 236
The Marrow of Divinity, 45
"The Religion of Christianity," 192f.
To the Religious Public, 204f.
Trinity, paper on and doctrine of, 178f.

U

United Irishmen, 40f.
United Presbyterian Church, 68

V

Visit to Indiana, 181

W

Walker-Campbell Debate, 185f.
Walker, John, 48f.
Washington, Pennsylvania, 69ff., 77, 92, 96, 101
Wellsburg, Virginia, 175, 184, 195, 219f., 221
Western Reserve, The, 196ff., 199f.
Wilson, William, 74ff., 84

Y

Young, John, 27

www.ingramcontent.com/pod-product-compliance
Lightning Source LLC
Chambersburg PA
CBHW050338230426
43663CB00010B/1909